THE SECOND BOOK OF
SOUTH BRENT

A Miscellany of 'out avver, in and roundabout' this Dartmoor Community

GREG WALL

HALSGROVE

First published in Great Britain in 2008

British Library Cataloguing-in-Publication Data
A CIP record for this title is available from the British Library

ISBN 978 1 84114 787 1

HALSGROVE

Halsgrove House
Ryelands Industrial Estate
Bagley Road
Wellington
Somerset TA21 9PZ
T: 01823 653777
F: 01823 216796
e: sales@halsgrove.com
www.halsgrove.com

Frontispiece photograph:
The pool at Brentmoor House. (THE WADDAMS COLLECTION)

Printed in Great Britain by CPI Antony Rowe, Wiltshire

Preface and Acknowledgements

When *The Book of South Brent* was published in 2005 there were still many photographs that had not been used. Its publication prompted many people to offer fresh information about many aspects of life in this community, which straddles the moor, the 'out-awver', and the 'in-under', the northern part of the South Hams. So *The Second Book of South Brent* was born. As its subtitle suggests, it is a miscellany rather than a chronological history. It takes another look at Brent but as a miscellany there are bound to be things that have been left out. In compiling it we have had access to over 600 photographs and many personal reminiscences, only a representative sample of which we have been able to include here. We are sure that when you see this book you might well say, once again, 'I could have told you about...', but that is the very nature of this very special community.

When people collect their personal 'archive' they include cuttings from newspapers and magazines, many of which are anonymous. We have tried to acknowledge sources of photographs and reminiscences in the text, but thanks go to everyone who, in any way, has supported the production of *The Second Book of South Brent*. We have tried to acknowledge all sources of information in captions and in the text. We would particularly like to express our thanks to the editors of the *Western Morning News*, the *Ivybridge and South Brent Gazette* and the *Times* group of newspapers for their support in the production of this volume; to Lucy Simister of 'The Mare and Foal' shop by again allowing us the use of her shop window for the display of photographs; to Keith Male for allowing us access to the vast resource of photographs of activities and for taking photographs especially for inclusion here; and to John Giles, who has been the 'critical friend', spending many hours collating the illustrations and proof reading the text.

The original Brent Band. (The Hayman Collection)

Richard A. Mumford

As a QUEEN'S SCOUT you have
prepared yourself for service
to God and your fellow men
and have shown yourself a
worthy member of the
great SCOUT BROTHERHOOD.
I wish you God-speed on
your journey through life;
may it prove for you
a joyous adventure.

Elizabeth R

January 1984

Richard Mumford is one of the South Brent Scouts to receive the Queen's Scout Award.

CONTENTS

Robert Hard and John Helmore, nineteenth-century 'village songmen' whose songs were collected by Sabine Baring-Gould and included in his Songs of the West.   (THE BRAMIDGE COLLECTION)

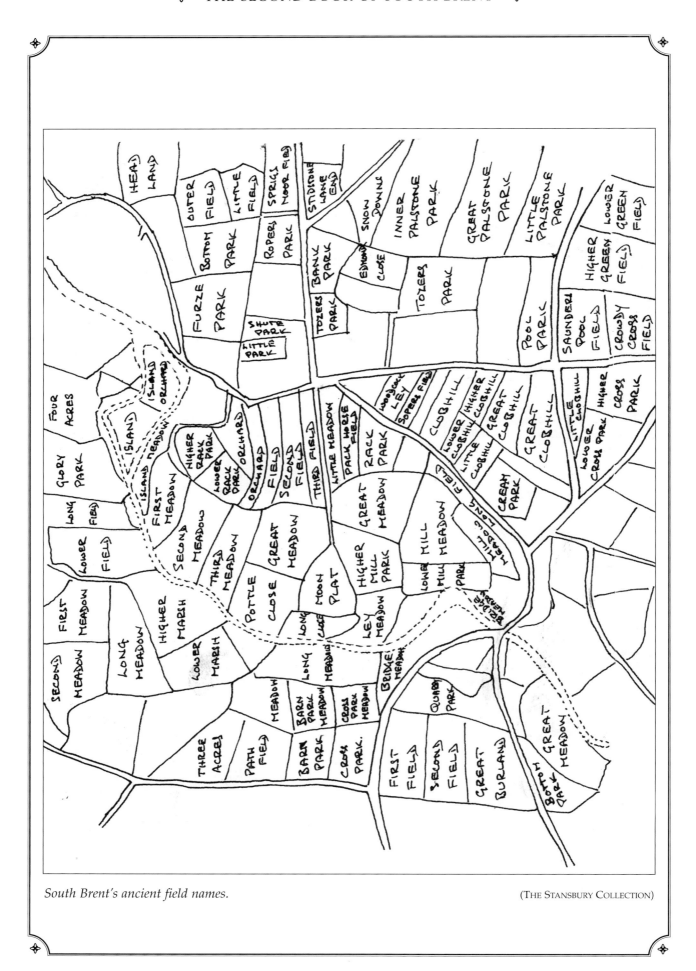

South Brent's ancient field names.

CHAPTER 1

Another Look at the Growth of Brent

South Brent, or just Brent, as she is known to the locals, stands where the Avon leaves the bleak and dangerous southern Dartmoor heights and begins its journey through the tranquil South Hams. It is on the moors that the story of South Brent begins, with Bronze-Age man.

(The Book of South Brent)

Cromlech on
Brent Fore Hill
near
Corringdon Ball Gate

The Early Years

Ken Smith has a great interest in the early history of Brent. He writes:

Evidence of early human activity on Brent Moor comes in the form of a Palaeolithic hand-axe, found near Petre's Pits during 1931 by R.H. Worth, presently housed in Torbay Museum. The axe is dated at circa 200,000 years old, and was probably made by the precursors of Neanderthal Man.

The earliest signs of modern man on Brent Moor date to c.4000BC in the form of a chamber tomb and circular pound just outside Corringdon Ball Gate. The remains of large granite slabs at its entrance are thought to have formed a 'dolmen'-type structure. This was a major construction project. The tomb is contemporary with a Neolithic settlement a few miles south, on Hazard Hill. Excavations at Hazard during 1950/51 found many forms of flint implements and pottery used by a hunter-gatherer/ farming community with trading links from

Lands End to Maiden Castle and beyond. These early 'Brentonians' were great travellers.

The Neolithic period slowly progressed into the early-Bronze Age; c.2700BC Brent Moor now begins to see its first true farmers. These early farmers (the Beaker Culture) were responsible for constructing the circular burial mounds, together with their associated stone avenues, found near Glasscombe Corner, Corringdon Ball, Brent Fore Hill and Black Tor. The reasons for this form of burial, which has been the subject of much scholarly debate, are unclear, with speculations ranging from astronomical alignment to mystical significance. Whatever their purpose, they are well worth a visit.

From about 2000BC the population of Brent Moor increases to an estimated 700 souls living and farming between Dockwell Ridge and the Glazebrook Valley, the highest concentration being in the Avon Valley. The wild woodland was now replaced by enclosed walled field systems called reaves, the remains of which are still clearly visible on Aish Ridge and between the head of the West Glaze and Three Barrows. Bronze-Age track-

ways leading to the 'Moor Gates' at Corringdon, Owley and Dockwell are still in use to this day. The huge clearance cairns at Three Barrows, Whitabarrow and Knattabarrow were built at this time. Go to any high place on Brent Moor when the sun is low in the autumn sky and you can clearly see the remains of the late-Bronze-Age hut circles and pounds on the valley sides. Numerous Neolithic and Bronze-Age artefacts have been found all over the parish of South Brent. These finds range from flint arrowheads, scrapers and stone spindle whorls to a more exotic bronze spear head and ferrules found at Bloody Pool. The most elaborate of these finds are two beautifully crafted bronze axe-heads found at Corringdon Farm and Shipley. Most of these finds are now in private collections.

Large-scale human occupation on high Dartmoor slowly came to an end during the first millennium BC. Brent Moor came to be used for summer grazing by the lowland farmers. The 'clearance' coincided with a dramatic change in climate, from almost Mediterranean weather to the cold, damp conditions we experience today. A number of factors contributed to this clearance, including deforestation, leaching of minerals from the soil, the formation of wet bog land, over-population and the introduction of the iron plough, which enabled the heavier valley soils to be cultivated. The moorland dwellers moved into the sheltered valleys, signalling the birth of such Dartmoor villages as South Brent. The clearance heralded the coming of the Iron Age. Early Brentonians were able to manufacture more durable tools both for farming and, alas, for war. This cultural change is amply illustrated by the Iron-Age fort on the top of Brent Hill, from which the name of the village is derived.

The Abbey Era

The Book of South Brent records that the first real written description of Brent is in a medieval document of Pope Nicholas among the records of the Petre family, where it is noted that, in 1247, 'there stood at Brent seven houses and a church'. It is likely that two of these seven houses were Island House and the Church House.

The Church House, as one of the oldest buildings in Brent, will have witnessed the growth of the community like few others, and its history was recorded for Mr and Mrs John Stanyon when they were owners of the property. It is typical of a Devon longhouse and was probably constructed to house the builders of St Petroc's, the churchyard of which the house abuts. This could indicate that the Church House might have been in occupation as early as the eleventh century, at the time of the Domesday Survey, although it is not specifically mentioned in the Domesday Book.

While the manors of Brent were in the ownership of the Abbey of Buckfast, monks and their lay brothers would have occupied the building, and it is very probable that when the first known vicar of South Brent, Richard of Teyngmuive (Teignmouth), was appointed as vicar, he would have lived in the house.

The Petre Era

Christopher Saxton's map of Devon, *Devoniae Comitat*, of 1575, shows 'Brent' sitting on the river under the hill but gives no indication of any roads. In 1570 Saxton began a survey of the whole of England and Wales on the commission of Lord Burghley. This was a significant undertaking at the time, and yet by 1574 the first plates had been engraved and in 1578 the survey was complete. The size of the 'logo' suggests that the community was quite significant in the area and we believe that by 1600 the community had spread out around the Fore Street crossroads and down Plymouth Road to at least as far as the Pack Horse.

In 1601 the Church House was occupied as the village parsonage by the Revd Nicholas Gibbs, who had become the incumbent in 1599 and who stayed until 1632. An inventory of 1601 calls the building the 'Vicaria de Brente', and describes it in great detail. The ground floor had eight rooms, including a parlour 'planked and ceild'. The hall was 'paved with broad stones', as was the kitchen. The buttery – something of a misnomer as this was frequently used for the storage of beer and other alcoholic provisions – had an earthen floor, as did the cellar. (By 1771 this had been pebbled over.) There were three other rooms on the ground floor, two of which are not described in the inventory, while the third was a dairy, which, as one would have expected, had an earthen floor. The upper storey consisted of a chamber and an adjoining study over the parlour. There was also the 'long chamber' – where the occupants would have taken their exercise in inclement weather – and 'another little chamber adjoining'. Other first floor rooms in 1601 included the 'porch chamber', the 'middle chamber', the 'curate's chamber' and the 'kitchen chamber'. The Church House was built of stone with a roof of shingle. The terrier also makes mention of three outhouses – a stable with hayloft above, a barn and a pound house containing a cider-press.

The pound house afterwards fell into a ruinous condition and in 1793, on being found unsafe, was demolished. The Revd John Amyatt – described as 'red of neck, short and stout, but features displaying withal good breeding' – who instigated the demolition of the pound house and who occupied the Church House from 1782 to 1810, was probably the last parson of South Brent to do so until 1971, when it became the home of Revd and Mrs Vesey.

The Church House would have been a rambling, somewhat inconvenient, but essentially comfortable place divided into two areas – one for service, one for

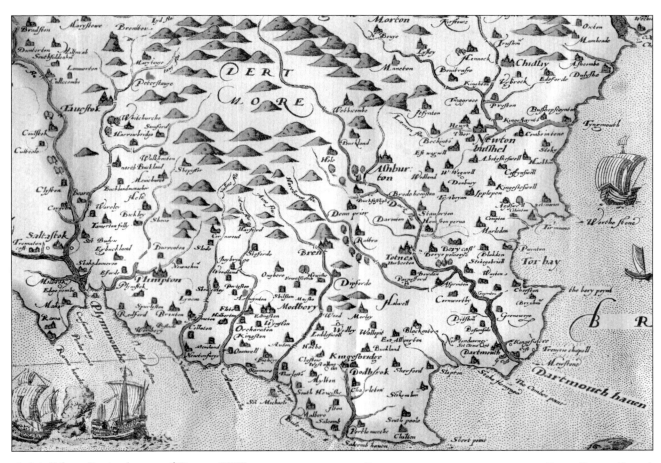

A detail from Saxton's map of Devon, 1575. (REPRODUCED WITH PERMISSION FROM THE DEVON RECORD OFFICE)

A modern photograph of Island House. Like the Church House, Island House is one of the oldest homes in Brent. A priests' hole, used for hiding Roman Catholic clergy during periods of persecution, was found during renovations in the late-twentieth century.

living. The former would have included rooms for brewing, dairying and laundering. At the very least, the latter would have been represented by a parlour, used on high days and holidays and for funerals. Bridging the two and serving as the chief focus for the house would have been the kitchen, where, sooner or later, all occupants met.

There is a tradition that Island House was the vicarage in the early part of the nineteenth century, but more recent documents contradict this. It may be that this building did once serve as the incumbent's residence in the late-eighteenth and early-nineteenth centuries, when it was owned by the Revd George Baker, the vicar of Brent between 1810 and 1845. It does appear as Baker's tenement in the 1840s.

In 1832 the Land Tax Assessment shows that the Church House was occupied by John Elliot, whose son, also called John, was lord of the manor at the time of his death in 1870 and to whom the east window of St Petroc's Church is dedicated.

Many of the cottages in Church Street date from the late-eighteenth or early-nineteenth centuries. For example, Peppercorn Cottage, at the time of writing, is about 200 years old, evidence of which can be found on an indenture dated 27 March 1812. Peter Ford the elder, a local builder, granted the leasehold of the property to his son, Peter Ford the younger, for the annual rent of peppercorn.

Another Look at the Railways

Stationmaster Arscott with Roy Sparkes, Mark Roper and Bill Reynolds unloading a Landrace boar from the Kingsbridge branch for the onward journey up the line.
(THE ROY SPARKES COLLECTION)

The staff of Brent Station just before the start of the Second World War. Left to right, back row: 'Nobby' Clarke, Ernie Wall, Jack Garland; front row: Tom Pitts, William Hack, Stationmaster Charles Matthews and Jack Reynolds. (THE GRAHAM JORDAN COLLECTION)

Above: A passenger train waits to pull away from Brent Station in the early-twentieth century.
(THE GRAHAM JORDAN COLLECTION)
Right: Ticket for the last train to Kingsbridge, signed by the guard.
(THE GRAHAM JORDAN COLLECTION)

A small crowd waits as the Flying Scotsman passes Brent signal-box. (THE FIELD COLLECTION)

An express train at Brent station. Because of its position at the head of the Kingsbridge branch line, many of the through trains between London and the West would stop at Brent Station. (THE ROY SPARKES COLLECTION)

Another Look at the Railways

This early photograph of Brent Station can be dated several years prior to 1910, as neither the 1910 cemetery or the Village Hall can be seen.

(THE SHARVILLE COLLECTION)

Building the higher railway bridge.

(THE ROY SPARKES COLLECTION)

Above: *Filling the branch-line engine with water on the up line at Brent Station in the early-twentieth century.*

(THE GRAHAM JORDAN COLLECTION)

Right: *Ponies being prepared for transporting up the line after Brent Pony Fair, c.1900. The importance of the fair can be gauged by the number of wagons in the train and the number of coaches on the branch-line train on the station platform. The branch line opened in 1893.*

(THE GRAHAM JORDAN COLLECTION)

Detail from a map of South Brent, dated c.1880, reproduced, with permission, from the Ordnance Survey map of around that date.

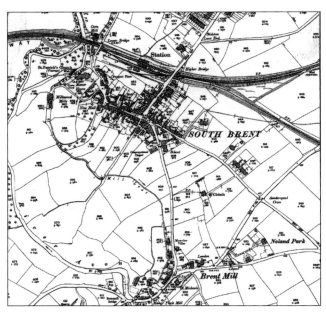

Ordnance Survey map (second edition) of 1906, reproduced with permission.

The Elliott Era

The above map shows the main railway line but not the branch line, which opened in 1893.

We can see the beginning of development along Hillside. There are the first houses in Moorland Park, then called Springfield Villas, built about 1877, and further up the road are Hillside Cottages, which date from the mid-nineteenth century and were part of the manorial lands. Further up the road, on the corner of Underhill, is Whinfield, the home from 1898 of the Collier family. John Collier, who lives there in 2008, writes:

The house is not particularly old. It does not feature on the Tithe Map, although there is evidence of an earlier farmstead which is referred to on the Tithe Map as Three Corners, which to this day is the shape of the garden. I believe Whinfield was built after the coming of the railway in the 1850s and was probably in the ownership of the Carew family from Marley and Haccombe, possibly as a hunting lodge.

Yonder Cross dates from 1905 and was built facing the way it does to get a favourable view of the railway. The map shows no other developments in the area. There are also no developments at all along Totnes Road, beyond where the Chapelfields entrance is at the time of writing, or along Plymouth Road past the Pack Horse. Clobells House is shown.

In 1878 the Church House, or Manor House, as it had become known, was put up for auction at Arscott's Royal Hotel in South Brent at three o'clock on the afternoon of Friday, 21 June 1878. The Manor House formed the first of eight lots sold and was described as being 'the dwelling-house known as the Manor House, now in the occupation of Mr Ford, a yearly tenant'. So another connection with the lordship of the manor ended. In 1881 it was occupied by a young farmer named William Pearse, 28, a native of South Brent, who described himself as 'farmer of eighty acres'. In 1892 it became the home of William Charles Gregor, who was 'jockey and trainer' for a number of families, but chiefly the Mildmays of Flete.

The Kingwell Era and Beyond

The Ordnance Survey map (second edition) of 1906, reproduced with permission, shows that by the early part of the twentieth century developments along Hillside had greatly expanded.

The developments along Hillside took place towards the end of the nineteenth century. Springfield was built in the field called Spriggsmoor Field, along with Belmont and Greenbank, around the late 1870s. Jervis Veale, the builder, was very involved in their construction. They were built according to demand in blocks, as is most clearly shown in the picture of Greenbank Terrace, where

Greenbank Terrace.

Springfield Terrace, just after it was completed towards the end of the nineteenth century, photographed by W.R. Gay, the Brent photographer. (THE CRANCH COLLECTION)

Belmont Terrace.

An early view of the villas towards the top of Hillside, another of W.R. Gay's photographs posted as a postcard to Teignmouth in July 1914. (THE PANNELL COLLECTION)

Clifton Terrace.

Crowder Park.

the houses have distinctly different façades. Farnborough and Pitsani have gable ends facing the road, whilst the others do not. The villas further up the road – Wayside, Firleigh (1893), Manadon, Nethermoor, Pengersek (1888), and Lostiford – are slightly later, whilst Hillside Cottages are earlier.

Brent Mill is a completely separate community and there is still no building further along Plymouth Road after the Congregational chapel and the school. Along Totnes Road, Airlea and Sands House have been built, as have Windward and the houses opposite Clobells House. It is also interesting to note the mis-dedication of the church to St Patrick (understandable with cartographers from afar, who may well never have heard of Petroc!). By this time the vicarage had moved to the large house now known as the Manor.

On the road to Glazebrook, another of Brent's larger houses, Melbury House, formerly known as Beggar's Bush, dates from 1911, when John Kingwell sold 1.5 acres of land to John Goodwin for the 'purpose of erecting a house, stables and outbuildings'. In 1919 the size of the property was enlarged with the purchase of a further two acres of land known as Little Cross Park.

Clifton Terrace appears on the 1906 Ordnance Survey map, whilst Woodhaye Terrace was constructed in 1912/1913. Mons Terrace came after the First World War, as its name suggests. The first major local authority housing on Brent was Corn Park, constructed in 1928 by T. Brook and Co. Ltd of Totnes. Among those who were involved in the construction were Cecil Wilkinson, Cyril May, George Wilkinson, Gordon Hobbs, Bert Pomeroy and Mike Quaintance. Mrs Lillian Chandler lived in one of the houses that her father and brother, the Wilkinsons, had built, for many years. Chapel Fields

The top end of Corn Park.

Courtenay Park.

Sanderspool Cross.

4 ONLY MODERN SEMI-DETACHED 3-BEDROOMED
SPLIT LEVEL HOUSES AT SOUTH BRENT
Further particulars apply to
DENNIS HOARE, builder on site or J. W. SOPER, Sopers of South Brent Ltd., Phone 2222 or Estate Agents, LUSCOMBE, MAYE & CO. LTD., South Brent 3108

The original advertisement for the Clobells and Sanderspool Cross developments.

Bishopsmead, 1972.

Brookwood Close.

also dates from this period, Mrs Nano Wood having rent books which belonged to her parents going back to November 1928.

Courtenay Park was originally built in the years after the Second World War but had to be demolished and rebuilt because of concrete cancer. Slightly later came Crowder Park, named from the original field on which it was built, Crowdy Cross Field. It follows the road plan of the wartime camp. The Church House was still called 'the Manor House' when it was acquired by Miss Florence Rex, who lived there until 1953. It was then purchased by Hugh Montagu Butler MA and his wife, Annie. When the Butlers left Devon for Gloucestershire in 1971, the building came full circle when Revd A.L. Vesey petitioned the diocese to purchase the house as the vicarage. The old vicarage by the river then took on the name 'The Manor, and the Church House returned to its original name. When the Revd David Niblett retired, the Diocesan Parsonages Board, following their policy that clergy houses should not be more than 50 years old, sold the building to John and Kathleen Stanyon, who moved in on 11 January 1991. It is now in the ownership of John and Mary Shepherd.

In the second half of the twentieth century there was an expansion of house building around the old A38 between the centre of Brent and Crowder Park.

Brakefield.

Fairfield.

Pool Park.

In 1968 came the construction of the first large housing development in South Brent, at Clobells and Sanderspool Cross. Mr Jack Soper, the proprietor of Soper's of South Brent, one of the two garages in the community, developed the area in the grounds of Clobells House. Clobells is a derivation of Clobhill, the name given to all the fields in the area. In the same year, Hillside Close was built on the remaining undeveloped field in higher Hillside. The first residents of Woodhaye Close, built on the site of the post-war prefabs, also moved in in 1968.

The early 1970s saw the construction of two further developments in the Hillside area. Brookwood Close was also constructed by T. Brook and Co. Ltd of Totnes. The planning consent states, 'The carrying out of the project, (Brookwood Close) shall be begun before 20th. October 1969.' The bungalows were built first and the houses were first sold during December 1972. There were several additions and variations to the original plans, causing delays in completion following various objections. The project was finally completed during the early eighties, Nos 15 and 16 being sold off. Bishopsmead was built by the South West Construction Co. of Kingsbridge in 1972 and was first occupied early in the next year.

The next area to be developed in Brent was the area to the south and East of Sanderspool Cross. Crouch Homes completed Brakefield in 1984. The planning agreement between Mr Bill Goodman, the owner of the fields, and the South Hams District Council was signed on 30 September 1977.

Pool Park was put up in the early 1980s, Higher Green in 1986 and Fairfield (built on Lower Green Field) designed to fulfil local housing needs and being part local authority and part housing association, was the last to be developed, on the site of the last village sheep fair.

There have been other, smaller, developments within the community whose names reflect Brent's past. Manor Court, built in 1986, is on the site of Manor Farm, which then became Manor Garage, the home of Sopers of South Brent. St Michael's Terrace occupies the site of a large house of that name in Brent Mill and the houses at School Gardens are built on exactly that – the former school gardens, where many Brent boys caught the gardening bug!

Paddy Mullen describes the character of South Brent.

One More Step

Ancient breeze blows softly on trees,
as mother nature asked for.
Slowly unwind the gates of time,
a place of character and awe.

Faces come and faces go,
young and old, in this place we know.
A fable here and a fable there,
amongst old friends, and grey of hair.

Take one step closer to reality's line,
through an age-old village that's friendly and fine.
Good food, good laughs, good pints and good halfs,
there's plenty of places to dine.

So take one more step, and close your eyes,
take deep breaths, under these Devon skies.
There is a place that's so heaven-sent,
this little old village called South Brent.

Explore South Brent

The village of South Brent offers you a warm welcome. Take time to discover its historic buildings, ancient church and range of individual shops.

A Beacon for Brent

Rising above the village is Brent Hill. It is composed of ironstone, which attracts lightning. In the past iron was mined here, also magnetite which was used in compasses. In Drake's time a beacon was lit on top to signal the approach of the Armada.

Take a Stroll

• To the island, a wildlife haven just steps away from the main street.

• Along the riverbank to watch the Avon cascade beneath Lydia Bridge. Originally built for packhorses, its name is a Saxon word for white water.

Lydia Bridge

Friendly Village Shops

There is a wide range of shops in the village. You'll find a clockmaker, chemist, DIY store and organic foods as well as everyday items. Refreshments are available at a variety of local establishments.

St. Petroc's Church

Ancient and Modern

St. Petroc's church is dedicated to the 6th century saint who founded it and probably Buckfast Abbey too. Inside you can see a beautiful millennium embroidered panel which depicts the parish in thousands of stitches.

Produced by South Brent Parish Council with support from the Coast & Countryside Service and Dartmoor National Park Authority.

(THE PARISH COUNCIL COLLECTION)

On the way to Market

Take a look in the Toll House Information Centre to find out more about the area and local events. On the wall outside you can see the tolls charged at South Brent fairs. Animals to be sold were kept in pens nearby before going to be sale ring in Wellington Square, then to Station Yard and onto the trains.

The Toll House

Lydia Bridge

KEY
Not to scale

🏠 Shops
🏠 Pubs
- - - - Footpaths

Elise Willisson

Map labels: Hillside, Station Road, Station Yard, Village Hall, The Island, St. Petroc's, St. Dunstan's, Wellington Square, Church Street, Methodist Church, Post Office, TOLLS, Plymouth Road, Old School Centre, Totnes Road, Exeter Road, Primary School, SOUTH BRENT

A map of South Brent painted by Elise Willisson for visitors to the community and placed strategically around the centre.

CHAPTER 2

Another Look at Brent as a Local Centre

The Dartmoor National Park Local Development Framework, published in 2007, describes South Brent as a local 'centre' acting as 'an important service centre for the local area extending outside the National Park'. Throughout its history Brent has been such, a busy commercial community. Its place as a significant centre for trade is reflected in the various *Directories* for Devon, published in the nineteenth and first half of the twentieth centuries, which list the commercial activities in the parish. These are reflected in the on-line directories of the present day.

The Turn of the Twentieth Century

Imagine living in Brent a century ago, when King Edward was on the throne. The reign of his mother, Queen Victoria, had been commemorated by the Victoria lamppost set in the centre of the 'square'. Brent was part of a thriving local area with a market that rivalled any thereabouts.

By far the most important activity in the parish was farming. The names found at this time amongst the farming community are still reflected in the names of much later years – Cleave, Luscombe, Mead, Savery, Smerdon, to mention but a few. The major industrial employment in this period was at the flock mills at Manor Mills.

Edwin Luscombe had traded as a butcher continuously since at least 1893 and would do so until the First World War ended. John Codd ran a butchery in Station Road and the Goodmans had their shops first in Wellington Square and later, after the fire which destroyed the properties at the bottom of Church Street in 1904, in the premises now known as No. 4 The Exchange.

Mr Jasper Hard had been baking bread since at least 1890 and was one of two or three bakers, not counting the various people who baked bread in the many bread-ovens to be found in the older properties in Church Street. Robert Gill, at the Post Office, is described as 'a baker, confectioner, grocer, stationer and printer and agent for the Sun Fire Office.' Mrs. Elizabeth Cole, with her son Frederick, was baking in 1893, and Richard Pinhey is recorded as a Church Street Baker at the outbreak of the First World War in 1914.

Then there were the other 'provisioners', the grocers, or greengrocers. In 1893 there were no less than six of these trading in various sites in the village centre, from Maunder & Co to William Doddridge,

The centre of South Brent at the turn of the twentieth century. (THE SHARVILLE COLLECTION)

William Soper, William Farleigh, William Collins and Mrs Sybil Hosking. Nicholas Wakeham, in 1915, is also described as the agent for Barclay's Bank.

Milk was provided by the various farmers and smallholders in the village, the Pearses at Manor and Town Farms and the Damerells, to name but two.

The other trades and professions that appear in directories in the years up to the end of the First World War reflect the way of life that existed at that time. George Ball was a blacksmith from at least 1893

Left and above: *A moorland farm – three views of Zeal Farm before the Second World War.*

(THE SAVERY COLLECTION)

Sheep at the show on the allotment field with 'Headlands' in the background. In the picture are Barbara Heathman; John Walter Symons of East Sherford; Jack Wotton and Den Harvey and son of Hexdown, Bigbury; Tom Brooch of Dorsley; R. Garland Rogers; Sam Horton of Fillham; Georg Sorge; Robert Savery, aged about nine; Herbert Coker of Venn, Ugborough; Victor Coker of Rattery and his nephew; Courtenay and Gladys Pedrick of Waterman, Ugborough; Mr Andrew of Wisdom, Cornwood.

(THE SAVERY COLLECTION)

The sheep fair of 1954. In the picture are Tom Broach of Dorsley; Jack Sprague of Chagford; Garland Rogers, Robert Savery, Georg Sorge; Harvey; Den Harvey of Hexdown; Pearce Dawe of Tavistock; Jack Bowden of Chagford; Norman and Reg Coker of Bittaford; Norman Colwill; R.H. Perraton; H.C. Coker of Venn, Ugborough; Jack Mead of Bullhornstone, John Mead. (THE SAVERY COLLECTION)

Another sheep fair in the field behind the Village Hall. Among those pictured are Harold Ellis of Dunsford; Ernie Hext of Cornwood; Dick Honey of Plympton; Jack Bowden of Chagford; John Walters-Symons of East Sherford; Mr Chilcott of Tavistock; Tom Brooch of Dorsley; Bill Endacott of South Brent; Walter Cleave of Stidston; Mr Lewis of Manor Farm, South Brent; Norman Colwill; Sidney and Eunice Wakeham of Hillside, South Brent, who were the secretaries of the association; Ron Andrew of Kerry Downs; Victor Coker and R. Garland Rogers. (THE SAVERY COLLECTION)

right through until at least 1919. John Brown had joined him by 1914. In the days before there was much motor traffic, Henry Clancey and Walter Langler were successful wheelwrights, and George Crimp and Walter Walke traded as saddlers. Whilst John Hosking was for a time a 'Chaise Proprietor', Charles Hingston is described as an 'Assurance and Cycle Agent'. It is not until 1914 that Charles Chenhall appears at Brooklands as a 'Motor Engineer'.

In the days before widespread travel and out-of-town shopping centres, Brent was well served by drapers such as the Peach family and tailors such as William Tope, John Bunker of Church Street and Salter's of Station Road. Miss Mahalah Edmunds at Brent Mill and the Misses Codd were the local dressmakers, and for many years

Above and left: *Three advertising blotters from A.W. Cranch & Son. Note the two-figure telephone number 26, which was issued to them on 23 January 1923.*

(THE WOOD COLLECTION)

Charles White traded as a boot and shoemaker in Church Street. He was not alone. Henry Veale also traded in Church Street and Henry Blight in Bowling House and, for a shorter time, John Farleigh also traded in the same field. Mrs E. Wills had a drapery and china dealership. Practically anything the population needed was available locally.

The years around the turn of the twentieth century saw a considerable amount of building taking place, so it is not surprising to find many associated with this activity. Jarvis Veale and later

The Manorial Court of South Brent meeting outside Cranch's shop in Church Street on 17 November 1913.

(THE INEZ JORDAN COLLECTION)

The Royal Oak Hotel, c.1910.   (THE CRANCH COLLECTION)

One of the many Pack Horse signs.

(THE WILKINS COLLECTION)

The London Inn sign, bearing the arms of the city.

his son, Richard, built a lot of the properties along Hillside. The Hosking brothers were also very active in the trade, as were Robert and Richard Codd. The directories describe the Cranch family as painters and glaziers, whilst John and, later, Frederick Preston plied the trade of carpenter. Both William Edmonds and then William Elliott were thatchers. William Edmonds is also listed as a basket maker. George Knapman Soper and later Thomas Knapman were the local hauliers.

With all the commercial activity going on it is not surprising that various banks had sub-branches in Brent. The Cornish Bank, listed in 1902, was taken over by the Capital and Counties Bank, which finally became part of Lloyds Bank. The Naval Bank, which in its turn became part of Lloyds, was listed in 1914. Barclays also had a presence in the community in Fore Street.

We would expect to find in a local centre, especially one at an important railhead, individuals who today would be considered part of the 'leisure industry'. Four public houses – the Royal Oak, the Anchor, the Pack Horse and the London Inn – were trading, and Mr Sydney Hill traded as an 'ale and stout merchant'. Mrs Mary Codd, and later Miss Annie Codd, ran 'refreshment rooms' in Fore Street, but

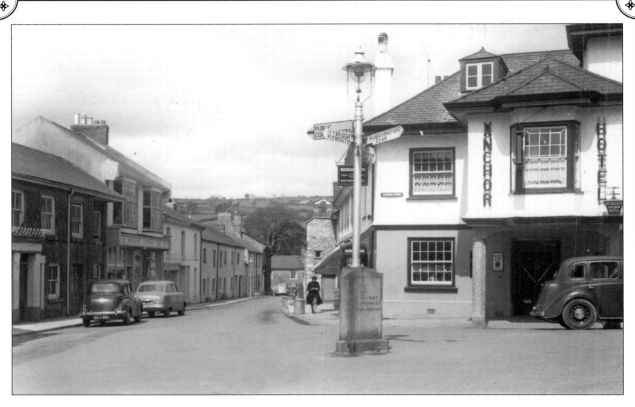

The Anchor Hotel and Church Street in the late 1950s. The jubilee lamp dominated the 'square'.

(THE SHARVILLE COLLECTION)

The centre of South Brent in the 1950s.

(THE ANDERSON COLLECTION)

what is really interesting is the number of people running what are described as 'apartments'. These appear both in the village itself, for example at Albert House, Culloden Villa and several houses in Nelson Terrace, and in Hillside, Belmont Terrace, Greenbank Terrace and Hillside Cottages.

Amongst the other activities listed at the beginning of the twentieth century, we find W.C. Gregor at the Manor House (now the Church House), who was a 'jockey and trainer'. The 20th Century Poultry Food Co. operated in Brent. W.H. Hawke is described as both a water miller and, latterly, as a corn and coal merchant, while John Maye was practising as an auctioneer and surveyor by the outbreak of the First World War in 1914.

With a local school, various private academies, doctors, dentists and other services present, we find a commercial centre that served the needs of the immediate area at a time when mass private transport was yet to arrive.

The Mid-Twentieth Century

At the beginning of the second Elizabethan era, South Brent was still a significant centre, although people had begun to travel outside the community for some goods, and deliveries to the village were being made by such as E. Dingle from Plymouth and E.B. Stoyle of Totnes.

Robert Savery, whose family have lived and farmed in the area for centuries recalled:

It is safe to say that practically every farm in this area 50 years ago was a mixed farm. They had a few milking cows, a few fattening cattle, some sheep, some pigs and some poultry on every farm. It was also far more labour-intensive, with hedges being trimmed and laid by hand and root crops hoed.

Soon after the last war farmers had 'friends they never knew they had'. Quite a number of the richer people from the towns came out and befriended farmers in the hope of perhaps buying a leg of lamb, a chicken or a duck or some eggs on a 'private basis', as they were in short supply and on ration. Many farmers found themselves with visitors on Saturday or Sunday afternoons – so-called friends who could see what they could get.

Mr Savery also recalled:

... a story I heard many years ago when a postmaster from one of the towns and his wife used to do an excursion out to a farm on Sunday afternoons. They had one child and always lingered around to have afternoon tea at the farm. The mother of the child used to stuff him with cream, obviously thinking it would be good for him and to help top him up. The farmer's wife got annoyed with the mother and one day she brought the cream out of the dairy and put it on the table. At the same time she looked across at her husband and said, 'Hey George,

I wish you'd do something about they rats in the dairy. They ate more'n 'alf the cream last night!' It had the effect of slowing the cream consumption down.

He also remembered another anecdote told him at this time:

In the days before mass veterinary medicine many farmers had a reputation for producing effective animal lotions and medicines. One such family were the Pearses at Manor and Town Farms. A farmer from the Harbourneford area came into Town Farm to get something to relieve his cows' constipation, which was often a result of red water. The laxative was given to him in a clay jar previously used for gin. The farmer and his friend decided that before they returned home they would avail themselves of the hospitality of the landlord of the Pack Horse next door. Suitably refreshed, they bought a jar of gin to take home. The jar was identical to the one in which the laxative was stored. The two jars got muddled and the men partook of the wrong one. You can imagine the result!

Another anecdote concerned two farmers who were having a race in their pony-drawn traps on the way home from Ashburton Fair. As they approached Rosary Corner halfway to Buckfastleigh a policeman suddenly tried to stop them. The first trap swerved and went on. However, the policeman managed to catch hold of the back of the second. The farmer turned to him and used his whip until the policeman let go. He was subsequently arrested. When the case came to court the farmer pleaded that the policeman had frightened the pony, which had bolted, and that the only way he could slow the pony down was to get the policeman to let go. He convinced the magistrate of this and was released!

Mrs Nano Wood and Mrs Joy Hayman recalled the centre of Brent in the mid-twentieth century:

In the middle years of the twentieth century the Brent branch of the Buckfastleigh Co-operative Society in Church Street was the largest retailer in the community, having within its building grocery, butchery, bakery, haberdashery and hardware 'departments'. Church Street also boasted Luscombe's butchery, which at various other times served as Soper's cycle shop, a boutique and the first home of the Treasure Chest. Opposite the Co-op was the pharmacy run by the Brockington family, then by Mrs Marian Woodhouse, and next door was the grocery run by Mr and Mrs Tidball. Further down the street the chip shop and general store was run by the Andrews family, whilst at the bottom of the street there were White's the butchers, run since 1922 successively by Mr Clarence White and then by his brother Geoffrey, a shoe repair shop and another chip shop. When the chip shop ceased trading, Mrs Sheila Wall moved into No. 1 The Exchange and from there operated as a dressmaker..

The façade of Miss Violet Manning's newsagency in Station road, March 1975. (THE VERA JORDAN COLLECTION)

Chenhall's Garage at Brent Mill. (THE SPARKES COLLECTION)

Fore Street was the home of the Post Office, with Gill's grocer next door run by Mrs Tucker and famous for its 'dough-buns', baked on site. Further along was Mrs Hayman's haberdashery, later run by Mrs May. On the other side of the road there have been, at various times, a barber/hairdresser run by Mr de Fueck, then, latterly, by Mr Phil Moore and his wife. In the mid-twentieth century the grocery/greengrocery run first by Mr and Mrs Wakeham and trading later as the Central Stores also operated in Fore Street. It later became the Russell Gallery, selling quality hand-made pottery.

Along Station Road one would find Manning's newsagency, Winzer's the butcher's, later to become the second home of the Treasure Chest next to Lloyd's Bank, and Mr and Mrs Durbridge's grocery shop. Then came A.W. Cranch's hardware business. At various other places at this time were Salter's the tailor, Moysey the electrician and Mrs Vickery's secondhand shop.

They recalled that:

At this time most of the people who plied their trade in the various building trades tended to work for one or other of the building firms, such as A.W. Cranch or George Preston, both of whom were also undertakers, as well as the nearby firm of Blight & Scoble, based in

Soper's Garage in Totnes Road. Mr. Jack Soper opened his original garage near the junction of Palstone Lane and Exeter Road in 1929 before moving to Marley Head, where his wife set up a Transport Café. From here he managed his agricultural business. In 1948 he bought Manor Farm and created the garage, extending the land by buying land from Mrs Luscombe and creating better access by buying and then demolishing a cottage in Totnes Road belonging to the Cranch family.

Buckfastleigh and Ivybridge. There were few, if any, full-time 'independent tradesmen'.

By this time Brent boasted two garages, Soper's of South Brent and Chenhall's at Brooklands in Brent Mill, and Manor Mills continued to be the centre of industry in the parish.

The Early Years of the Twenty-first Century

Even 100 years on Brent is still seen as an important service centre, which the Dartmoor National Park Development Framework describes as a 'town'.

At the heart of the centre of Brent over 80 years on we still have the Co-op, albeit in its twenty-first-century form as a local supermarket. We still have our local butcher, working in the same shop that the Luscombe family used. The pharmacy, now run by Kay Reynolds, still operates in the same shop used by the Brockingtons. The Home Bakery, first operated at No. 1 The Exchange by Mr and Mrs Woodley, is now located on the Brent Mill Industrial Estate, with its retail outlet at The Crumb and Cuppa. The newsagent also provides the services of a small grocer and off-licence, whilst Brent still boasts an independent grocer, The Pantry. This is on the site of the original Co-op and Mr and Mrs Durbridge's premises in the 1950s and follows the tradition of the mini-market set up by Brian and Valerie Wollington in Fore Street. A century ago John Maye was the sole 'estate agent'. Luscombe Maye has grown into one of the largest agencies in the South Hams and has been

Rachael Timmins, pharmacist Kay Reynolds and Trish Luker in South Brent Pharmacy, 2007.

joined by Everett's, which opened in 1984, and Bradleys, whilst John Ellison continues with surveying and letting. Brent also has two architects, Moxley Macdonald and Kevin Shotter

Brent can still boast a hardware store in Wakeley's in Station Yard, which also covers the haberdashers and footwear traders of 100 years ago, and Wendy Etherington is now Brent's dressmaker.

Wakeley's, in its capacity as a builders' merchants, also provides for the needs of the many builders working in the area. Alan Lake and E.D. Ashfield trade as builders, whilst Francis Sparkes is a roofer. Paul Hedges, Robert Illman and Chris Palmer work in the realm of 'property maintenance services'. Grant Ford describes himself as a stonemason, John Seager works in the field of green oak framing and Duncan Stewart trades as a carpenter. Dave Ayres at Electroporto advertises the firm as 'Designers and Installers of Plumbing and Heating Systems. General Plumbing and Heating Repairs, Renewals and Alterations. Established 1972.' Plumbsure, Corgi registered, offer a full heating and plumbing design and installation service. Kate Stubbs, a City and Guilds qualified painter and decorator, offers wallpapering, paint effects and customised stencilling, and Andy Steer Decorating also works in this field, as do Staybrite. Brent still has a thatcher, Alan Prince.

One building service that would not have been found 100 years ago is provided by Kingswood, aluminium seamless guttering specialists. Peter

Brian and Val Wollington when they took over the mini-market. (THE WOLLINGTON COLLECTION)

Crimp and Barnan Electrical provide electrical services, which would not have been in high demand in 1907 but are needed today.

Whereas 100 years ago the concept of 'interior design' would have been alien to most people, Brent can now boast the firm Floor Solutions, 'domestic and contract flooring specialists', and Keith Holder, who personally runs his small business supplying quality rigid or flatpack kitchens and bedrooms. Peter Sings is a bespoke furniture maker and repairer.

A century on Lloyds TSB is still here and the mobile NatWest Bank comes once a week.

Mary Jane, one of the staff at The Crumb and Cuppa in Station Road, part of the Home Bakery.

Patrick Benacer and Ken Austin, with (seated) Claire Austin, Aminah Benacer and Linda Austin in the Stables Tea Room.

South Brent Flowers is a very successful business in Church Street owned by Jackie Lugger. Her grandmother, Mrs Moysey, started a small flower shop in Station Road which Jackie took over before moving to Church Street. Here Jackie (left) is with Cathie Pannell, who works in the shop. Both Jackie and Cathie, along with Debbie Burnitt, who has also worked in the shop, have won national awards for floristry.

Right: The staff of The Mare and Foal. Left to right, back row: Elaine Pengelly, Pam Honeywill, Avril Kelly, Eileen Blockley with Tess, Natasha Cooke, Joan Brown; kneeling: Mary Bradford, Anne Carter and Lucy Simister (manageress).

Jane Wellens and Penny Wainwright at the doorway of Artworks in Station Road. There have been outlets for local artists at various times in South Brent. In the late 1970s Alf and Gladys Russell opened the Russell Gallery in Fore Street. It was reported in 1978 that, 'Usually if a business closes down after only a short time it's a sign that things may not be going too well but the opposite is true of the Russell gallery in South Brent. Now they are closing the Gallery because it has become too busy for them. They did not think there would be such a large demand for hand-made pottery that a project which started as a retirement project would grow too big.'

The staff at Moortek. Founders Richard Cleave and Tracey Cleave with Neil Edlin and Kevin Chamberlain.
(PHOTOGRAPH BY GREG TAYLOR, FROM THE CLEAVE COLLECTION)

As well as having a large primary school, health centre and dental practice, South Brent is also served by Ann Ellison, a registered osteopath who has been working in the community for many years, and Sally Blades, an acupuncturist. In the same building, John Bevan works as an accountant.

Of the public houses in Brent, only the Anchor has ceased trading. Today's refreshment rooms are The Crumbs and Cuppa, attached to the Home Bakery, and The Stables Tea Room, part of the Pack Horse. There is the addition today of the Friary Fish and Chip shop. Today accommodation is available not only in some of the pubs in the village but also in several hotels and guest-houses such as Glazebrook House, Didworthy House, Clobells House and Church House, as well as at caravan parks.

At the beginning of the twenty-first century, there is a wide range of businesses serving the needs of today's inhabitants which certainly would not have been found 100 years ago – Moortek for IT needs, Antastic, the one-stop print and design shop, RM Services Fabrication and Welding services, PECS electrical control systems and PD Devices, who manufacture surge protectors. Simon Fox operates in television aerials and electrics, while Paul Timmins runs a taxi service.

Robert Savery noted that:

Today's farming has changed. We have four farms which until quite recently didn't have any dairy cows, while a fifth farm had as many dairy cows as all the farms of 50 years ago put together, if not more. There are now only three farms in the parish that actually milk cows.

Farming today is now more specialised, some beef, some feed, some sheep, but there are not many pig farmers in this area now. In this area there are plenty of sheep farmers but not many farms, as the farmsteads are becoming valuable places to live.

Postwar agricultural production increased so much that we went from a severe shortage to a glut. That was shown in the relative prices of sheep. In 1955 a worker could buy two sheep with his wage. Today it is more like ten.

The Post Office

A lot is spoken today about the importance of the Post Office as the centre of community life, and so it has been in South Brent.

As long ago as 1850 William White mentions a Post Office in Brent at R. Mitchell's, with letters coming and going via Ivybridge. By 1870 the Morris and Co. *Directory* tells us that Henry Veale was the postmaster, as well as being a boot and shoemaker. Letters from Ivybridge arrived at 8.25a.m. and were dispatched at 4.50p.m. The Post Office was also a money-order office and Post Office Savings Bank. Brent Post Office was also responsible for the sub-

post offices at North Huish, Avonwick, Diptford and, from 14 November 1901, Aish. It was a busy place. Between 18 and 23 October 1897 the Post Office log-books record that 2,495 letters were delivered from the Brent Post Office.

The 1902 Kelly's *Directory* records that R.H. Gill then ran the Post Office. By 1914, Brent Post Office also had responsibility for the Board of Trade Unemployment Insurance. In 1903 Mr Gill secured the contract for the supply of bread and flour to the Devon and Cornwall Sanatorium at Didworthy

A daily mail delivery to the Carew Arms started on 1 February 1903, and postal deliveries to Rattery were transferred to Brent in May. Sometimes special deliveries were arranged for special events. Brent races took place on 24 May 1904, and 53 forwarded telegraph messages and nine press messages are recorded as having been dealt with. When the Plymouth Company Boys' Brigade held their camp at Corringdon Ball between 29 July and 6 August 1910, two deliveries were granted daily. Fred Hannaford, who undertook the job, delivered 496 letters and 19 parcels during this time. The following notice appeared in the press on 10 September 1906:

Post Office Telegraphs
Pursuant to the Provisions of
The Telegraph Acts 1863 to 1904

NOTICE IS HEREBY GIVEN that his Majesty's Post-Master-General, having obtained the consent in that behalf of the body having control of the public road between the Great Western Railway, near the Station, and The Rock, South Brent, intends to place a telegraph over and along the said public road, and for that purpose to erect and maintain posts in and upon the said public road under the powers conferred on him by the Telegraph Acts above-mentioned
H. BABINGTON SMITH, Secretary
General Post Office, 8th September 1906

In May 1908 a newspaper report described a situation which could almost be paralleled today:

South Brent Post Office
Although the external appearance of the South Brent Post Office has not been altered, the interior has for several weeks been undergoing renovation and extension. During the last ten years, the work has developed by leaps and bounds. The amount of mail work has increased enormously and the establishment of the Public Telephone Exchange recently has compelled the Postmaster, Mr R.H. Gill to provide more accommodation.

The adjoining cottage [the old Post Office until 1894] has been secured on a lease and a doorway connecting with the present office has enabled a bag and basket room to be made where the parcel post can be dealt with separately from the letter mails. This will be

a great advantage at Christmas time. The postmen's sorting room has been provided with separate benches for nine men at each delivery, apart from the sorting tables for the clerical staff. The rooms over the added portion have been converted into store-rooms. The whole premises are now spacious, light and airy. Gas light has been installed in place of oil lamps. All the telegraph and telephone wires have been removed from their terminals on the house and connected with an immense pole at the rear of the building so fixed as to take subscribers' wires from every direction. The alteration is very satisfactory and will suffice for future developments for some time to come.

In July 1911 it was reported that:

Mr A. Catt of the Royal Oak stables has secured the contract for carrying Post Office mails between Brent and Kingsbridge. The work has so far increased as to necessitate a double-horsed carriage instead of the single one as heretofore.

Sunday apparatus duty, introduced from 31 December 1911, was undertaken by postmen Davis, Soper, Hard and Moores.

Discipline was strict in those days. Mr J. Lemon, one of the postmen, was suspended from duty for being drunk on 18 November 1911. He was summoned for drunkenness at Totnes magistrates' court on 8 January 1912. Mr H. Veale was summoned for salmon poaching on the same date. The first had his wages reduced, the second had his stripe deferred for six months.

On the other hand, the postmen did find time to celebrate. It was reported in May 1904 that:

About a dozen of the employees and friends of the South Brent Post Office met at the Assembly Room, Anchor Hotel, on Saturday night when a smoking concert was arranged and presentation made to Mr E.W. Matters (town postman) on the occasion of his marriage... which took the form of a beautiful coal cabinet and fine brass lamp. It was handed to Mr E.W. Matters with the best wishes of the postal staff generally. Subsequently a very enjoyable evening was spent and songs were given by Messrs G. Clark, J. Knapman, A. Weymouth (2), R. Codd, and A. Elliott.

In November 1912 another newspaper report reads:

About 20 members of the Post Office staff assembled in the sorting room on Thursday evening to bid farewell to Miss E.A. Tope, clerk, who is leaving to take up another appointment in Cardiff. The postmaster, Mr R.H. Gill, who made the presentation, said he regretted to lose such a good and trustworthy officer as Miss Tope, who added one more to the list of those who had been trained at South Brent and were now making good progress in the service. On behalf of the Staff and himself, Mr Gill

handed her a brown leather dressing and travelling bag bearing a suitably inscribed silver plate.

From the early 1900s postmaster Mr R.H. Gill was president of the National Federation of Sub-Postmasters' Devon Branch and as such was required to attend presentations to members of the profession from all over Devon.

In July 1915 there was yet another presentation, this time a retirement:

In the sorting room of South Brent Post Office all the staff assembled on Monday night for the purpose of presenting Mr Henry Blight (postman) with a testimonial on his retirement. In asking Mr Blight to accept the gift of a beautiful armchair, Mr R.H. Gill (Postmaster) referred to Mr Blight's long official career, which extended over 40 years. During that long period, he had honestly and faithfully carried out his duty and now retired with unblemished conduct. He hoped that the chair would be a great pleasure to him and always remind him of the pleasant associations with the South Brent postal staff. Mr W.H. Veale (senior postman) also referred to Mr Blight's good qualities and wished him many years of peaceful retirement.

The motor mail from Totnes started on 1 March 1923

The postbox at Lydia Bridge, the oldest surviving postbox in South Brent. Registered as No. 30, it was installed on 24 December 1894, with collections at 7.15a.m., 11.00a.m., and 7.50p.m. However, this was not the first box to be installed, that was No. 11 at Brent Mill, which was put in on 3 February 1875, again with three collections a day. It was replaced with a more modern box.

Description	No	When erected	Place of Box	Collections
wall	11	February 3 1875	Brent Mill	8.30am,11.30am.8.10 m
"	30	December 24 1894	Rock Bridge	7.15am,11.00am,7.50pm
bracket	31	April 14 1897	Brent Station	7.10am,10.20am,3.15pm,8.00pm
wall	58	August 30 1897	Aish SO	7.35am,7.45pm
"	33	November 22 1897	Gara Bridge Station	7.25 pm
wall	66	June 1915	Diptford SO	Early closing days
wall	20	March 14 1898	Hillside	7.45am,10.50am,7.40pm
wall	6	February 14 1899	Harbourneford	6.45pm
wall	34	Transferred from Ivybridge	Wrangaton	7.15pm Sundays 8.10pm
wall	41	Transferred from Buckfastleigh	Marley	6.55am,6.30pm Sundays 7.55am
wall	42	October 30 1903	Bennicknowle	6.40am, 6.15pm, Sundays 9.25am
wall	43	October 10 1904	Rattery Mill Cross	8.20am,5.00pm, Sundays 9.15am
wall	44	March 8 1905	Stidston Cross	6.15am,6.45pm,Sundays 9.30am
wall	45	April 3 1905	Lutton	6.30am,6.00pm
wall	49	May 16 1906	Carew Arms	6.15am,7.20pm,Sundays7.15pm
wall	55	November 10 1909	Didworthy Cross	
wall	80	December 2 1927	Wrangaton Manor	
	84	September 1 1930	Cheston	
	88		Rattery SO	

The above list of postboxes comes from the Post Office Log-book of the time.

at the same time as the Kingsbridge mail cart ceased.

A report of 12 March 1925 tell of the expansion of the telephone service at Brent:

Telephone Extension at South Brent

So rapid has the telephone developed at South Brent, doubtless due to the energy of the local manager, that a fourth switchboard is now being installed at the Post Office exchange to cope with the daily expansion. The Post Office department are alert to the situation and anticipate great things according to the plant they are laying down. Over a hundred wires leading from the four entrance roads are being put underground in lead cables enclosed in earthenware pipes. The new switch-board is of the latest type and is said to be the first installed in the West of England. Provision has been made for near on four hundred subscribers and for about 20 trunk and junction circuits. The limited space in the Post Office has needed reorganising the fixtures to accommodate the apparatus. The old form of obtaining the power from le Clanche batteries is to be scrapped and the generating power will be provided by the installation of gas engine power at the rear of the building. The work will take some months to complete, but when accomplished South Brent Post Office will be one of the most up to date telephone exchanges in the West of England. It has already direct communications with all the near towns and the new machine is capable of providing whatever may be required. At first some skill will be required in the manipulation of the intricate machinery, but Mr Gill, the local postmaster, says the difficulty will be easily overcome.

The early log-books make frequent mention of the upkeep of the handcarts. A new station handcart was made by Mr Langler on 5 December 1898 at a cost of 30s. using the old wheels and axle from the previous one. On 15 May 1900 the wheels were repaired at a cost of 8s. On 12 November 1902 Mr Langler fitted the apparatus wheelbarrow with two new sides for 12s. Again, Mr Langler repaired the wheelbarrow – one new side and painting on 19 August 1911 – for 9s. The station hand-cart was repaired and repainted by Mr Langler on 31 August 1912 for 15s.

Aish sub-Post Office, situated in what is now Box Cottage, opened on 14 November 1901. On 25 January 1904 the cash reserve held there was increased to £20. On 14 May the residents of the

Lydia Mill, South Brent, c.1900. (THE SHARVILLE COLLECTION)

Around the Square

Three photographs showing the Dartmoor Hunt meeting in South Brent. Hunting has for centuries been part of Brent life. 'The Square' is the venue for the annual Boxing Day meet for the Dartmoor Hunt. It continues to draw large crowds of supporters from the area. (THE RUSH AND CRANCH COLLECTIONS)

Around the Square

The Royal Oak, c.1900. The outlet of the leat that came down from Hillside can be seen in the centre of the picture. (THE CRANCH COLLECTION)

Fore Street is known locally as 'The Square', being in the heart of the community. This early-twentieth-century view from the top of Stockbridge Lane shows Station Road. (THE SHARVILLE COLLECTION)

Left: Station Road in the 1950s. Note the newsagency run by Miss Manning next to the Anchor, with Barclays Bank next door.
(THE MILLER COLLECTION)

Below: This photograph of the top of Plymouth Road by W.R. Gay, the Brent photographer, was sent as a postcard to Mademoiselle M. Revol in Valence, France, by the 8.30pm post on Thursday 26 June 1913. The picture was taken before Woodhaye Terrace was built, the buildings ending at the School and Congregational chapels. Notice Mr Blight's shop on the corner of Bowling House.
(THE SHARVILLE COLLECTION)

hamlet received their first Sunday delivery. The Sunday delivery to Didworthy started on 3 September and that to Diptford residents on 12 November. It was not until 14 February 1909 that Wrangaton got a Sunday delivery, with Harbourneford following just over a year later, on 13 March 1910.

On 12 January 1902 the telegraph messenger was established. In May 1905 the telegraph poles to the Carew Arms were renewed and on 9 February 1906 a Morse sounder instrument was installed in Brent Post Office.

The Post Office, from a painting by Christine Raikes.

Communications reached new heights when, on 20 June, the trunk telephone call office opened. The operator, Miss Cook, came out from Plymouth and 'attended 13 calls on the first day'. It was not until 15 December, however, that the first residence came on line, Mr Prince in Somerswood being the first subscriber. It was some time before the second subscriber, Mr W.H. Hawke, was connected, on 29 February 1908. The hours of telephone duty were decided upon as 8a.m.–8p.m. on weekdays and 8.30a.m.–10 30a.m. on Sundays.

In April 1911 it was estimated that telephone rental in Didworthy would be set at £7.10s.6d. and that there would be a special charge of £1.17s.6d. for new pole work.

Somewhat surprisingly, the Police Station was not connected until 7 August 1912 with the number Brent 5. The following October the South Brent exchange was transferred to the Exeter telephone district. By 1913 the trunk charge to Totnes, Buckfastleigh and Ivybridge had been reduced to 2d.

On 1 December the South Brent exchange, along with Avonwick, Bittaford, Diptford and Ugborough call offices, was brought under the control of the Plymouth district manager.

A new telephone switchboard was fitted on 2 December 1922 and the continuous telephone service

Post Office staff in the 1980s. Left to right, standing: *Ian Addison, Ian Andrews, Trevor Newman, Alan Kempster, Conrad Heath, Tim Martin;* front row: *Margaret Bannister, Christine Kempster, Trisha Crosbie, Carol Heath, Jackie Newman, Linda Newman, Val Addison.* (THE BANNISTER COLLECTION)

The site of the new Post Office, to be constructed by Mr and Mrs Foley on the site of the old sorting office.

Keith Male , photographer, who, along with John Presley, is successor to W.R. Gay, who took many of the photographs of early-nineteenth century Brent.

(KEITH MALE PHOTOGRAPHY)

Mrs 'Flip' Foley and Mr. Linda Newman in the Post Office in 2007.

Simon Coulton, who now runs his clockmaker's business in A.W. Cranch's former shop, follows in the tradition of Charles Mason of 100 years ago and Mr Arnold of Springfield Terrace in the mid twentieth century.

started on 1 August 1923, by which time both Ugborough and Bittaford had been transferred to South Brent. The telephone kiosk outside the Anchor Hotel, which opened on 11 June 1935, is now a listed building.

For many years the Post Office was run by the Holloway family.

A series of articles in the parish magazine in the 1980s described some of the various businesses in South Brent, and in April a profile of the new faces in the Post Office appeared:

Val and Ian Addison, the new owners of the Post Office Stores, have only been in the Village for a few months,

but already they feel at home. They had often thought about owning their own business one day, but the ambition has been realised sooner than they expected.

In June 1986, after viewing about 30 unsuitable businesses, they heard about the Post Office Stores, and decided to drop in to view it on their way to view another in the Saltash area. As soon as they saw it they knew that it was what they had been searching for, and they moved in on 14 January.

The Pantry, run by Steve and Carol Fogg. Left to right: Kay Mullen, Carol Fogg, Steve Fogg. Denise Langdon was also present.

The Post Office side of the business is Ian's responsibility, while Val runs the shop. His day starts at 6.00a.m. in the sorting office and finishes at 7.00p.m. except on the evenings when they go to the cash and carry. The Post Office closes on Wednesday afternoons. They sell sweets, tobacco, stationery, soft drinks, toys, some general household things, and are agents for the West of England Dry Cleaners. They intend to expand the video library and will be applying for a licence to run an off-licence, for which they are collecting signatures in support. Patsy Tidball, Marilyn Bullen and Shirley Livermore staff the shop and Post Office and there are five postmen – Roy Baker, Tony Bird, Terry Fiveash, Eddie Chapple and Trevor Newman.

There follows a poem written by Tom Anderson to 'celebrate' the laying of the new water main in 2007.

South Brent
Oh, Paddy, South Brent is a wonderful place,
As you walk through its streets you'll fall flat on your face,
With roadworks and ditches and burst pipes galore,
If you think you can drive through – you can't any more.

They've closed all the roads for a month at a time
With dirty great diggers stretched out in a line.
There's six men or more formed up in a band,
But the only one working has a spade in his hand.

The holes that they dig they just sit all forlorn,
They've been there so long that they're growing a lawn,
But let's hope by summer they all will have gone
And the village once more will be South Brent's own home.

CHAPTER 3

Another Look at Civic Matters

South Brent Parish Council was set up under the Local Government Act 1894 and replaced the Ratepayers' Vestry and Parish Meetings held regularly prior to that date. The first meeting of the Parish Council was on 4 January 1895 at the Board School. The minutes of Ratepayers' and Parish Meetings from 1870 and Parish Council meetings to 1985 are kept at the Devon Records Office at Exeter. This list of Parish Council Chairman was compiled by Roger Elford. Historically, the head of parish 'government' in South Brent has been known as the Portreeve, Roger Elford writes.

Beating the Bounds

The custom of beating the parish bounds has been taking place in South Brent since time immemorial. Because the parish is very large it is the custom to beat the bounds in two sections, the moorland or outer bounds on one occasion and the inner bounds on another. On 6 July 1978, the title deeds for the lord of the manor of South Brent were conveyed to the Parish Council to be held by them as trustees on behalf of the parish. The responsibility for maintaining and upholding the ancient customs associated with this title therefore falls squarely upon the shoulders of those elected to serve on this Council. The Council could therefore claim that they have the right, however tenuous, to beat their bounds whenever they please, and that's exactly what they do.

In 1985 the following report of the Beating of the Inner Bounds appeared in the parish magazine for October:

On Saturday 7th September, a total of about 40 people took part in the beating of the inner bounds of the Parish from Gidley Bridge to Bullhornstone, although only half that number actually walked all the way. The party set out from Gidley Bridge at 9.30a.m. and walked to Marley Head, Hatchlands Farm and on to Westmoor

CHAIRMEN
of South Brent Parish Council

Jan 1895 Cllr W Pearse	April 1955 Cllr E.W. Nicholls
April 1900 Cllr R.J. Kingwell	April 1957 Cllr R. O'Shea
April 1907 Cllr Revd H. Speare-Cole	May 1959 Cllr A. Jefford
April 1910 Cllr J.W. Wakeham	May 1961 Cllr E.G. Pascoe
April 1914 Cllr J. Veale	May 1964 Cllr Mrs M.E. Collier
April 1919 Cllr E.W. Mead	May 1967 Cllr G.B. Preston
April 1922 Cllr R.H. Gill	May 1969 Cllr Maj.-Gen. V.D.G. Campbell
April 1925 Cllr W.F. Northmore	May 1972 Cllr L.R. Hard
April 1929 Cllr F.W. Shute	May 1974 Cllr Brig. J.S. Vickers
April 1931 Cllr C. Mead	May 1977 Cllr P.A.W. Moore
April 1934 Cllr T. Wakeham	May 1978 Cllr C.J. Eales
April 1937 Cllr A. Jefford	May 1979 Cllr P.A.W. Moore
April 1940 Cllr W.H. Soper	May 1987 Cllr Mrs A.V. Chapman
April 1943 Cllr C.L. Churchward	May 1991 Cllr P.A.W. Moore
April 1945 Cllr R. Damerell	May 1999 Cllr P.E.H. Kelly
April 1946 Cllr W.H. Soper	May 2003 Cllr Mrs I. McNevin
April 1948 Cllr C. Mead	May 2005 Cllr G.D. Richards
July 1949 Cllr G. Preston	
April 1953 Cllr F. Tidball	

South Brent Parish Council, elected on 3 May 2007. Left to right, back row: *Greg Wall, David Mould, Mark Copleston, Ron Akehurst, Kevin Chamberlain, Peter Kelly, Donald Wiseman;* front row: *Cathie Pannell, Glynn Richards, Jill Elms, Susan Jozsa, Julia Willoughby (Clerk to the Council). John Summers was unable to attend.*

(The Parish Council Collection)

Farm after crossing the Totnes- Avonwick road. Near the farm was a mud or slurry pit which was about two feet deep in places and some unfortunate walkers managed to fall in, much to the amusement of their companions! The route went on to Lincombe, where one of the posts which had been put in the river-bed during the last beating of the bounds was found. It had the name 'South Brent Parish Council' stamped in Dymo tape still intact, and it looked as though it had been there for only a short while rather than seven years – being in such good condition. It was a very warm day and by the time the walkers had reached Diptford Green they were

Beating the bounds in the early 1960s. Leading the group is Cllr Giff Pascoe, Chairman of the Parish Council, and in the party are Cllr John Johns (centre) and Cllr Norman Hard (second from right) with his daughter Melba, Christopher Westcott, Michael Hard, Peter Hall, Brian Bewsher, Nicholas Collier, Brian Hughes, and Lester Hard.

(The Hard Collection)

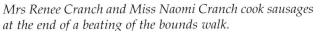

Mrs Renee Cranch and Miss Naomi Cranch cook sausages at the end of a beating of the bounds walk.

(THE SAVERY COLLECTION)

well ready for the lunchtime refreshments which were so efficiently provided by members of South Brent Youth Club. The afternoon's route wound through Charford, Horsebrook, past the Woodpecker Inn on to Owley and finally Bullhornstone. When the party was nearing the Woodpecker Inn three of the younger members decided that they would cross the A38 by means of the culvert which takes the river underneath the road (the boundary actually goes through the middle of this tunnel). The three (all girls) could not persuade the boys, some of whom had walked all the way, to join them. So Joanna Smith, Dominique Davy and Catherine Harris set off, accompanied by Michael Harley, who had also decided to have a go, and managed to get through to the other side despite some deep water. Arriving at Bullhornstone at 4:30p.m., the party was ready to sample the roasted lamb which had been given by Mr John Mead and roasted at the bakery in Loddiswell because the baker's oven in South Brent was not large enough! (Mr. Peter Moore had arranged the transportation of the lamb to and from Loddiswell.) This was the perfect end to what had been an enjoyable day.

It will be another seven years before the inner bounds are beaten again, but the outer bounds, from Bullhornstone across the moor to Gidley Bridge, are due to be beaten in two years' time.

The Inner Bounds were last beaten in August 2006.

Cllr Peter Kelly, then chairman of the South Brent Parish Council, wrote in the parish newsletter of

Top and above: *The 'Little Petre' boundary stone, together with what is thought to be the remains of 'Petre's Cross'. Little Petre is close to Western Whittabarrow and the cross is on Western Whittabarrow. You can just about make out the shoulders of the cross before it was beheaded!*

(THE SMITH COLLECTION)

October 2002 of the Beating of the Outer Bounds in that year:

The 8-10 mile walk began at Dockwell Green shortly after 9.30a.m., following the loyal address by the Chairman of the Parish Council, Cllr Peter Kelly (who was also one of the bus drivers for the day, along with Cllr Irene McNevin).

The 76 walkers found the first of many boundary stones, where Joseff Parke was 'bumped' very gently five times, once for each of his five years, so that he would remember the extent of the parish boundary in years to come.

The party included our Vicar, David Winnington-

Ingram, who had to leave at the Avon Dam to return to South Brent for a wedding service. Tea and coffee were gratefully received, while everyone had the opportunity to be guided through a passageway inside the dam, where the parish boundary is marked.

A party of 63 stalwart individuals continued on the walk, led by Tim Ferry, with members of the Dartmoor Rescue Group on hand, if required. We passed the remains of an old farm, usually covered by the water in the reservoir, ate lunch near disused tin workings and walked along part of the boundary which has existed since the Bronze Age.

At 4.15p.m. we reached Bullhornstone Farm, where Mr John Mead made a field available to the weary walkers, and pasties and drinks were provided by the Parish Council.

Ken Smith has researched the origins of the ceremony and in 1996 wrote an extensive essay, 'The History of Beating The Bounds of South Brent', from which the following extracts are taken:

Let all men know that we, parishioners of South Brent, in whom are vested the title, rights and privileges of Lord of the Manor, will this day, the 16th of September in the year of our Lord, one thousand nine hundred and ninety nine, beat the bounds of our ancient parish in accordance with precedent and time honoured custom. Thus demonstrating to all men for a further term of seven years, the limits and boundaries of our parish, God save the Queen.

This proclamation is issued by the chairman of South Brent Parish Council at the commencement of every beating the bounds ceremony.

The parish boundary of South Brent was determined, or 'mered', by the Ordnance Survey during 1883. The work of 'mereing' the parish of Brent was performed by one Sergeant James Ford (Royal Engineers) on behalf of the Government. He was assisted by a Mr William Henry Heath, Meresman for the Parish of South Brent. A boundary change on 1 April 1950 altered the original Parish by excluding a large area at Avonwick and placing it within the Parish of North Huish. Apart from this alteration the South Brent parish boundary has remained unchanged since 1883.

Beating of the Bounds is an ancient ceremony that has lasted for over 2,500 years, and in its own way conveys a story about certain aspects in the development of rural parishes. As with all folklore and legend, this old custom carries with it elements of truth about our forefathers and the life they led, and as such I firmly believe that it should be preserved and understood.

During his researches Mr Smith visited the archives of Devon County Council and studied many volumes written on the history of Devon and Dartmoor but was not able to find a definitive answer. He continues:

The Chairman of South Brent Parish Council, Peter Moore, kindly gave me access to the parish files on this subject. Within them I found comprehensive details of the perambulation ceremonies dating back to 4 August 1919. I must say that it gave me great pleasure

Chairman of the Parish Council Cllr Peter Moore with his wife Pearl lead the South Brent Carnival procession in a 1930 Morris Cowley driven by Mr Stephen Morris in 1980. (THE WOODHOUSE COLLECTION)

searching these records. So many young faces in the old photographs. Village characters, many of them sadly no longer with us. To me this was more than just a file on boundary beating. Within is an excellent record of the way that a village progresses or evolves and what a community does on its day off. Landlord, farmer, shopkeeper and poacher, all mixing together with a common cause of setting their boundaries for the coming years. Some on horseback, most on foot, hound and hare together in harmony. Nowadays this ceremony is usually terminated with a ram roast and cider for the participants. Years ago there are records of the usual feasting and drinking coupled with showground activities, a village fair. However when the parishioners of South Brent beat their bounds they have fun! It is still one of those occasions that is treasured by its participants. It's still an occasion for the youngsters of the village to leave their sound systems and TVs at home and learn something they perhaps didn't know about their surroundings. They still get the 'bumps' when crossing a bridge, and are dumped into the rivers when they are crossed.

While reading the files I came across a scrap of information from an old parish magazine. It was difficult to put a date on, but I believe it to have been printed during the sixties. Its contents are as follows:

'This ancient custom was done as a duty before the days of ordnance maps. It is said that at each important landmark a boy would be beaten, so as to impress upon his mind the position of the boundary between Brent Parish and those adjoining it. Presumably it was a different boy at each landmark! And if some had a ducking when crossing a stream, it only helped to memorise the route.'

Mr Smith was also given information by local people:

One local gentleman informed me that the reason for beating the bounds originated in the Dark Ages. Villagers gathered all the broomsticks they could lay their hands on. They then proceeded around the village, shouting at the tops of their voices, beating the ground, shrubs and just about anything that got in their way. They slowly moved to the outskirts of the village, kicking up one hell of a racket. The purpose of this was to scare away evil spirits (it would also scare away rats if plague was about). The spirits would leave the village in peace for a year or so and then it would all have to be done again.

Another, similar, suggestion was that on certain days during the year villagers would again gather broomsticks. This time they would perambulate the village or manor boundary. They would beat down all vegetation so that nothing could overgrow it, thus making a pathway all the way round. This exercise would ensure that the inhabitants of an area would all know where the limits of the land held by their Saxon or Norman lord and master extended.

During the late Saxon period penalties for a slave or bondsman were very harsh indeed if it were proved that they had strayed onto another man's land without permission. Every year the youth of a village or manor were taken by their elders and shown the limits of their lordship's land. The elders would beat the young boys and girls at every prominent landmark, such as a tree, river or bridge. This would instil from a very young age, and in an unforgettable manner, the limits of, for want of another word, freedom, for these lowly peasants.

Another ceremony similar to Beating the Bounds was, and sometimes still is, performed at Rogationtide, which falls on the fifth Sunday after Easter just before Ascension Day. Ken Smith writes:

These outdoor Rogation Processions were suppressed in England in 1547. The Act of Suppression must have had an undesirable effect on the Crown in some way, because in 1559 Queen Elizabeth I issued a Royal Injunction reordering the perambulation of the Parish at Rogationtide. I can find no record of the Royal Injunction ever being rescinded. Does this mean that priests are still obliged to Beat the Bounds every Rogationtide?

Be that as it may, Revd John Harper performed the ceremony during his incumbency. He and his congregation walked 'round the perimeter boundaries of a farm blessing the crops and other produce to ensure a good harvest.' Revd David Winnington-Ingram again revived it in 2007.

Policing

Mike Major writes of his time as a police officer stationed in Brent:

The current Police Station at South Brent was built as the beginning of the 1960s. Prior to its location at Sanderspool Cross, the Police Station was at the bottom of Church Street.

I moved to South Brent from Sidmouth in 1972, on 7 April, to be precise, and it snowed! At that time there were four police officers based at South Brent – PC Dick Morrish, PC Phil Joyce, PC Pete Rockey and myself, PC Mike Major. Three of us provided 16-hour cover with a panda car, as they were known then, and PC Rockey had a motorcycle covering the subdivision.

The South Brent section comprised the parishes of South Brent, Rattery, North Huish, Diptford and Ugborough, and formed part of the Totnes subdivision, part of Plympton 'G' division. The sergeants, an inspector and a chief inspector were all based at Totnes. This meant daily trips to Totnes to hand on all the necessary paperwork, and there was always plenty of it, even in those days.

At a rural station you dealt with everything from domestic incidents to public order, missing persons, crime, road traffic, firearms enquiries and licensing –

PC Mike Major outside the new South Brent Police Station with the new police Landrover. The vehicle was much better suited to the rural area, particularly in bad weather. (THE MAJOR COLLECTION)

Sergeant Ted Fowler, long-serving Brent police officer. (THE GOSS COLLECTION)

In the late 1930s this Brent police constable lodged with Mrs Maud Hard at Victoria Cottage.

PCSO Vicky Gummow joined the police team in South Brent in early 2007. She can be seen on street patrol in the community, making regular contact with the public.

Successful pupils from South Brent Primary School who were awarded their Cycle Safety and Awareness Training ertificates. The course was run by PC Jacqui Hopper and Robert Taylor, a member of staff at the school. Left to right: Jordan Finch, Duncan Taylor, Alistair Wiseman, Jack Chatwin, Mr Robert Tayler, PC Jacqui Hopper, Maddie Budden, Paige Lavers, Cassie Matthews, Kerri Dardis, Jack Underhill. (THE HOPPER COLLECTION)

The South Brent police team. Left to right: PC Jacqui Hopper, SPC Andy Phillips, PCSO Jay Vasey, SPC Bob Eddie, PCSO Paula Frain, Spc Paul Fardon, SPC Lisa Julyan, SPC Jon King, SPC Steve Thornhill, SPC (section officer) Jason Webb, PC Alan Lowe. (THE HOPPER COLLECTION)

there used to be 14 licensed premised in the South Brent section. We were also coroner's officers, making enquiries and preparing reports for HM Coroner on any sudden death, such as fatal road traffic accidents, industrial fatalities or deaths where a doctor was unable to issue a certificate as to the cause of death. The job was varied and interesting – you never knew from one day to the next what you would be dealing with. Dealing with such a wide variety of things you got to meet and know lots of people and, importantly, they got to know you.

I joined the Devon Constabulary as a police cadet in 1962 and became a police constable in 1964. Being a 'country boy', I wanted to work in a rural station, and this was fulfilled when I arrived at South Brent and remained here for 20 years until retirement.

Living and working in a rural location meant that you were able to become closely involved in the community. PC Dick Norrish was involved in setting up and running the Cricket Club. PC Phil Joyce was involved in setting up and running the Loft Youth Club in the old building which used to stand next to the London Inn. PC Pete Rockey was involved with the Parent Teachers' Association. I was first involved with the Scout Group as a committee member and then as Group Scout Leader, with the Primary School teaching Cycling Proficiency and in the Produce Association – being returned as Chairman for 27 years. There was also involvement with carnivals, fair days and the Village Hall Show! This was all done with the generous support of many people and would not have been possible without them.

When I first moved to South Brent the A38 ran through the village and much of the police work was related to traffic, which rapidly increased in the summer time with all the holiday traffic. Crossing the A38 at Sanderspool Cross from Kerries Road into Totnes Road could be quite hairy at times in the summer. I recall one wet summer's day when every holiday-maker decided they should visit Plymouth via the A38 (no dual carriageway then), and the tailback of traffic from Plympton reached Sanderspool Cross.

The building of the A38 dual carriageway made a great difference to the work. Accidents were greatly reduced and more serious traffic-related matters dropped dramatically. Unfortunately the better road meant that the criminal fraternity could move about more easily and the crime rate figures went up considerably.

I enjoyed my time as a Community Police Officer and got to know many people, which I think is essential in the role of a police officer. Personally, it was a privilege and a pleasure to be stationed at South Brent.

As with all communities, Brent has had, and still does have, many personalities. Below and overleaf we present just a small selection of those that have come to light.

Paul and Simon Wonnacott outside TC2. Paul writes: 'Between Nos 8 and 9 Station Road is a short lane leading to three buildings. These originally housed two blacksmiths and a slaughterhouse and served the stagecoach passengers who arrived to stay at the Anchor Inn. Of late ladies now long in the tooth themselves have recalled bringing their ponies to the last blacksmith, Mr Stan Stevens. His premises were adapted for the motor car and Bill Thomas ran Station Road Motors before Douglas and Pat Johnston bought No. 9 with two of the outbuildings, changing the shop from Winzer's Butcher shop to the Treasure Chest. I rented the old smithy and, in keeping with its history, it became a bicycle store and workshop. After more than a quarter of a century the area remains a resting-place for steel horses!' Paul is often seen 'treading the boards' for SBADS at the Village Hall (THE WONNACOTT COLLECTION)

Another Look at Some Brent Personalities

Irvy Wood and Malcolm Tidball take a rest during a Christmas carol sing at the Pack Horse. Irvy was an accomplished tailor working for many years at Salter's in Station Road. Malcolm founded and ran The Friary in Church Street and was involved in many Brent activities. (The Wilkins Collection)

Mrs Lillian Wakeley enters into the spirit of a pre-war carnival with her impersonation of Charlie Chaplin. (The Wakeley Collection)

Ben Wilkins pulls his first pint at The Pack Horse watched by his parents, Alan and Sylvia. At the time, Ben was believed to be probably the youngest pub boss in the South West - at the tender age of 20! (The Wilkins Collection)

Brent Chelsea Pensioner Cyril Gove with Larry Wooton, one- time Brent horological expert. (The Wilkins Collection)

Left: *Fred Milton, another Chelsea pensioner.* (The Church Collection)

Church Street looking towards Fore Street in the early 1900s. The motor-car would have refuelled underneath the Pratt's petrol sign immediately behind it. (THE CRANCH COLLECTION)

Miss Bentley's School in Hillside in the early part of the twentieth century (THE WAKEHAM COLLECTION)

CHAPTER 4

Another Look at Growing Up in Brent

Growing Up in the Early-Twentieth Century

On 2 August 1993 Evie Hard, Rosalie Smeeth and Anita Perkins recorded their memories of growing up in Brent in the early-twentieth century.

Evie Hard, born and married in Brent, lived at No. 3 Wellington Square from the time she was married. She was 79 years old at the time of the interview.

Rosalie Smeeth was born in Somerset and came to Brent when she was 12 months old. Her mum lived down by the river but was worried that her children might drown in the river or the leat for the mill. The only place she could find to move to was No. 26 Church Street, which was where Rosalie still lived. She spent the first years of her married life in Plymouth but was blitzed out and came to Brent. She was then widowed and stayed. She was 88 years old at the time of the interview.

Anita Perkins was born in Wrangaton but came to school and was married in St Petroc's in 1934. She recalled those early days:

There were six of us and my father worked on the railway and we lived in a house that belonged to the railway and he used to have to go a quarter of a mile to fetch our drinking water and he used to carry it in buckets. He walked all the way down the garden path, which was such a long way, and back along the railway bank and up a big slope – like carrying buckets up and down a mountain to get drinking water. We used to get washing water from the end of the cottages. You used to have to dip it up and we caught rainwater, of course, but drinking water was a treasure to us. It was always kept under the stairs covered up with a cloth so that the flies, etc., couldn't get in. It was very precious to us because of the length of time it took to collect it and how far it was to walk. He didn't use a yoke. He made sure he was well balanced.

Evie could also remember fetching water from a well across Wellington Square.

Rosalie Smeeth recalled her schooldays. The boys and the girls had separate entrances. They had to behave. If they didn't behave they would have to go 'in the line' and were not allowed to go out to play. The toilets were outside. The children in each class were of about the same age and stayed in Brent School until they left at 14 years old. Evie Hard noted that there was no 'advanced teaching'. They could all remember Mr and Mrs Hull, the headmaster and his wife. Anita Perkins could remember being pushed to school as she was not well as a child. 'The worst bit was pushing home.' The ladies could recall Mr Bidmead taking singing lessons. Rosalie Smeeth remembered him saying:

... who'll come out and sing so and so. All of a sudden a boy, who lived up at Wrangaton, shouted out, 'Rosie Soper will, sir!' 'I beg pardon,' I said. 'I don't think so.' Well us both had to go out and sing then. It was so funny in they days.

Anita Perkins remembered the capes that were purchased with the Feoffee money. They were black capes with a red number on them. 'You put your name on the list and brought the cape back the next day.' She also recalled having cocoa during the lunch hour when the other children went home:

For years I was the cocoa lady. We used to buy Cadbury's cocoa. I was allowed to keep the coupons and

Miss Doris Manning in service in the early-twentieth century. (THE GOSS COLLECTION)

I sent them away. I had three helpers. We had a big box of chocolates and I can remember a big ceremony to divide those chocolates between the four of us. That was our wages for making the cocoa and washing up, of course. The cocoa was heated on a gas stove in the kitchen, which was also used for cookery classes.

On leaving school Evie went into domestic service. It was either live in or by day. She first went to Kerries to Mrs Maddock and then went to General and Mrs Armstrong, where she stayed until she was married. 'I lived in and had a nice bedroom. They used to take me on holiday to places like the Tidworth Tattoo. It was very educational.' She was a cook general:

I was taught cooking by Mrs Armstrong – she was a great cook. They used to have a woman come in two or three times a week to do extra jobs and they had a gardener. You were allowed out and if you went out you had to be back by six to help get the evening meal. You had your half a day a week – not the same day every week. I went home to my mother and she had a few jobs for me to do, having a family. I wore a uniform and cap and a white apron. When I had a green dress, not a navy blue one, I was extra posh because most wore black or navy blue. I didn't have to wear black stockings. [When she was talking in 1993 black stockings had become very fashionable but those who had to wear them in service hated the sight of them.]

Anita was not able to work because she had a leaky valve in her heart and in those days it was not operated on:

I went down to be a nursemaid to a farmer down to Dean. They were farmers down at Cheston and they moved from Cheston to this farm down at Dean, right at the top of the hill. My mother thought that would be very nice because she knew the woman and I was just to help her with anything I could. She'd feed me for it but I didn't have very much pay. I was there a couple of weeks and I didn't go home because it wasn't very easy. My sister was sent out to see that I was alright and when she told her (mother) where I was living she sent her poste-haste to bring me back because it was in the back of beyond. But it was very nice. It was a pity really because I was quite happy there. I remember it as if it were yesterday.

Anita then went as a help to Cornsclose, where she lived in. As time went on she got more medical help, which helped terrifically.

Rosalie worked at different places in the village then. 'I went down to the London Inn serving in the pub. They took in visitors, you see, so I did anything there that I could do.' She then went to a friend's place in Plymouth – a fish and chip business. Just before she got married she went to Ilfracombe on seasonal work: 'At the end of the season I expected to get the sack but I was offered longer term employment in a restaurant. She never worked on Sundays and lodged out.'

She recalled that there were a lots of things like swimming to do. 'It was like going on holiday for me.'

Childhood Around the War Years

Growing up in and around Brent during the war years and just before is recalled by Pam Honeywill,

A view of Church Street at the turn of the century. Traffic is conspicuous by its absence, except for the wagonette at the top of the street. The Co-op has not yet been built.
(THE SHARVILLE AND CRANCH COLLECTIONS)

Joan Ayres, Margaret Eales, Sally Newman, Betty Vallance, Nano Wood, Mary Bradford and Sheila Cockings. Their reminiscences reflect the need in those days for children to amuse themselves. They recall coming home from school and having a cup of tea, then changing and going out to play, mainly in the roads. Mary Bradford remembers playing donkey and two-ball on the wall outside Andrews's Fish and Chip shop. Children would skip or play with tops and hoops made by Stan Stevens, the local blacksmith. Pam Honeywill recalls playing hide and seek in Fore Street and the base (homey) was the old jubilee lamppost that stood in the centre of the junction. Mary Bradford also recalls playing with the kneelers from the Catholic Church on the grass outside. Her parents were the caretakers. Pam Honeywill and Sheila Cockings remember the concerts that the children put on for their peers. They recall that one of their pieces was a rendering of 'There I was waiting at the church'. The audience would be charged a penny to watch, but they cannot remember what they did with the money!

Sally Newman recalls that Saturday evenings were spent at friends' houses. The children would sit around the fire whilst their parents and their friends played darts. Families would play darts and card games for amusement.

Children all had their specific jobs to do. Margaret Eales remembers delivering milk to the top of Corn Park in two cans, one on either side, whilst Nano Wood can remember going to fetch milk from Mrs Emma Hard, and recalls the day when she dropped the jug and had to go home and get another one. Joan Ayres can remember going with Joyce Pulleyblank when she delivered the *Evening Herald* to houses. Other tasks included fetching gas mantles from Mr Giggs at the gasworks, and accumulators, the forerunner of the modern battery. The danger with gas mantles was that they could easily be broken and the accumulators would run down quite quickly so that those listening to the wireless would have to strain to hear to what was going on.

Water was collected from various communal taps around the village. One such tap was in Station Road. Joan Ayres recalls one man going up to the tap complete with soap and towel and washing in the cold water in the morning.

During the primrose season many children recall going out to pick primroses that were then sent off to London.

Nano Wood recalls that during the Second World War her family was living in Chapelfields. Whenever there was the possibility of an air raid during the summer, when there was double summer time, the warden would come around blowing his whistle as a warning. All the residents would come out of their houses, sit on their steps and watch the aircraft on the way to bomb Plymouth as they got caught in the searchlights. She can recall that her grandfather, who

was an elderly gentleman at that time, said that if he was going to die he would die in bed, and so would not move.

As they grew older both Mary Bradford and Pam Honeywill remember belonging to the Junior Air Corps for a short while.

Two of the ladies recall having told their parents that they were going to Totnes, but instead took a train from Brent Station to Kingsbridge. When they came to go back to Brent they found that they had missed the last train. They were scared at finding themselves in Kingsbridge, not knowing anybody. The Kingsbridge stationmaster told them how naughty they were. Fortunately, there was a goods train about to go up to Brent and so they were allowed to travel home in a cattle truck. Needless to say, when they got home they were not the most popular young people in Brent!

Another activity in their youth was attending dancing classes in Avonwick.

A highlight of the year for people in Brent was the race meeting at Stippadon. Pam Honeywill recalls how many people would go up to the races on the edge of the moor, hanging onto the side of the dust-cart. They would also walk all the way to the races at Buckfastleigh. Sometimes Gordon Wakeham would pick up the youngest ones and take them over in his car, while on other occasions they would go by horse and cart.

A Church Street Childhood in the 1950s

This section, produced by the author for the South Brent Parish Council newsletter, was first published in October 2005:

Those of us who have spent a large part of our life living in South Brent are often asked how much it has changed over the years. Many of you know that I come from a family that has roots in Brent, which go back over many generations into the aeons of time. My own younger days revolved around Church Street and Wellington Square. We lived first in Victoria Cottage, which my grandfather, Alfred Scott Hard, had created from several cottages off Church Street, and then, on my grandmother's death in 1954, we moved to No. 1 The Exchange.

Church Street has not greatly changed physically since my childhood except that the cottages on the corner at the bottom have been demolished, except for one, which, vastly extended, is now known as Stag's Head House. Its garden occupies the site of another three cottages. Cedarholme sits where another three cottages stood. At the bottom of the street was the Police Station, but apart from change of use most shops still exist. Wellington Square has undergone a 'facelift' – the final resting-place for the jubilee lamppost base – but is basically still the same.

A later picture of Church Street, probably in the 1950s. The Co-operative Society Ltd is on the left-hand side of the street. Mr and Mrs F. Tidball's grocery shop has its window covered against the sun and next door is S.F. Brockington's pharmacy. Halfway down the street, just above the car, is the Andrews's fish and chip-cum-general store. The lack of traffic and people suggests that this picture was taken on early-closing day – Wednesday.   (MRS. V. JORDAN'S COLLECTION)

Wellington Square at the beginning of the 21st century. In the 1950s Church Street children would play ball games in the square. The paved area was level with the road and rough surfaced, and the jubilee lamp, which now holds a sun dial, was set in the centre of the junction of Fore Street, Church Street and Station Road as a functioning lamp.

(THE FORD COLLECTION)

In my childhood, what traffic there was travelled quite happily in both directions. Like many children all over the country, we played in the street. We would play marbles in the gutters or 'chalk' on the road using the slate from the bridge underneath Hawke's Bridge (the lower station bridge). We would stop if a car went by, or if Mr Marks, who lived in a caravan where St Dunstan's car park now is, came by in his chain-driven wheelchair. Sometimes we would see Frank Rogers on his way to church with his crutches stretched out until they took up a large part of the road.

Yes, it rained in those days just as it does now, but on sunny summer afternoons we would often go down L'Aune to play in the river, or sometimes go with Miss Bessie Heard, who lived at the top of the street, out for a 'picnic' in the meadows down Somerswood Lane, or along the path fields below Aish. Sometimes we would go along Crackhill's path (now it would appear to be known as 'Fat Man's Alley') to Weir Pathfields. Then there was the train-spotting on Station Bridge, complete with Ian Allen books. Summer evenings would see a whole group of children playing rounders or some other form of ball game in Wellington Square, using the manhole cover as 'home base' and lampposts and other features as the posts. I cannot ever remember a window getting broken! A truce would be called if a car came by. The yew tree in the churchyard served as a hiding-place when necessary.

Many of the men who used to stand on Anchor corner lived in Church Street or Wellington Square. Jimmy Garland, Bill Endacott, John Scott, 'Jack' Hard could be found watching the goings-on in the 'Square', as well as, of course, Arthur Manning, Brent's famous blind organist. At various times during the day he would make his way down to the Church, feeling his way along the edge of the pavement with his white stick or holding the shoulder of one of the others to practise or just sit. Frank Watts, the sexton, lived in Sunnyside with his wife, Gladys. Such was the community feeling in Church Street that when my mother, who had been born in one of the cottages, told him that we were moving to Springfield Terrace, he was quite upset that a 'Church Street maid' was moving 'over the bridge'. We would also often see Mr Knott on his way from his cottage in Brent Mill to do his duties as verger at St Petroc's.

And then there were Nora and Lottie – Miss Andrews and Mrs Knapman – who ran one of the two fish and chip shops in Church Street. Many Brentonians will have their own memories of going into the shop, which was also a general store and sold everything from groceries to pens and paraffin, as well as lighting sticks and, of course, fish and chips. In the back room sat old Mrs Andrews, keeping a keen eye on the shop and watching television – one of the first around – the blue hue from the screen visible in the shop. Many of the Church Street children would go to Mrs. Briggs's to watch children's television when she bought her first black and white set.

Hot summer Wednesday afternoons were not the best time to be around. That was when the offal lorry arrived from Exeter to take the residue from Mr White's slaughterhouse behind The Exchanges. The waste was collected in open bins and loaded onto the back of the lorry to be taken away. The animals would be delivered on Monday for slaughter and butchering. The slaughterhouse was adjacent to our garden plots and I can remember not being allowed down there whilst the process was taking place, but it was a far cry from the sterile conditions that we have today.

South Brent Playgroup – the Early Years

Geraldine Gould, who founded the South Brent playgroup, recalls the early days:

The playgroup came to the village shortly after they began to appear in towns throughout the country. Reasonably new to the village, with a toddler who wanted friends to play with, I had invited parents and children to an informal group in our house. Peter Feloy, the new headmaster, was keen to introduce 'family grouping' for the younger classes in the school, and a playgroup would make a helpful lead-in to this. He called a meeting, and, as no one else volunteered, I offered.

Playgroups then were organised by groups of mothers with their children. The Village Hall, a very different place in those days, was the obvious venue. A group of us got together for the first essential, to scrub the floor! The hall was dauntingly large for small children, so hundreds of chairs were used to divide the hall up into areas – a painting area, a book corner, a home corner. The mothers brought their own children's toys.

The early years of the South Brent playgroup. Children playing in the 'car' made from an old cabin trunk by the woodwork class at Ivybridge Secondary Modern school.

(THE RUNDLE COLLECTION)

The indoor slide. **Left to right:** *Mary Honeywill holds her daughter Wendy, Gary Wilton, Molly Wilton, Helen Levett, ?, Andrew Field.* (THE RUNDLE COLLECTION)

Regulations had just begun to be brought in. Somewhere a child-minder had allowed toddlers to play around a portable oil stove, with the inevitable result. The government weighed in with a typical blanket of rules. An essential course was being organised in Torquay, but without a car I had to manage on the bus for ten evening sessions. The number of hand-washing facilities for the children was specified - bowls of water on chairs met this one, allowing one to reflect that the bureaucrats who frame these things have very little practical experience. As a holding measure, my husband went into Exeter and read up the new regulations and, for a while, we opened for one hour 55 minutes and so were exempt.

The South Brent Art Exhibition at Ivybridge Secondary Modern School, staged by Ken Fernee. The exhibition was first staged in the Royal Oak. (THE RUNDLE COLLECTION)

Heating was difficult in the winter months, as the Village Hall was 'warmed' by two coke-fired heaters. When lit they belched out fumes, necessitating the opening of windows and nullifying their effect. The cost of fuel was a problem on which we disagreed with the hall authorities, and I recall on one occasion taking up my kitchen scales to weigh the amount we used!

All the mothers helped on a rota, though at times the reverse was almost a problem. Some children seemed to need an experience of being without mum for a while, but it was a long walk from Crowder Park down to the hall; we needed to arrange somewhere for them out of sight. Two exceptions to this being an all-mothers affair need mentioning. One was Phyllis Rundle, who had worked in nurseries from way back during the war. With her own children now teenagers, she came and offered to help and was a Godsend, the kind of person who did all the hard work, taking children to the toilet, washing painty hands, but standing back and letting the mothers take all the decisions.

Another was Lucy Moore, who then lived up at Lutton, and came in each session with homemade

South Brent Playgroup were regular entrants in the summer carnival. Here Katie Taylor, Hannah Murgatroyd and Lorraine Peard portray three of Snow White's companions. (THE MURGATROYD COLLECTION)

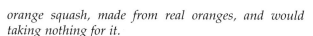

orange squash, made from real oranges, and would taking nothing for it.

One of the things that escaped us for a year or so was that playgroups normally made a small charge. Rent for the hall was raised by a cake stall under what was then the Anchor and the usual other fund-raising events – I still have a poster from the First Anniversary May Fair. A less usual way was a duplicated magazine entitled Bravo Brent. *Apart from items about the play-group there were articles on such diverse subjects as 'The Mills of Brent' and 'Local Place Names'. The first cover, by local artist Sally Cottis, showed a number of the children in the playgroup 'car', whilst the second had a charcoal drawing by Ken Fernee. It was dupli-cated, in the then common foolscap size, free by Jack Soper on his garage machine and sold for one shilling. Sadly, it only ran to two issues.*

Lack of funds also led to parents making equipment for the new group. This was the age of 'good' toys, when firms like Galt and Abbatt began, and their simple, solid designs could well be copied. One father made wooden boxes with doorways cut in them that piled up to make a large dolls' house; my husband made his first wooden jigsaws, little thinking he would still be doing this 40 years later. The playgroup 'car' was an old cabin trunk fitted with casters and a large steering wheel. The woodwork class at what was then Ivybridge Secondary Modern School made a large indoor slide, a very impres-sive affair that folded in half, but which sadly was in time dispensed with as too bulky – all the equipment had to be put away each day. One exception, however, was a sand pit in the grass area outside the hall, made from four old rail sleepers.

Kenneth Jameson had just published his definitive book on Pre-School art, showing how children should be allowed to develop naturally from their first 'big head' pictures; colouring books with adult-drawn outlines and stencils inhibit this and lead to the often-heard 'I can't draw'. I still fight against these things. It was decided to put on an exhibition of our playgroup children's art that would demonstrate how their natural skills develop, and were offered the free use of the room at the back of the Royal Oak for a Saturday. Unfortunately, the room, the present skittle alley, was needed on the Friday evening. We got around this problem by pinning all the paintings on sheets so we just had to go in and hang them up. One mother who offered to come in to be there during the day said she would take her knitting, feeling it would all be boring. She was amazed to find how it was all so fasci-nating. Ken Fernee was then the art master at Ivybridge and had a gallery in the school where he invited local artists to exhibit; he asked us to take the pictures, now more suitably hung, there, and it was surprising to note how interested the teenage pupils were. The exhibition finally went to County Hall and, of course, the children went along with their mothers to put the display up. An official approached to say that the children's voices could be heard in the august Council Chamber – you can imagine the mothers' reply!

Most of the children from those early days are now themselves parents with children in playgroup, but it is interesting to reflect on those enterprising early days.

Rosemary Stansbury writes:

When we moved to South Brent in October 1973 the playgroup was in the Village Hall and was run by Mrs Murphy, an experienced playgroup leader married to a doctor in Totnes. She came out twice a week to run the playgroup. I went along to see if I could help and I assisted for two years. She then wished to leave, and felt it was time the people of South Brent ran the playgroup themselves. I was asked to run the playgroup and, with Sue Norrish and Doreen Horan as assistants, the play-group continued. There were normally 20–25 children, and all the equipment, including a large slide, a play kitchen and artists' easels, was stored in the basement and had to be brought up the stairs and then put back in the basement at the end of each session. The playgroup could use the Patch in suitable weather for a short session after milk and biscuits. A Rising Fives group was started once a week after playgroup, run by Sue Norrish, usually for 3–5 children. In about 1982 I left, and Ginny Murgatroyd took over.

In March 1977 it came as a distinct shock to learn that the playgroup was in some difficulty and faced with the possibility of having to close down. Numbers had been dropping, even though there was a large number of pre-school children in Brent. Mrs Horan, the Secretary, told the editor of the parish magazine, Olive Dodd, that she was sure that it was due to the bad weather, but for whatever reason it meant that all the children on the register were not turning up, and therefore the income for the group was dropping. The immediate worry was to pay the hall rent and replace some worn equipment; their financial state would hardly allow both.

In May 1982, despite the rain, the playgroup held a very successful open morning at the Village Hall. Lots of children and adults came to take part in play-group activities and to see the displays, and about 100 children joined in the Teddy Bears' Picnic. We were very pleased to raise over £70. Playgroup and Toddler Group had an enjoyable outing to Sparkwell Wildlife Park on 15 June 1982. We were now looking forward to a party and sports on the last day of term. At the end of the term, Ginny Murgatroyd left to take up a teaching appointment in September.

Everyone settled well into the second half of the Summer Term of 1984. The weather was beautiful, so the children were able to get outside and play. Even so, the 'craft' section had been using different types of materials – lentils, peas, glitter, polyfilla, unused lollipop sticks and dolly pegs – for collage, and many varied items had been produced. The annual outing, on 5 June, was to Paignton Zoo, and a great day was had by all. Val Meek wrote: 'The weather was extremely kind and the rain held off. Although we took upwards of 40 'monkeys' with us, not one wanted to stay behind with the real ones!'

Later Mrs Meek summarised the year:

All too soon it's the end of yet another term and another successful year at Playgroup, fun and academic wise anyway. Fund-raising has been necessary again during the year but this too has been well patronised. Many of the children are leaving at the end of term for pastures new and we wish them well. We also have to say a fond farewell to Diane Marment, who is also leaving us at the end of term. Thank you, Diane, for all your valuable help and assistance. We wish you every happiness for the future; the kids will miss you and so will we. Francis McCarthy is, as from September our new leader.

As well as a new leader the autumn of 1984 saw a new assistant supervisor, Dympna Gorrie. The group continued to run during normal term time on Mondays, Tuesdays and Thursdays from 9.30a.m. to 12 noon. Wednesday mornings were for the mother and toddler group. The playgroup was run by mums with guidance from the Pre-school Playgroup Association.

The term saw the usual round of fund-raising activities. A coffee morning was well patronised and did very well for the playgroup's ever-increasing demand for funds. Another fund-raising event was held on 3 November, when the group held a 'Fun, Family and Firework' party for playgroup families.

In the spring of 1985 a most welcome visitor to Playgroup was PC Steve Hopper, not as a parent helper for once, but in his role of policeman. The children enjoyed seeing his car, trying on his helmet and generally being 'entertained'. The group was most grateful to him for giving of his time.

South Brent Playgroup continued to flourish.

The highlight of April 1985 was the visit to Judith and Simon Hill's farm to see the lambs. Once over the shock of so many people, Mr Hill took us to see the birth of a lamb, which was a most moving experience. We then toured the lambing shed and saw lambs from half an hour to seven weeks old. The children were allowed to wander round and get close to the lambs; indeed, two children helped with bottle feeding, and three lambs were removed from their pens for the children (and mums) to stroke. Playgroup continued to run smoothly in spite of the work in progress at the Village Hall and, amongst other things, the children made nesting boxes, ably assisted by Steve Hopper.

The unusually cold and wet summer of 1985 meant there was little opportunity to hold playgroup in the open air, although the weather was very kind for our summer outing to Paignton Zoo, a most enjoyable day. Postman Pat and Jess (courtesy of Torquay Post Office) also visited the group in June.

The children were able to see his van (although unfortunately not from the inside); and all received a badge from Pat, who then spent some considerable time talking to them, and was very well received. The playgroup, which went from strength to strength, were pleased to report a second prize in the carnival for our 'Box of Sweets'.

The September 1987 AGM of South Brent Playgroup marked the conclusion of another successful year for the group. To ensure that 1987/88 would be equally enjoyable and rewarding, the new committee were soon busy launching a publicity campaign around the village.

At Christmas, remembering that Christmas is both a time for receiving and giving, the children filled used Smartie tubes with pennies to donate to Cot Death Research and raised £44.

The playgroup was at full capacity in early 1988 and there was the possibility of the number of days available being extended to four. Parents of children approaching three years old were encouraged to book a place for their child to ensure the day of their choice. Beth Merriman took over the organisation of the mother and toddler group from Sally Crees, who was attending a training course. The fund-raising went on with a 'nearly new' sale, together with a sale of Usborne Books. Later on in the year we hoped to compile a 'quick and easy' recipe book and welcomed any contributions of favourite recipes popular with children.

South Brent Pre-School

After many years in the Village Hall the Pre-School moved on to its current site in the Old School Centre. Sherida Mould writes:

To this day Pre-School children are learning in the happy environment that their parents, grandparents and previous generations have enjoyed.

The availability of the Old School Building for a Pre-

A visit by the Dartmoor Rescue Group to the South Brent Pre-school. The children of the Pre-school have frequent visits from outside agencies. (THE PRE-SCHOOL COLLECTION)

School was made possible by the foresight and generosity of local benefactors, without their help some twenty years ago Pre-School as it is today would not exist.

Since arrival at the Old School Centre the Pre-School has proved a success and, with the expansion of the village and the dedication of the staff, Pre-School has continued to progress.

With the promotion of pre-school education by central government the statutory requirements have grown enormously, but South Brent Pre-School has always maintained the philosophy of 'learning through play'.

This philosophy has produced an excellent standard of achievement by the youngest members of our village and equipped them well for successful integration into primary education. This has been made possible by the close working relationship between Primary and Pre-School.

The facilities at Pre-School have continued to be improved. The outdoor play area (seen from the Plymouth Road), opened in 2004, includes a large covered sand pit, Wendy house and covered benches.

In 2007 the 'Playbarn' was opened. It was formally the primary school toilets and store room and is, by covenant, for the use of the children of South Brent.

The generosity and commitment of our village community and businesses have made these superb additions possible. At the time of writing all employees live within the parish, endorsing the spirit and commitment of South Brent.

When South Brent Pre-School was inspected by

Ofsted in November 2000, when there were 38 children on roll. The report concluded that:

... the children make good progress towards the early learning goals at South Brent Pre-School. Good teaching ensures that children learn effectively in all six areas. A very supportive partnership with parents and carers effectively helps children work towards the early learning goals. Children's personal, social and emotional development is very well fostered.

Each time the Pre-school has been visited by Ofsted, the reports have been very favourable. Juliet Hartridge commented in 2003:

South Brent Pre-school provides good quality day care for children. Children are happy, secure and well cared for. They are presented with an interesting, stimulating and imaginative range of well-planned activities and stimulating resources which meet their developmental needs and encourage their creativity.

Heather Morgan noted that:

South Brent Pre-school provides high-quality nursery education and children are making very good progress towards the early learning goals in all six areas of the curriculum.

And in 2006 the report was similar. Sally Hall wrote that the provision for the 49 children was good in all aspects, and management were also considered to be good.

The Montessori School

Another school for younger children, opened by Jane Tuson, was based on the educational principles of Maria Montessori. Mrs Tuson had been introduced to the Montessori method by a friend many years

Children from the Pre-school sit in the shelter in their outside area with their leader, Sherida Mould.

(THE PRE-SCHOOL COLLECTION)

Mrs Jane Tuson prepares to cook at the Montessori School.

(THE TUSON COLLECTION)

Maypole dancing at a School Association Fair in the 1970s. Headmaster John Wain commented: 'The dancing was very well done and it went down very well with the spectators.' The evening began with the traditional maypole dance by a group of 10 and 11-year-olds. This was followed by a number of games and stalls in the school. 'People seemed very willing to part with their money,' Mr. Wain added. 'The whole evening went very well and was well supported.'

(The Stevens Collection)

Matthew Toogood and Melissa Hard holding the winners' shield at the 1984 School Sports.

(The Toogood Collection)

Sports Day at South Brent School. (The Reed Collection)

The School Association Shrove Tuesday pancake races. Left to right: ?, Pan Mitchell, Ginny Murgatroyd, Mary Wonnacott and Jenny Prince, who won the race.

(The Wonnacott Collection)

The School Association jug band at the Village Hall concert, 1982. Left to right, back row: Sally Luscombe, Pat Luscombe, Cy Sampson, Norman Saunter, Neil Toogood, Jan Goss, John Wain (the head teacher), Brian Dent; front row: Paul Edginton (deputy head teacher) Jenny Prince, Robin Horan.

(The Toogood Collection)

Left: *The School Association often took part in the summer carnival. Here we see, left to right, Neil Toogood, Norman Saunter, Robin Horan and John Wain.* (The Toogood Collection)

Two former pupils of South Brent Primary School, Christopher and David England, who both graduated from Plymouth University with Applied Chemistry degrees, are two of the many former pupils who went on to greater things. One former pupil even became Chairman of BOAC.

(THE ENGLAND COLLECTION)

before in Drayton. She trained in the Montessori method and then, eventually, after many years, opened her school in 'Little Orchard' on Exeter Road. Olive Dodd the editor of the parish magazine wrote of 'the newest school in Brent':

I recently spent an interesting and enlightening afternoon at 'Little Orchard' seeing the alterations and innovations that Jane Tuson has made to her home, and hearing her plans for the Nursery School she intends to open on 7 September.

Jane has been trained in the Montessori School tradition and has planned her school along those lines. Everything possible has been done to comply with the health requirements, even to the extent of having a special low toilet installed, together with the right-size hand basins.

Looking at all the equipment she has installed and listening to the enthusiasm with which she described the various activities that are planned I could only envy the youngsters who are going to absorb knowledge while playing. If it is truly the case that naughty children are really only bored children I feel she will have no troubles on that score. Outside there is a nice grassy garden, a sandpit, and a swing and climbing frame to be erected, and twelve little patches for tiny hands to cultivate.

South Brent Primary School

Just as the other educational establishments have received accolades from outside sources, so South Brent Primary School, founded way back in 1874, has been described as 'a good school with some very

South Brent dinner ladies celebrate Christmas in 1981. Left to right: Ena Stephens, Rosemary Hillman, A. Sobey, Marilyn Bullen, Sally Luscombe.

(THE BULLEN COLLECTION)

good features', confirmed more recently as 'a good school with outstanding features'. It boasts a basic Skills Agency Quality mark, an Artsmark Gold Award from the Arts Council and a School Achievement Award. In June 2006 the following

The dinner ladies at South Brent Primary School. Left to right: Sally Luscombe, Anne Wakeham, Frances Roche. Lil Chandler. (THE ANDREWS COLLECTION)

press release was issued from David Hutchings in the Devon County Council Press Office concerning the school:

A SOUTH HAMS primary school has become the first in the country to offer a prestigious national education qualification. South Brent Primary School has been chosen to host the course, aimed at anyone working with children and young people. The course leads to a Certificate in Emotional Literacy and will run at South Brent later this year. It can lead on to a full Master's Degree in Education. This is the first time that the prestigious Institute for Arts in Therapy and Education (IATE) has allowed one of its courses to be run on an outreach basis instead of at its base in London. South Brent was chosen to host the course because of the work it is doing on a pioneering pilot scheme with the Department of Health to look at children's emotional health and wellbeing. The school has developed an alternative creative provision that runs alongside the national curriculum to support children's emotional health and wellbeing and early results are showing a significant impact on children's learning.

South Brent headteacher Helen Nicholls said that she was delighted with the news:

Never before has an organisation as prestigious as IATE allowed any of its work to be done on an outreach basis.

Mr. Robinson's Class, 1981. Left to right, back row: *Fiona Rooke, Darren Hannaford, Eleanor Cudmore, James Norrish, Richard Buckpitt, Catherine Harris, Paul Smith, Lisa Stitch, Nicholas Morgan;* third row: *Debbie Newman, Edward Ashfield, Natasha Sutton, Gary Kelly, Louise Ellison, Robert Crannis, Joanne Goss, Caroline Warne, Tamsin Rockey, Victoria Sampson;* second row: *Steven Popham, Christopher Lake, Katie Halliday, Ian Vinecombe, Mr Bill Robinson, Lee Bullen, Kate Wild, Gillian Bartlett, Matthew Smith;* front row: *Shawn Biddis, Elaine Buckpitt, Amanda Tidball, Tracy Hannaford.* (THE KELLY COLLECTION)

Mr Edginton's Class, 1981. Left to right, back row: *Jo Sitch, Andrew Cleave, Pamela Venor, Peter Morgan, Craig Stickland, Wendy Mugridge, Lizzie Sparkes, Mark Norrish, Gary Down;* third row: *Carl Neil, Kirsty Pakes, Matthew Froggatt, Jo Vooght, ?, Tracy Honeywill, Jo Tolchard, Shaun Teague;* second row: *Mary Harris, Rosalind Smeeth, Rory Stevens, Charlotte Farrell, Mr Paul Edginton, Jo Kelly, Alison Reed, Adrian ?, Maxine Nimmo;* front row: *Trevor Chandler, Robert Lavers, Paul Vinnicombe, Stephen Hawkins.* (THE KELLY COLLECTION)

Class of '67. Left to right, back row: *Julie Eales, Robert Steer, Ernie Chapple, Richard Rundle, Nigel Caudwell, Timmy Reeves, Phillip Hill, Rodney Male;* third row: *Irene Newman, Evelyn Johns, Jane Bristow, Wendy Mead, David Underhill, Craig Chapman, John Gallagher, Michael Wakeham, Jennifer Stevens, Gillian Bishop, John Bowden;* second row: *Colin Jones, Martin Stewart, Peter Slade, Muriel Sowden, Ian Clements, Nigel Eastley, Peter Hawkins, Maria Bond, Ashley Reevey, Paul Wills;* front row: *Marilyn Field, Alan Coker, John Widdecombe, Phillip Wakeham, Lillian Hard, Ivor Watts.* (THE EALES COLLECTION)

Mrs Murgatroyd with Helen Lock, Daniel Beddington, Bertie Prosperi, Tina Lock, David Williams and Marie Fox. (THE GINNY JONES COLLECTION)

South Brent's answer to Top of the Pops – 'Trogs' – in the summer of 1965. Left to right: Ian Burrows, Chris Blackler, Dave Ayres, Basil Smale. (THE BULLEN COLLECTION)

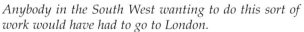

Caroline Nimmo, June Rundle, Elizabeth March and Margaret Grill on the gate at Glazebrook Lodge.

Anybody in the South West wanting to do this sort of work would have had to go to London.

The Every Child Matters agenda, which is looking at developing the whole child, is increasingly important for everyone working with children and young people. This course will equip them to address Every Child Matters in practical ways.

Course directors Lynne Gerlach and Julia Bird said:

This is the first time IATE has given permission for one of its established courses to be offered as an outreach course. It is a pilot project that will be subject to review. Whether the full MA will be available in the South West will, to some extent, depend upon the outcome of this pilot project.

Bert Field, Peter Crockett, Cecil Crockett and Mossy O'Connell enjoy a pint in 1948. In the background is May Osborne. (THE FIELD COLLECTION)

Paddy Mullen has written about Brent:

Where Life Trundles On
Among the hills, and rivers and moors,
through the trees and chanting words,
there is a village of kindly kin,
where people laugh, and welcome you in.

The Village of Brent is old and steady,
the pubs, the life, the enjoyments ready.
Full of wisdom, and boisterous chaps,
a place to dream in your mind perhaps.

Through crooked spires, and open fires,
the folklore will live long,
as pints are passed, and wines are glassed,
Brent Village where life trundles on.

CHAPTER 5

Another Look at Young People and Their Activities

South Brent Youth Clubs

Many people who were growing up in the mid-twentieth century remember the youth club that was held in the Vicar's Hall at the junction between Church Street and Millswood Lane. This one closed on the sale of the building. In the late 1960s there were two youth clubs in Brent. Miss Audrey Westmoreland formed one, which was held in the then Church Hall on Monday evenings and had links with St Petroc's Church. The second was held in the Methodist Church.

There was great excitement in 1978 when the new landlords of the London Inn, Frank and Joyce Fletcher, proposed to re-open the Loft Youth Club, housed in an outbuilding behind the inn. Mr Fletcher hoped that the brewery would pay for the structural repairs and then he would redecorate the inside. The Parish Council greeted the news with 'delight'. However, the project did not come to fruition because the expected funding was not forthcoming and it left the village youngsters with nowhere to meet.

In 1984 Malcolm Barnes, the founding chairman, handed over the reins to Steve Hopper. At this time there was a request for any adult with a couple of spare hours now and again to assist in the running of the club, especially anyone with specialist knowledge in such activities as sailing, rock climbing, photography and craft work.

The youth club hosted the Action Van at the school playing-field in July and, inevitably, discos were a great success, as was the annual trip to Butlins and the many other activities that took place. In 1985 six of the members took part in the annual 50/50 Sponsored Walk organised by the Devon Youth Association in Tavistock and walked 16 miles. Also in 1985 there was a fund-raising 24-hour 'bike ride', the money raised being used to buy life jackets for use on the Mirror dinghy which was being built at the time. The ride, on a 'fixed' bike, took place outside the Anchor Hotel from 10a.m. on Friday, 9 August, until 10a.m. on Saturday, 10 August. Mr Paul Wonnacott of TCII arranged this event, which raised a superb £230. The total distance covered was recorded at 377 miles, and 46 children took part.

A new youth centre opened in Brent in April 1996. The club, in the cellar of the former Anchor Hotel, was the culmination of a three-year campaign by the local community to provide a meeting-point for

The London Hotel and Brent Mill with views towards Ugborough Beacon. The Youth Club was between Chenhall's garage and the London Hotel. At the time that the picture was taken the road, the A38, was the main trunk road in the area.
(THE SHARVILLE COLLECTION)

The Anchor Hotel and Station Road in the 1950s.   (THE WOOD COLLECTION)

village youngsters and was run by a committee of the teenagers themselves. The centre in Fore Street was called The Anchor. According to initial reports:

The room is an empty shell at the moment, and plastering, plumbing and rewiring are taking place.

Then the youngsters will go in and decorate it themselves, with help from various sections of the community, including an art group offering to help with murals.

Mr Ken Smith, chairman of the steering committee which fought the long campaign to set up the centre, commented:

It's great. It's really good. The youngsters will run and police it themselves. It's quite unique. They will make all the decisions and will be running it themselves carefully on a very small budget. The whole village has recognised there was a problem, and this will give youngsters somewhere to go. I have found the young members' committee to be very polite and sensible. They will be left to sort out their own policies.

South Brent Youth Fishing Club

As well as the usual youth clubs, a Youth Fishing Club was formed in the 1980s, initially using facilities at Merrifield. The members, as well as taking part in the sport, also supported village activities. As part of the Village Street Fair attractions, the club held several fishing competitions with both junior and senior divisions, the winner of each heat being the member who caught the best fish.

The carnival fishing competition in 1985 went off very well and even produced a couple of brown trout of just over 1lb, which the organisers did not know were in the ponds. In the same year, during the school holidays, a sponsored '24-hour fish' was held, with the juniors fishing during the daytime hours and the seniors taking the 'night shift'.

A fishing club still exists, although its members are now more senior than junior.

Brownies and Guides

The Brownies
A report on the 1977 Thinking Day gathering sums up the underlying foundation of the Brownie movement in South Brent:

The South Brent Guides and Brownies turned out in excellent numbers for their 'Thinking Day' in Totnes, 29 out of 35 Guides being present, and about 30 Brownies. Other companies and packs in the district did not do quite so well. Of course, South Brent have a wonderful example in the matter of service and dedication to follow, for this year marked the 50 years that Miss Naomi Cranch has given to South Brent as Brown Owl, and during the proceedings an inscribed silver tray was presented to her from the Totnes District. When one thinks of the number of girls she must have influenced and set on the road to Guiding, 'the mind boggles'. South Brent Guides provided a colour party, and ten of them read out the Guide Laws; standing on either side of the County Commissioner, Mrs Harley, tea and a camp-fire sing-song followed, and everyone had a thoroughly enjoyable afternoon. The South Brent Guides were particularly pleased that the Vicar (Revd David Niblett) was able to join them and take part in their Thinking Day.

Later that year, Miss Cranch held a reunion in the Village Hall. She had enjoyed her 50 years of Guiding so much that she wanted to meet as many old Brownies as possible!

In 1981 there were two packs of Brownies in Brent. The South Brent Brownies attended a Teddy Bears' Picnic to celebrate 75 years of Guiding at Ashburton Country Park on Saturday, 8 June 1985. Annie Snelson, Brown Owl of the second South Brent Brownies, reported:

There were well over 1,000, and maybe more than 2,000, Brownies. There were so many you could not count them all. There were many races with teddies, and competitions such as the best-dressed teddy, the teddy who had the biggest smile and the oldest teddy (who I think was 59).

The mid-1980s found the South Brent Brownies in desperate need of adult help. One pack had to close due to the lack of adult leaders and the other now had only one Guider. However, the Brownies survived and there is still a Brownie pack in South Brent to continue the tradition begun all those years ago by Miss Cranch.

The Girl Guides

Miss Naomi Cranch was also instrumental in the reformation of the Guides in South Brent. The South Brent Guides had been in abeyance for a long time. Mrs Unity Harley remembers how Miss Cranch gave her the Guide Handbook in one hand and, with six Guides on the other, the Second South Brent Guides came into being. They met at Mrs Harley's house in Aish. Mrs Harley had to get a camper's licence to take them away, but the group flourished. In 1972 Patricia Crosbie became the first member of the 2nd South Brent Guides to reach the rank of Queen's

Julia Stevens receives her Queen's Guide Award from Mrs Unity Harley in the Church Room. (THE HARLEY COLLECTION)

Brent Guides on parade in the mid-1960s. Left to right: *Diane Reed, Yvonne Wills, Melba Hard, Joan Goss, Carol Goss, Mrs Gray (District Commissioner), Margaret Knapman, Miss Audrey Westmoreland Leader, ?, Marion Wills, ?, Nancy James, Wendy Luker.*
(THE REED COLLECTION)

Brent Hill viewed from the top of Penstave Copse.

Colette Crosbie, aged 14, and Jane Karkeek, with their Queen's Guide Awards. (THE HARLEY COLLECTION)

St Petroc's, the Parish Church of South Brent, where many events take place.

Guide and received her certificate from Mrs Malsom, wife of the Vicar of South Brent. Other members who received similar awards in those early days were Colette Crosbie, Jane Karkeek and Julia Stevens.

Amongst their achievements were triumph in a singing competition and a visit to Adelboden in Switzerland

By 1981 there were two Guide companies in the community, run by Mrs Judith Morris and Mrs L. Wakeham. As the units were fast growing in size help was urgently needed, so in September 1984 the 3rd South Brent Guides joined with the 2nd South Brent Guides to form one company.

Mrs Joyce Howitt, Captain, wrote:

I would like to thank all those who have given the company their support, and especially the girls, who have been keen, enthusiastic and hard working. We look forward to working with our friends from the 2nd South Brent and feel sure that the interests of Guiding will be better served by one company with two qualified Guides than by two separate companies each with only one qualified Guider.

In July 1985 Mrs. Howitt described the activities of the group:

So far, 1985 has been a busy year for us and it promises to continue to be so for the next couple of months at least. At the beginning of February, 26 girls took part in a sponsored silence and, as a result, £108.85s. was raised, half of which has been donated to the RSPCA, the charity of the girls' choice. It was some feat to have 26 normally vociferous girls in complete silence for 1.5 hours, and they are to be congratulated for their self-control. Later that month we took part in the District Thinking Day Service, which this year was held in St Petroc's. During the Easter holidays some of the girls spent a day helping the Dartmoor Ranger to clear litter at Shipley Bridge, unblock a stream bed and tidy up an old camp site . It was a day of work and pleasure, and wet feet. If anyone was looking out of their window in the vicinity of the village square at 5.00a.m. on Sunday, 5 May, they would have seen a little group plus a dog, in the rain, on the way to climb Brent Hill! The intention had been to climb the hill to watch the sunrise as part of an Outdoor Challenge, but it rained. Nevertheless the stalwart few decided to climb the hill in any case. The rain stopped and we had some satisfaction in standing on the top, in the biting wind, looking down on the quiet, sleeping village (except for those few people to whom 5.00a.m. is part of a normal

Some of the many participants in one of the 'Gang Shows' held in the Village Hall. Scouts, Cubs, Guides, Brownies and Venture Scouts all combined to provide acts for the shows – the leaders did their bit as well!   (THE MAJOR COLLECTION)

working day). At the end of half-term week, 13 girls spent an enjoyable three days at a Division Training Camp at Wadstray, near Dartmouth. It was perfect camping weather, a picturesque site, and the opportunity to learn or perfect skills.

We helped at the Parents' Association Jumble Sale and Coffee Morning at the beginning of June, had a stall at the Street Fair and have entered two teams in the netball competition.

The year 1985 was the 75th Anniversary of Guiding and, in commemoration, a county tree-planting ceremony was held in March at Pear Tree Cross, Ashburton. Representatives of all the divisions in Devon were present, and South Brent had the honour to be asked to represent the Totnes Division. The three girls who took part were Young Leader Beverley Newman, Guide Dominique Davy and Brownie Carla Saunter. It rained, but the 350 trees were planted and covered by their plastic shelters. It is hoped in time this will be a pleasant grove for sitting in or picnicking. A further celebration was an anniversary thanksgiving service at Exeter Cathedral, which was attended by Guiders, young leaders and other adult members of the movement. It was described as 'a very moving service' and one which all were proud to be part of. South Brent's own jubilee celebration was a barn dance.

From 28 July to 4 August 1985, Mrs Anne Harris

and four members of the 2nd South Brent Guide Company, Mary and Catherine Harris, Suzie Ellison and Anne Clarke, together with other members of the South Brent District (Diptford and Modbury) took part in the 75th Anniversary Badger Camp at Bicton Arena. The camp was divided into 29 sub-camps, of which South Brent District was one, and contained 900 guides from 98 Guide units in Devon. It was officially opened by Lord Clinton, the great-grandson of Lady Clinton, who started Guiding in Devon in 1910. On Tuesday, 30 July the campers were joined by another 1,500 Guides from all over Devon, who had come to take part in the rally day, which included activities such as knockout sports, tug-of-war, blindfold tent pitching and orienteering. It was a super day, enjoyed by all. The campers had a most enjoyable week and made many new friends, and those of South Brent District were particularly pleased to gain third place (out of 29) in the camp competitions, and to bring back a 'Good Camping' certificate as well. Incidentally, the name 'Badger' was derived from: B – Bicton; A – Arena; -D – Devon; G – Guides; E – Encampment; R – Rally.

Mrs Howitt also described Guide Week, from 24 to 29 June:

It was celebrated in the South Brent District (Brent, Diptford and Modbury), by a District Camp Fire and a

District Barn Dance. The former, held at Mothecombe beach, proved to be most enjoyable. Each Company had a sausage sizzle on its own camp fire, the girls were able to go for a dip, and then everyone gathered around one fire to sing. After days of rain it turned out to be a lovely warm evening. The Barn Dance at the Village Hall was attended by Guides, ex-Guides and Guiders. Candles surrounding the Jubilee cake were lit from the light which had originated at Buckingham Palace on the Monday. An exhibition of Guiding mementos was displayed, and this proved to be most interesting.

A few weeks later, the South Brent Company had another special event to celebrate. Patrol Leader Mary Harris was awarded the Baden Powell Trefoil badge, which is the highest award a Guide can earn. She was the first Guide in the district to gain the award, for which she had worked extremely hard. District Commissioner Mrs Leonard presented the badge and certificate at a special ceremony, which was followed by a celebration tea for the Company and invited guests.

In August, a few members spent the day on Holne Moor helping the Dartmoor Ranger to pick up litter. It was an enjoyable day out, even though at times they were nearly blown down by the wind, and never knew what they would find next.

In 1986 the Devon County Commissioner, Mrs. Rosemary Howell, came to the meeting to present Catherine Harris with a certificate and a book for completing the '75' Challenge in Jubilee Year. Catherine decided to walk 75 miles during 1985. This she did both at home and on a family holiday in Scotland and was the only Devon Guide to complete this challenge.

Thinking Day is an important event to Brownies, Guides and Rangers. In 1988 Mrs Howitt reported that:

The South Brent District Brownies, Guides and Rangers held their District Thinking Day Service at St Petroc's Church, on Sunday, 21 February. There were representatives from the Diptford and Modbury Brownie Packs and Guide Companies, the Rangers, and the local association, as well as members of the Brent Brownie Packs and Guide Company The readings were very clearly delivered by Brent Guide Rebecca Ingram, and Modbury Ranger Jane Timmis, while Brent Brownies Gillian Ross and Louise Hedges said prayers. District Commissioner Mrs Lyn Leonard, from Modbury, led the rededication. We owe many thanks to Revd David Niblett for taking the service and to organist David Langton for playing for us at rather short notice. The service was followed by a Thinking Day ceremony in the Village Hall, during which Brownies and Guides remembered Brownies and Guides in other countries, especially those where there is trouble or persecution. Refreshments were provided by members of the Parents' Association, to whom we are

grateful. Special thanks to Mrs Liz Jordan, who baked a lovely Thinking Day cake for us all.

The Scouts and Cubs

The present Brent Scout group began in 1975. The minute in the Parents' Book, which records the founding, notes:

Mr Stansbury reported that 24 boys, from 11 to 15 years of age, turned up for the first meeting of the Scout Troop in February. The numbers had since risen to 29 and the list would close at 30. A waiting list would then be started. Only one boy had already been a Scout. Twenty-seven boys had already bought their uniforms. Two 17-year-old boys had come along as instructors. The District Commissioner thanked the Scouters for their work in starting the Troop, and the City Commissioner for Plymouth commented on the amount of support the boys were receiving from the village and wished them well.

Rory Stevens wrote in his log-book for the 1980 Cub Camp, Cadiho:

29 August 1980. *We arrived yesterday, Thursday 28th, at about 7p.m. Last night hardly anyone got to sleep until 2.00a.m., partly because Paul Williams lost his Monkey Mickey's trousers and partly because Daren Wallington kept on making funny rude noises. This*

August 1980 saw the International Scout Jamboree held at Crediton. The South Brent Scouts built and slept in the tower. A picture of the structure, with mention of South Brent, appeared in the Times newspaper at the time of the jamboree.
(THE MAJOR COLLECTION)

morning we played on the swings that the Scouts put up for us. Then we had Keep Fit, where we ran around the field and did several other exercises. Then we had breakfast. After that we had inspection, where we got the best score of the pack – 9 out of 10. Then we had a wild game in the woods, where Peter Morgan almost got lost. Anyway, we lost him for a bit. After lunch we went to the police headquarters in Exeter, where we went for a swim in their pool and played football in the gym, and we won, so we got eight points for that. Also we had a look around the museum. We went back to camp, had tea and went for a walk to collect wood. We came back, had some hot chocolate and biscuits and went to bed.

30 August 1980. *We got up and went to wash. I was the first one up and first one down. We are just about to go to breakfast, so I better leave now. We are just about to have inspection. This afternoon we are having a Knockout, and we have to make a Joker.*

Description of where our camp is and what it's like. We are in a field surrounded by forests, where we can play lots of games. We eat in a lovely cottage (farm). There is a field next door where Scouts are camping.

Our journey to Cadiho. We all were meant to get to the station car park by 6.00p.m. (or, if you like, 18.00); I went with Mr Norrish and we got to camp 3rd, in front of Baloo, which is an achievement. We arrived at about 7.00, or 19.00.

The most fun thing. I think most things are fun, but jumping off the diving board was especially fun. I've got to go now – goodbye. At the moment, we are doing our Joker for the Knockout; it is a wine bottle. We also have to make our country's flag. Our Knockout was great fun and there were games. Like 3-legged holding water stilt races, the mini-marathon was trying to catch and burst a balloon with water in which one of your six threw to you, but if you did not catch it, it would not count and several other races which were fun. We came second over all. I have just had tea of fish finger, baked beans and spaghetti and some cake. We are going to have our camp fire tonight, but that is not the only thing I am looking forward to, the other thing is Tuck of Tic Tac and chews.

31st August 1980. *Last night was great fun, with the fire and midnight feast. For our tent's entertainment was a striptease down to our swimming trunks and the cooks, Mrs Burgess. N. Simon and Mrs Neal (N Mickey) did it with us. N = nickname. The midnight feast was also great fun.*

Today we played rounders, adults against cubs. I scored a rounder but the adults still won 6-3.

Mr Major is taking up the tents and has to pack and take everything out of the tent.

Dinner is just about to be served. The End

In January 1981 Graeme Taylor became the fifth Scout from the troop to gain his Chief Scout's Award. This award was only gained with dedication and hard work, and Graeme showed these qualities during his years with the troop. He led the successful 'Adventure' competition team and helped to win the City of Plymouth cooking competition for Brent. It is usually thought that Scouts eat only baked beans and sausages at camp, but this was certainly not true with South Brent, where savoury pancakes and steak and kidney pudding are more likely to be the expected standard, and Graeme's interest in cooking certainly contributed to this standard. His skills at first aid, learnt with the St John Ambulance Brigade, were extremely useful to the troop, and he has worked hard to gain the Royal Life Saving Society award.

For the Scouts the most memorable event of 1980 was their week at the Scout Jamboree at Crediton in August, which was attended by over 6,000 Scouts, including many from abroad. Brent managed to make their mark, however, by building a large tower, five storeys high, in which all 25 boys slept in hammocks. This attracted a lot of attention, featured on BBC Spotlight and, much to everyone's amazement, appeared in the *Times* newspaper.

Other notable occasions for the Scouts during the year were their first Gang Show, in which they joined with the Guides, Brownies and Cubs to provide two evenings of entertainment, and winning the City of Plymouth Scout swimming competition. In April 1981 Group Scout Leader Mike Major reported:

The Group now comprises a mixed Venture Scout unit (boys and girls), a Scout troop and a Cub pack. Just over 80 young people in the village are actively engaged in Scouting. The newly formed Venture Scout unit, under the leadership of Mrs Sue Sampson, has indeed been very active on various projects around the village. In the week following Easter, 'Job Week' will be with us and the whole group will be busy raising funds. As a group, we have to pay a sum of money per head to the National Scout Association as a membership fee. This year 1st South Brent has to pay ever £400 – this is over and above any funds we need to run the group locally, and we have many expenses. So, as you can see, Job

The Scouts and Cubs, always entrants in the summer carnival, with their entry 'Gulliver's Travels'. Left to right: PC Mike Major, Brian Grieves, Paul Mitchell, Mrs Stone, Rod Tidball. (THE MAJOR COLLECTION)

Mike Major receiving his Group Scout warrant from District Commissioner Ron Snell. (THE MAJOR COLLECTION)

A fund-raising stall at one of the Scout Pioneering Days. Libby Major was running the stall with helpers. Sid and Gladys Mercer, who are in the foreground, supported many activities in the community. (THE MAJOR COLLECTION)

South Brent Scouts Pioneering Day, held in the 'Sheep Sale Field', now Higher Green. The tower was used for abseiling. Mike Major comments: 'This was before Health and Safety came along. Incidentally, no one was ever injured at the Pioneering Days.' (THE MAJOR COLLECTION)

Richard Male and Jamie Wiggam representing South Brent Scouts at No. 10 Downing Street

(THE RODNEY MALE COLLECTION)

thank you for your past support and look forward to even more support in the future.

In 1982 Andrew Smith gained his Chief Scout's Award, the sixth Scout in South Brent to achieve this coveted prize. Rosemary Stansbury, Group Scout Secretary, noted:

Andrew has been a loyal Scout and an excellent patrol leader, and his sporting prowess has, over the years, helped us to win quite a number of sporting trophies in both City and District competitions, particularly in football. However, cross-country is perhaps his best sport, and last year he won the City of Plymouth under-16 Scout cross-country competition, and this year, just two days too old to compete in this again, went on to win the under-21 competition, coming in four minutes ahead of the Venture Scouts and others in this competition.

Week provides a challenge which the boys and girls enjoy. It provides satisfaction and pride knowing they are doing their bit and pleasure in the reward for the job done. If you receive callers during Job Week, please remember 'small boy, small job'; you would be surprised at what some Cubs and Scouts are expected to do. Also, the week is now called 'Job Week'. 'Bob a Job' disappeared with the arrival of inflation long ago. May I

The South Brent Scout entry for the Scout Car Challenge, the pedal-powered 'Brent Bullet', appeared on local television news. Greg Phillips is the driver, with Simon Woodhouse, Gerard Stubbs (standing) and Roy Major (kneeling). The parent chief engineer was Brian Phillips and the race driver was Simon Woodhouse. Sadly, the chain broke during the heats on Plymouth Hoe and the team had no spare! (THE MAJOR COLLECTION)

Also in 1982, cross-country was one of the group's best sporting events of the year, as Malcolm Mant won the individual medal for the under-13¹/₂s competition.

The group were also runners-up in the district five-a-side and six-a-side football competitions, and in the City Swimming Gala, and came sixth in the County Backwoods Competition against very formidable competition. Other successful ventures of 1982 were the second Gang Show, and the second Pioneering Day, when the Scouts were able to show their abilities at building a monkey bridge, abseiling tower and other structures, which provided a lot of fun for village youngsters once built. They also entered the National Scoutcar Races, held on Plymouth Hoe that year. These events are held in different parts of the country every year and attract a lot of entrants from as far afield as North Yorkshire. It was noted that:

... it's no use pretending we were the fastest – we certainly weren't – but our car was quite an achievement for a first attempt, and under the guidance of Brian Phillips the team of boys who built and drove the vehicle learnt a lot about its construction, including welding. They also appeared on Westward television, showing their car and talking about the event.

The 1982 summer camp was held near Glasbury in the Wye Valley, at a beautiful, remote site 1,000 feet up on the edge of the Black Mountains. Perfect weather certainly contributed to the success of the camp, and two overnight canoeing camps on the River Wye, in which eight boys participated, were much enjoyed.

In August 1984 the Scout troop in South Brent stopped collecting newspapers and magazines, etc. They had been collecting for five years and during this time found it a steady, helpful form of fundraising. However, due to storage difficulties and the increasing amount of time that a few people have devoted to it, the troop decided to cease collecting.

Each year the Cubs went on summer camp. In 1984 Andrew Beer wrote in his log:

On the first day we had a packed lunch. We got here 11 in the morning. After dinner, when we finished putting up the tents, we went down to the beach. It was fun getting the water from the tap. We put all the rucksacks in the tents. Then we put the ground sheets, then the sleeping bags in. I put my pillow down the end of my sleeping bag. When we got back from the beach we got changed and played till it was tea time. Then we had our tea of beefburgers and bread. For afters we had a piece of cake. After tea we washed our hands and our dishes and dried them. After we dried them we rinsed them out. When we finished we played some games. Then we had some tuck to eat, and we had to do a log.

Modern Scouting

Outdoor activities – canoeing on the River Tamar.
(THE SCOUT COLLECTION)

Andrew Cook, Kyle Hodge, Jenny McMurran, India Creed, Sam Smith and Luke Williams at Gypsy Bank.
(THE SCOUT COLLECTION)

Fiona Harvey (ASL), Josh Karkeek, Ruth Oldershaw, Daisy Burris, Tom Chamberlain, Alistair Wiseman, Lucy Bushby, Stephanie Doree, Phoebe Clark, Michael Parker, Christopher Winnington-Ingram, Andrew Cook, Calum Langdon, Sam Smith, Tom Soper, Maddie Budden, Luke Rutley, Alex Smith, Iain Tinkler, Tim Harvey (SL) and Kevin Vickers (GSL).
(THE SCOUT COLLECTION)

The Beavers in preparation for the St George's Day parade.
(THE SCOUT COLLECTION)

St George's Day Parade.
(THE SCOUT COLLECTION)

The Youth Organisations at the Remembrance Sunday Service.
(THE SCOUT COLLECTION)

On the second day we had our breakfast and washed our dishes. We went for a walk around Salcombe. I spent 69 pence on a little duck and I don't know how much I spent on my power ball. Then we had our dinner of chips and sausages and a drink. After dinner we went back to the beach to have a swim. Then it was tea time. We got our plates and we had our tea of salad. When we had finished washing and rinsing our plates out we had to finish making our tents nice and neat. Then we had our tuck and to finish our log for today.

Third day. In the morning ,after breakfast we had flag break and inspection. We got more points than yesterday. After inspection and flag break we had to play for a little time. Before breakfast, at keep fit, we had to start by the marquee and go up to the gate and up to the top of the lane and back again. When we got back to the marquee we had to go around the field and back to the marquee. After we played for a little time we went from North Sands to South Sands. The footpath went up around by the sea. We saw a sheep in the ferns. Then we came to a wood sloping down. Then we went up to the South Sands beach. Then we went from South Sands to the camp site and we had our dinner.

Andrew Beer

In May 1985 Scout Malcolm Mant received the Chief Scout's Award from District Commissioner Ron Shell. During Job Week, Cubs and Scouts raised over £300 and this was by no means the final figure. A group of 20 Scouts enjoyed the week's annual camp, which was at Caddy Hole in the Ashcliff Forest near Exeter and of these, only three had previous camping experience. It was a very successful, enjoyable week, and the weather was good. The patrol competition was won by David McNevin's patrol. On the Thursday they were joined by 21 Cubs, who camped with them for the remainder of the week.

South Brent Young Farmers

Another group that has at various times thrived in South Brent is the Young Farmers. During the mid-1980s reports of their activities appeared in the local media.

In 1985 a Dairymaid and Dairyman dance competition was held in the Coach House Inn at Wrangaton, where Mr and Mrs R. Camp chose Susan Luscombe as the Dairymaid and Andrew Steer as Dairyman. The choice of a winner was described as 'difficult', and Denise Kendall was chosen as reserve Dairymaid. In April, the group held a sponsored cycle ride to raise money to purchase ophthalmic equipment for local hospitals. Two teams entered in the South Devon Groups Public Speaking competition. It was a competition for those under 26 years old. Both the teams were aged between 14 and 23 years. The A team members were: Miss H. Cooper (Chairman), Mr J. Grieveson (Speaker) and Mr R. Scott (Proposer). The B team members were: Mr A. Steer (Chairman), Mr D. Wakeham (Speaker) and Mr M. Grieveson (Proposer).

Jeffery Grieveson spoke about goat keeping with a speech entitled 'We're not Kidding about Goats'. Derek Wakeham spoke about rare breeds of birds, and his speech was entitled 'Eggs on Legs'.

The A team gained fourth place and the B team were placed sixth. Totnes B won this competition.

Then, in August, the group held a very successful whist drive at the Village Hall and was able to fill 16 tables. The prizes were from local shops and pubs, ex-young farmers and present young farmers. As well as this, the group held a clay pigeon shoot at 'Sopers', Horsebrook, Avonwick. Denise Kendall, the secretary wrote:

It was attended by about 70 people from far and wide, including Cheshire. The Cornish Champion was also there. This Open Competition, which started at 2p.m., continued until it became dark. In all £55 worth of prize money was handed out, including a voucher which was donated by Tuckers Seeds of Ashburton. The highest score of the day was a total of 39 clays out of 40.

South Brent Young Farmers whist drive, 11 February 1947. (THE MEAD COLLECTION)

Another Look at The Aune – Some Nineteenth-Century Views

The River below Brentmoor House.
(THE WADDAMS COLLECTION)

The Bridge at Brent Mill, ivy-covered and picturesque, as viewed from downstream. (THE WADDAMS COLLECTION)

The Aune as she tumbles over rocks at Shipley.
(THE WADDAMS COLLECTION)

The road leading to Brentmoor House following the River to Shipley Bridge. (THE SHARVILLE COLLECTION)

CHAPTER 6

Another Look at Wartime Brent

Evacuees

Children living in Brent during the Second World War have memories of the evacuees who came here. They generally got on well and many of them kept in touch long after the war had finished. Evie Hard often talked of 'the Dukes'. In an interview in the 1980s, she said:

I remember when war was declared. It was one of our family's birthday and I took two evacuee children from Acton.

They had a committee which said that if you had a spare bedroom you had to take a child. I was quite prepared because I like children. I only had one but these two children, they didn't know each other until they were on the train but they were about ten years old. They hung onto each other when they got to the Village Hall, where we had to go up and pick a child up. Jack Preston, he was doing them, and he said, 'Well there's these two children and they won't be parted,' so I said, 'Well, I'll have them.' There were such awful stories about these children arriving dirty and everything like that. A friend of mine was very concerned and she said she would help me bath them and everything and they were so clean and so sweet we never even... Well we washed them before we put them to bed and that was the end of that. We've been friendly with the families ever since.

Alan Jones, although born in Bristol, has, at the time of writing, lived in Brent for over 50 years. In his unpublished reminiscences he recalls being evacuated to Cornwall.

By mid-'41, children were being evacuated in large numbers to various parts of the country. Myself, I was evacuated to Cornwall. Many children were upset having to leave their parents. Dozens of very tearful Mums watched that train leave Bedminster Road Station, some, no doubt, never to see their children again. To me, with a small suitcase of clothes, my gas mask case and a name label around my neck, I went over 100 miles by train to Liskeard. It was the start of a big adventure.

When we arrived in Liskeard, we gathered in the town hall. Tea, buns and lemonade were provided, then we were split into various small groups, and directed to a number of coaches going to different villages. My group went to the beautiful sleepy little village of St Neots, (one church, two chapels, one school for infants, juniors

and seniors, one pub, one butcher's shop, one black-smith's shop, one Post Office-cum-general store) and, of course, the Village Hall, where another reception committee was awaiting our arrival. There was more tea, buns and lemonade. Many people from the village and surrounding area had gathered to collect and take us kiddies to our new homes. I was more than happy. With another lad from my own area, I was located with a farming couple who had a young boy of their own of our age. This could have been a recipe for friction, but not so, in no time we were accepted by and well integrated into our new family and a totally different way of life.

Every day we had a walk of about two and a half miles each way to school and back. The farmer did have a car but only used it for Sunday trips to chapel and on Mondays to go to Liskeard market. It was a hard, fair and happy way of life, we boys having to do our fair share of work. There were many jobs a young lad could do around a farm. During the harvest season, school became secondary. All hands were needed, there were no tractors or motorised machinery. Horses were used

Mary Woodward and Joy Lang at Albert House. Mary was an evacuee from Acton in London who came to stay with the Lang family. (THE HAYMAN COLLECTION)

The Ballad of Tippling Down *portrayed the arrival of evacuees in a sleepy rural village not far from South Brent!! It received its world premiere on the stage of South Brent Village Hall in 2007.* Left to right: *Emily Pinfield, Jo-Jo Parke, Sion Parke, Victoria Lannin, Robbie Thomas, Christi Terry, Caitlin Prosser, Jen Laity and Josh Antonio (Lucy Ridout is out of picture).* (THE SBADS COLLECTION)

Alan and Christine Jones after their wedding at St John's Church, Bridgetown, on 20 September 1952.

(THE JONES COLLECTION)

for hay making, corn cutting, harrowing, ploughing, etc., although an old tractor was used by the contractor when threshing and bailing. Man-power was increased with the aid of neighbouring farmhands, each farmer in turn helping the others out. When harvesting, lunch was brought out to the men. There was cold tea, cider, a true ploughman's lunch consisting of a great hunk of home-made bread, a lump of cheese and pickled onions. At the end of a day's work, a proper roast meal was provided by the host farmer's wife, always finishing with huge helpings of pudding and own-produced clotted cream. Perhaps as many as a dozen to 16 persons sat around the huge scrubbed-top table.

We went to school on most days. There was an occasional visit to market and twice in two years I remember a visit to the cinema in Liskeard. The opening music was 'When the lights go on again all over the world', and the closing music was the National Anthem. It was a real treat. On Sundays we attended the village chapel, both morning and evening services. School was nothing to shout about, but the most memorable thing in my mind was the arrival of the school dentist in a caravan parked in the playground. To us kiddies it appeared as if the dentist really enjoyed using the antiquated drill, operated by some form of pedal power. Weather permitting, on Friday afternoons there was a nature walk and a golden opportunity to slip away and so go home early. There were no school meals. Each day there was a packed lunch, more often than not consisting of a Cornish pasty and often exchanged for perhaps another lad's sandwiches.

There was an added attraction to us lads living on a farm. Our own farmer was by trade a professional blacksmith (an ex-farrier from the First World War). Consequently, on such occasions as his services were needed for shoeing our own or neighbours' horses, or ancillary works such as forging frames of various sorts as attachments to different agricultural machinery, us boys used to take turns to operate the forge bellows.

On the farm itself there was no electricity. We did have an accumulator-powered wireless. There was no gas nor running water. Lighting came from candles and paraffin lamps. Cooking and heating all came from a wood-burning range. Washing facilities were in a lean-to outside the back door and next to the pump. Bath night was in the old galvanised tub placed in the kitchen. The toilet, across the yard and into the vegetable garden, was a shed inside which was a plank with a hole in it, and a bucket underneath. The farmer himself cleaned that place up. Toilet tissue was 6in. squares from back numbers of The Farmer's Weekly *suspended on a piece of string on the door.*

Farming families produced most of their own food – butter, milk, bread, cheese and fruit preserves. Meat was plentiful, oneself and neighbouring farmers taking turns to slaughter a sheep, lamb, calf or pig and share out the meat. Chicken, goose, duck and rabbit were always available. Meat coupons were denied to these families!

When a big old fat pig was butchered us kids were given the job of shaving the carcass when it was hanging prior to being quartered and shared out. There were no freezer units; the meat was preserved in a layer of rock salt, then a layer of meat and so on in a large wooden barrel.

There was an occasional visit by the local community rat, rabbit and mole catcher who would arrive on his battered old bike loaded up with snare nets and ferrets, his loyal dog following behind, and once again us kids would try to spend a day with him, a very pleasant and informative time.

Nevertheless, for myself, it was a very hard but idyllic way of life. War to us was miles away, nearest awareness was in news bulletins on the radio. Our very own awareness was from our bedroom window, where we could see the sky lit up over Plymouth, Saltash and Torpoint (about 16 miles away as the crow flies), and if the wind was in the right direction could be heard the rumble of bombs and gunfire.

June 1944 saw the invasion of France and so the changing tide of the war.

As with most good things, those wonderful, memorable days had to come to an end. The tide of war was changing. Not my idea, and much to my regret – I went back to Bristol, Mum, Dad, now three sisters and city life. After two years, 11 years old and once again uprooted from my accepted and idyllic existence, the return journey from Liskeard to Bristol was not of my choice and I distinctly recall being very upset. So much so, as I sat in a corner seat of the carriage and was obvi-

ously very unhappy and miserable, an American soldier tried cheering me up and got me to open up. I broke down and related my thoughts and ideas, to me such a drastic change of lifestyle, not my style or my wish. From his luggage the soldier produced a bar of candy (chocolate), which did go quite a way as a consolation and, daft as it sounds, that bar of chocolate made the final miles to Bristol seem much brighter.

Off to War

Ken Fox remembered going off to barracks with someone who had never been on a train before and was very upset about it. Ken took him under his wing and 'he seemed to settle down'. They started talking and away they went to Colchester. They stayed together in the Army.

Ken was sent to Burma on a troop ship, the *Marnik*. At 6.30 on 4 November they were torpedoed in the Mediterranean Sea. He was picked up by a naval boat and taken to a hospital ship. The first man he saw on board was Reg Hard, a Brent man. He thought that 'amazing'. Ken was 'more than pleased to see him, I might tell you'.

They went to Phillipville in North Africa and were sent out more kit. It was very hot but when they woke up they saw a brigade of guards as if they were outside Buckingham Palace. 'I could have cried to

Ken Fox with his wife, Daphne, at the christening of their son, Simon, in 1966. Also in the photograph are Andrew and Sally.
(THE FOX COLLECTION)

see all that sight with those guards on parade.' They were picked up and sent through the rest of the Med to Port Said, where they stayed for a couple of days. They watched children diving for coins that they threw in. People were going up and down trying to sell trinkets. They sailed through the Suez Canal and across the Indian Ocean. 'It was a long, tedious voyage.' Ken would sit watching the sunset with a Welsh choir singing. 'It used to be lovely. I enjoyed that.' He saw flying fishes. The passage lasted for 14 days until they landed in Bombay, where they stayed at a transit camp for a week. Ken recalls it was very dirty. In Bombay he met someone who greeted him. Ken replied, 'Hello.' The other chap said, 'I think I know you. Aren't you from South Brent? I think so because you're called Ken Fox. I think you're a Brent boy.' He was Bert Chulk. They had a few pints over successive nights. He was on his way home because he was in the regulars. Bert gave Ken some good advice.

Ken went onward to Calcutta and Chittagong. It was fortunate that the war was almost over. Ken recalls that some ports were good and some were not so good. He was invited to Naval clubs for evenings out. They had a race meeting there and the guests were allowed to bet on the horses – 'Great fun'. They did not have a lot to do with the local people – each kept themselves to themselves – although Ken had an Indian chap to look after him. Ken moved to the Royal Corps of Military Police because they wanted a Quartermaster Sergeant. He enrolled in the Royal Corps of Military Police. Ken took part in motor patrols to make sure that the British people were not up to any trouble. If they were they would get put inside for a few months to cool them off. Ken did this for 18 months. He was then transferred home and served as a military policeman until demobbed at Aldershot, then returning to Brent.

In Calcutta Bill Kennard had given him a copy of the book *Tarka the Otter*, which made him a Henry Williamson fan.

The Camp

Stuart Draffen was one of the soldiers stationed in the camp, which occupied the site of the present Crowder Park. He was a member of the London and Scottish Regiment and recalls arriving at Brent on New Year's Eve in 1942, a Wednesday. When they arrived the soldiers were broke, but, as it was New Year's Eve and being Scottish, celebrations were a must. Stuart and his friends went down to the London Inn, where they spent the evening with the locals drinking scrumpy. He recalls that, as they went back to the camp, 'We could have taken the Germans on single-handed.'

The London Scottish Regiment was a training battalion and Stuart and his fellows were instructors, training men to join regiments for service all over the world. They spent a lot of time training on Dartmoor in all winds and weather. He recalls taking the men on 50-mile forced marches in full kit, and can remember on more than one occasion waking up in winter covered in snow!

A moment of relaxation at the Brent Camp.

(THE DRAFFEN COLLECTION)

Above: *Stuart Draffen* (far right) *and friends preparing for a wedding in Liverpool Scottish dress uniform.*

(THE DRAFFEN COLLECTION)

Left: *Stuart Draffen outside his quarters at the Brent Camp. He recalls standing here at night with his fellow soldiers watching Plymouth burn.*

(THE DRAFFEN COLLECTION)

The barracks were in Nissen huts, which housed 20 men, the instructors living with those they were training. They were of a much better standard than the accommodation British soldiers were used to, since they were built for the American troops to American standards. This is confirmed in the official records of the regiment, where it is stated:

New Year's Day 1943 found the Battalion in Devonshire. The noteworthy fact to record is that, for once, the camp accommodation was well built, with excellent facilities, although it was not quite finished.

Mr Draffen recalls the men standing at the door of the hut in the evening listening to the bombing of Plymouth and seeing the orange glow in the sky as the city burned. He also recalls travelling back from Scotland dressed in his best gear, getting off the train at Brent Station and being taken direct to Plymouth to help clear the debris from the bombings. When they eventually got back to Brent Camp their clothes were far from pristine.

The members of the Liverpool and Scottish Regiment socialised with the local Brentonians. Mr Draffen remembers the concert parties and dances in the Church Hall and the games of football against Brent that were held on Sunday afternoons. It was not long before the Brent people began to recognise the soldiers and greet them in a friendly way.

Mr Draffen stayed in Brent for just over a year before the battalion was moved on, as was the custom so that the German authorities could not pinpoint who was where, and eventually joined the Gordon Highlanders. He spent time on a course in Salcombe preparing engineers in the techniques of offloading vehicles from invasion barges without sinking in preparation for the D-Day landings.

Nano Wood, who was growing up in Brent at this time, can recall that whenever there was an air-raid siren the Liverpool Scottish soldiers would take all their lorries from the field at Sanderspool Cross, where they were parked, and drive them out around Aish, where there was less likelihood that they would be bombed.

Reminiscences of the Second World War

Gilly Hawes recounts her memories of living in South Brent during the Second World War:

My mother, Marion Hawes, was Quartermaster of the Brent section of the Red Cross. As soon as war was declared, she ran first-aid classes in the Vicar's Hall. I was taken along to be a patient and was bandaged up like a mummy. Mother also went to help at Totnes Hospital each week – using the train, of course.

My father, Charles Hawes, was home on leave from India and had to wait for a return passage round the Cape. He helped to organise the Home Guard and was known as 'The Major', though that was only a title from the First World War. He instigated the day-long watches on Brent Hill mentioned by Barbara Lodge. As a child, I enjoyed picnics up there.

There were several episodes of parachutists landing over the moor. To solve the mystery, father and Sergeant Badge went up to Marley Head and concluded when coming back down that it was the barrage balloons over Plymouth which appeared to descend.

Also to guard against invasion the Hunt organised riders (in twos) to patrol a great sweep of local moor

Mrs Marion Hawes, Quartermaster of the Brent section of the Red Cross. (THE HAWES COLLECTION)

Mrs Hawes in her Red Cross uniform on the front steps of The Sheiling during the Second World War.

(THE HAWES COLLECTION)

Left: *During the Second World War Millswood Mill was used as a munitions factory making aircraft parts. The local workforce was expanded by men brought out from Plymouth to help with this vital work*

(THE EALES COLLECTION)

Right: *The staff of the Army and Navy Stores which operated from the Church House during the Second World War.*

(THE EALES COLLECTION)

during the long, light evenings. Presumably, if they saw parachutists, they would have to gallop to Brent, because few outlying farms were on the 'phone.

In the First World War, sphagnum moss was used to dress wounds, so Mum had us all going to collect it from the bogs. We took a pony to carry the dripping sacks. The moss had to be picked over, washed and dried, a tedious business, and after all that, the authorities decide they didn't need it.

Everyone in Brent remembers Ugborough Beacon being lit up by Plymouth burning. There was the danger to us that a German bomber being chased might jettison its remaining bombs in order to beat a hasty retreat. Accordingly, my parents dug a shelter in our orchard – quite an undertaking and quite useless because the shelter rapidly filled with water. When one of our precious hens fell in and drowned the shelter was filled in again.

Anyone who could, kept hens to augment the ration of one egg per person per week. Dried eggs were not easy to disguise. When the hens got past laying, they were eaten – as were rabbits if you could get one. I was expected to take my turn skinning rabbits, plucking hens and de-gutting both.

In the war there was a ruling that one acre in seven had to be ploughed, even if the local soil and climate were unsuitable. There was a man, known to the farmers as Mr Gestapo, who had to inspect the ploughed land. We tried growing cereals and it was always too wet to harvest the crop in reasonable condition. In the end, we just grew potatoes.

At the start of the war, we housed a family of friends from India. At the same time we had a little girl, Ruth,

from London. Mum established that her hair was clean, but then she caught nits from some of the other evacuees. The poor girl was too ashamed to tell Mum so we all got nits and it was very hard to get rid of them. The final cure was to apply sassafras oil (very smelly) and wrap your head in a towel for three days. It took many more days of washing to eradicate the smell!

Ruth returned to London, and we had a family from Plymouth – the wife and three children, and a baby was delivered at home soon after they arrived. The husband was a bus driver and rarely spent the nights in Brent. On one memorable occasion he got drunk and his wife rushed in to Mum saying he was threatening her with a knife. Mum had to confront him, extract the knife and tell him he could never come back if he behaved like that again.

That family returned to Plymouth and we had the family from Guernsey mentioned by Barbara Lodge [in The Book of South Brent]. The wife became the local school doctor. She had a daughter and three sons, the eldest of whom was in the RAF.

If a Canadian ship docked at Plymouth and was due to stay a few days, a Canadian organisation, the Knights of Columbus, would telephone Mum and ask if we in Brent could accommodate a certain number of sailors. Mum had a list of housewives to call and see if they were able to help. Then she met the lorry transporting the lads and would go round dropping then off at their hosts' homes.

Once we had a Canadian sailor for several weeks. He was recuperating from an appendix operation and taught me to play blackjack.

A NAAFI canteen was set up in the house called St

Michael's – since demolished – and Mum had the task of organising shifts to serve the soldiers. If she had too few helpers she would press-gang me into assisting. One night she and I were just packing up when two breathless Tommies came in begging for a cup of tea. They said they had been chasing a naked man on Brent Hill, unsuccessfully it seems. So we put the kettle back on and made tea and they insisted on escorting us home in case we met the aforementioned fellow. Probably he had absconded from the psychiatric hospital at Bittaford, then known as Blackadon, later Moorhaven.

We had a pony and trap to go shopping, sometimes in Totnes but mostly at the Army and Navy Stores at The Manor (now the Church House). We did well when the American troops passed in convoy and they all threw candy into the trap – a welcome addition to our sweet ration.

One American, Joe Nardone, was a cowboy in previous life and he soon latched on to Mum and our bigger pony. One day, on an exercise on Ugborough Beacon, his fellow GIs challenged him to ride a wild Dartmoor pony. He promptly roped a pony, leapt onto it and was jettisoned in double-quick time! With a small pony there was nothing to grip. He often told the story against himself. On Thanksgiving Day he had organised the cooks to make us a special apple pie with a cheese topping. He was furious when the officers discovered it and scoffed the lot. He was in the military police escorting food convoys and would often appear with a tin of peaches or some such delicacy. He also adopted the Stones at Zeal Farm and rode their horses. He developed a great liking for Devonshire cream and would bring us some, too.

At that time I had my left leg in plaster from hip to toe. Joe appointed himself as my guardian to stop me trying to climb trees or ride my pony. Mum, always busy organising things in the village, was only too delighted to have his help. How many mothers today would trust a young soldier to look after their young

girl of 14? Alas, Joe did not survive Omaha Beach.

To train for the invasion of France the area of Slapton Sands was commandeered. During the evacuation of the civilian community the WVS was called upon to help. The Brent section duly reported for duty along with all the others. They helped run a mobile canteen so that the locals could be fed without having to take time to prepare their meals.

Mum was assigned to a farmer who had to kill and prepare all his poultry. Mum spent a week plucking geese and said she never wanted to repeat that performance. The fluffy down penetrated everywhere and she sneezed and sneezed.

In The Book of South Brent, *not much is said of VJ Day. Having been away at school for VE Day, I had felt cheated of celebrating. On VJ Day it poured all day. My sister Liz was on leave from the ATS and she and I loaded the pony trap with faggots and hauled them to the top of Brent Hill in readiness for the bonfire. We made two trips wondering if any of it would burn. It did.*

My father returned from India and arrived in Brent on VJ Day after an absence of more than four years.

Liz had joined the ATS in 1941 so she was seldom in Brent after that. She was on radar operations, latterly stationed near Portsmouth trying to shoot down doodle-bugs before they could get to London. After the war, while waiting to be demobbed, she took a commission and was stationed briefly at Denbury Camp. One day she was escorting two lorries full of troops on a local trip and had hinted that they might drop in to tea. I had just saddled up to go for a ride when she arrived with one lorry, the other having got lost. Liz immediately grabbed my horse, jumped on it despite her tight uniform skirt and dashed off to look for the lost lorry. Mum and I were left to produce tea for everyone, including the men in the lost lorry when Liz found it and guided it back to Sheiling. I felt pretty grumpy about my interrupted ride!

Brent Centenarians

Miss Ida Sherrell on her 103rd birthday. Remembered as an avid gardener and animal lover, even when she had passed her 100th birthday she still looked after the boxes and baskets outside her cottage in Station Road.
(The Miller Collection)

Mrs Anne Collier with her husband George in the grounds of Whinfield. (The Collier Collection)

Miss Violet Manning on her 100th birthday. For many years Miss Manning ran the newsagency in Station Road. (The Stephens and Wright Collections)

Mrs Ann Jones taking her favourite stroll along Hillside in 2001. (The Brooks Collection)

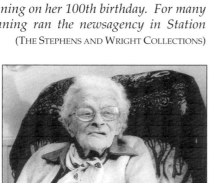

Mrs Wendy Turnbull on her 105th birithday. She eventually lived to the age of 107, spending her last years at Pinewood Lodge.
(The Everett Collection)

Mrs Ruth Hard, one of the Garland girls of Church Street, a very active member of the Brent community, on her 100th birthday. (The Timmins Collection)

CHAPTER 7

Another Look at Carnivals

One of the highlights of the year in Brent is the summer carnival. The carnivals in the late 1950s were very much village affairs, with local organisations and individuals spending the Saturday of the procession arranging floats and entries. The carnival itself ceased to function during the 1960s and the early part of the 1970s but was then revived.

Choosing the Carnival Queen

Carnival begins with the choosing of the year's royalty. In 1977 the dance to choose Miss South Brent was deemed a great success. The judges had difficulty in making a decision and the marking was very close. They chose Sally Fox as Miss South Brent and Jackie Towl and Julia Stevens as her attendants. All the girls who were brave enough to compete looked charming, and, under the friendly questioning of Monty Flashman, acquitted themselves well; it was a pity they could not all have been chosen. One thing was certain, Mr Flashman knew more about campanology (bell-ringing) when he had finished the interviews than he did when he started, since Julia was a member of St Petroc's Church bell-ringers.

Tracy Sings (née Miller) writes of her time as the 1980 carnival queen:

I was South Brent Carnival Queen in 1980. I had just returned from a long holiday to Australia with my parents. The carnival queen choosing was quite a busy affair back then. It was held at the Village Hall, as I believe it still is. I went in for the competition because all my friends were entering and because my mum had been a carnival queen back in 1957. She was the longest reigning carnival queen in South Brent due to the carnivals ceasing in 1957 and not recommencing until

A pre-Second World War South Brent carnival queen, Miss Doris Manning, and her attendants.

(The Goss Collection)

Carnival Queens Roll of Honour

Reigned	Carnival Queen	Reigned	Carnival Queen
	Freda Bishop	1989	Louise Copley
	Margaret O'Shea	1990	Michelle Male
	Serena Soper	1991	Donna Warne
	Pam Andrews	1992	Lisa Hooper
	Ruth Dodd	1993	Karen Soper
1957	Jean Uren	1994	Dawn Vinnecombe
	And then a break until	1995	Gemma Illman
1976	Linda Walters	1996	Melanie Tarr
1977	Sally Fox	1997	Kate Evemy
1978	Jackie Newman	1998	Ami Wilson
1979	Andria Hampton	1999	Megan Flett
1980	Tracey Miller	2000	Joanne Hanney
1981	Jackie Mitchell	2001	Alison Parr
1982	Tracey Mumford	2002	Lisa Illman
1983	Anya Cockings	2003	Rebekah Kirk
1984	Teresa Lake	2004	Bronwyn Thomas
1985	Louise Ellison	2005	Rebekah Kirk
1986	Amanda Tidball	2006	Samantha Taylor
1987	Nicki Andrews	2007	Kelly Turner
1988	Debbie Hellyer		

Choosing the 1957 carnival queen. (The Miller Collection)

South Brent carnival queen 1957, Miss Jean Uren, making her speech of acceptance. She 'reigned' from 1957 until the carnival was revived in 1976. (The Miller Collection)

Miss Ruth Dodd, the retiring carnival queen, with her successor, Miss Jean Uren, 1957. (The Miller Collection)

The 1956 carnival royalty. Left to right: Janet Nesaule, David Newman, carnival queen Ruth Dodd and Patsy Giggs. (The Newman Collection)

The 1957 carnival royalty, Avril Trundle, Jean Uren (carnival queen) and Marilyn Langdon. Margaret Hard, Len Watts and ? look on. (The Miller Collection)

In 1978 there were about 300 people in the carnival procession, which was led by the South Brent carnival queen and her attendants. Left to right: Loretta Bass, Jacky Newman, Heather Suddes. (The Sparkes Collection)

1975. I remember buying a bright red dress for the occasion. We had a panel of judges, one being the Chairman of South Hams District Council. We were all interviewed individually and asked our hobbies and ambitions. My ambition then was to become a nurse, which I have more than fulfilled as I am currently Matron of a local nursing home. I couldn't believe it when I was told I had won. My attendants were Wendy Rodgers

and Lorraine Bass-Twitchell. I remember winning £25, which seemed a lot to me then, as I was only 15. I was actually crowned on the night, which differs from today. I remember my Dad coming to pick me up and the front doors were locked, but the doorman said, 'If I have to let anyone in it has to be you.' Then I appeared with my tiara and sash. He was thrilled, as was my Mum when I got home.

My carnival float theme was a castle. My Dad was working for Slumberland Beds at Brent Mill at the time. They were on short time then, so my Dad made the float by himself on the days when he wasn't working. The manager, Mr Harry Doye, kindly donated the timber required. I was very proud of my float, as my dad made such a professional job of it.

I was the only carnival queen then to wear a short dress and we were penalised for it by some of the judges on the carnival circuit, as the float had an historical

Carnival royalty of 1976. Left to right: *Jane Widdicombe, Trudi Mugridge, Tracy Sparkes, Melanie Stevens, Nicky Smith, Teresa Smeeth.* (The Sparkes Collection)

Carnival royalty of 1983. Left to right: *Teresa Lake, Anya Cockings (carnival queen), Julie Towl.*

(The Sparkes Collection)

theme and we were in modern dress. When we were due to visit Totnes we hired medieval dresses, complete with Neil Suddes dressed as a court jester in tights!

The carnivals were hard work, especially for my parents; most Saturdays were tied up with them. We provided flower tubs from our own garden to decorate the float, and as the summer progressed, we had to rely on donations of flowers from neighbours and friends – Joy and Bill Hayman provided us with an endless supply. The part that I didn't enjoy was waiting to be judged. We would have to sit around in all weathers for hours on end, although, unlike today, we didn't have to paint our faces or dance, we just had to sit there, wave and smile.

I really enjoyed my year as royalty. My only regret is that, having a daughter of my own, she had no interest in entering herself when she got to that age. That would have really been something. I don't suppose many villages could boast they had three generations that shared the title of carnival queen.

Building the Float

Having chosen the carnival royalty, the next major event of the carnival is the building of the float upon which the 'royal family' will travel, not only through Brent but far and wide to other carnivals.

In 1983 the carnival hit a crisis when the local press reported, under the title 'Vandals Scupper Carnival Float', that:

Carnival committee members in Brent have appealed to heartless pranksters who stole important decoration from the carnival float. Chairman Mr Frances Sparkes and secretary Mrs Lucy Moore posted notices throughout the village in an attempt to 'prick the consciences' of those who may have threatened Brent's chances of winning prizes in carnivals throughout the district in the next few weeks. Members were busily preparing for Monday's Bank Holiday carnival at Modbury when it was discovered that the float had been attacked.

Mrs Lucy Moore, a carnival committee member for many years, preparing for a summer carnival procession.

(The Woodhouse Collection)

South Brent's award winning 'Swan Lake' carnival float of 1987. The carnival queen was Nicki Andrews, her attendants Amy Crago and Natasha Illman.

(THE SPARKES COLLECTION)

Mrs Frances Sparkes, Mr Gerald Cleave and Mrs Jean Cleave with the prizes won in 1987. The swan float is in the background. (THE SPARKES COLLECTION)

Velvet curtains, two old-fashioned spotlights, paint and ropes were missing. Mrs Moore said: 'The total value must be at least £100. At one time, it looked as if we would have to withdraw from the Modbury carnival but now someone has loaned us curtains and it looks as though we can go ahead. However, the float will not look as effective and a lot more work will be needed in time for other events this summer. It doesn't look as though we're going to get the things back but they are

valuable and it would be nice to receive a phone call letting us know where we could pick them up.' She said police had been informed of the theft. When the float was judged at Modbury, it actually came second!

In 1985 everyone was hoping that the Saturday carnival procession would not be washed out by the rain, which had hardly stopped since the Thursday evening. It did stop for a while – long enough to prevent everyone from getting soaked through. However, because of the rain and possible damage to the floats, only five of the expected ten visiting carnival queens arrived. The South Brent 'royal party' looked splendid on their float, which had been built by Gerald Cleave and decorated by Lucy Moore and Frances Sparkes. The girls' dresses were complemented with lovely hand-knitted capes and slippers: Valerie Newman had knitted them over the last four months (at times she had been working with over 300 stitches on the needles).

In 1987 Brent's 'swan' carnival float carried off top prizes at each of the carnivals it took part in. The massive blue and white swan entered 16 carnivals, took an impressive total of 11 first awards and came second in the remaining five. A trio of carnival helpers, Gerald Cleave, his wife Jean and Frances Sparkes, took three weeks to build the float and then took it all over the Devon carnival circuit.

Mr Dave Newman told the Ivybridge and *South Brent Gazette*: 'This is the best we have ever done with a float. It has been really terrific. It's a real credit to South Brent.'

South Brent's carnival float was also successful in 1988, winning many prizes including the premier prize at one of the West Country's biggest carnivals at Torbay. Before a crowd of hundreds in Torquay, South Brent's Dave Newman received the 2ft 6in high Prestige Trophy for the best float in Torbay Carnival procession. The float had earlier carried off the silver cup first prize for the best visiting queen. It was the first time the award for best float had gone to a visiting queen.

Dave Newman commented that: 'People were absolutely amazed to think that a small village could come along and win a major award. It was fantastic.' The float was made by Gerald and Jean Cleave, Mark Cleave, Mrs Frances Sparkes and Dave's daughter, Debbie.

Carnival Week

Carnival week begins with the street fair and lasts for a week, culminating in the grand procession on the following Saturday. The reports of the 1976 street fair reflect the popularity of the event at the time:

You had to arrive early to get the bargains. Brent's annual street fair, which traditionally marks the start of carnival week, yet again was a great success. After only

Mrs Sheila Wall, Mrs Lillian Wakeley and Mrs Eunice Vallance man the Mothers' Union stall at the 1977 Carnival Street Fair.

half an hour the empty stalls may not have seemed all that attractive to the passer-by, but you had to be there at the start to take in the atmosphere of the day.

The stalls were full of goodies and the smiles on the faces of the carnival queen and her attendants said that, even if the formula was the same as last year and the year before, there was no need to change the winning recipe for enjoyment and fun.

In fact, the organisers did even better this year and added to the afternoon's attractions. A crisp-eating contest and the Brent Hill Race brought in good entries. While youngsters queued up to send four packets of crisps tumbling into their stomachs in the shortest possible time, the runners trudged up to the top of the hill and tumbled down to the Anchor Inn.

Cream Coffee, the Brixham Band, provided the musical accompaniment and the rain held off long enough to ensure that the potency of the Brent Winemakers' Guild 'samples' remained, like the afternoon's entertainment, undiluted.

Carnival Week 1977 began on 1 July with a carnival dance in the Village Hall. Having chosen a 'Sweet Sixteen' Miss South Brent and attendants, the committee decided to have a 'Gorgeous Granny' parade at the dance.

At the end of the 1977 carnival season the carnival committee held the final meeting and invited the public to look at the carnival films that had been made and to hear the financial results.

About 70 people came to the Village Hall and all were delighted to learn that the carnival had made a substantial profit of over £400.

The committee very carefully considered all the requests from village organisations and decided to allocate the money as follows: the Girl Guides, Scouts, the Loft Youth Club, the Playgroup, the Cricket Club, the St John Cadets and the Football Club all received £30. The School Association was given £20. The Brownies, Cubs, St John adults and the Village Hall benefited from £15 each. Finally, the

The Scouts and Cubs were frequent participants in the summer carnival. Here a 75ft long dragon is led through the streets by Libby Major and Patsy Tidball. Scout leader Adrian Woodhouse was inside the frame supporting the dragon's head. A number of Scouts and Cubs were roped together under the cloth to make the body.

(THE MAJOR COLLECTION)

senior citizens had £10. That left a balance of over £1,140 in the funds to start the 1978 activities, and for any work to be done on the float during the winter.

The public meeting elected Mr Francis Sparkes ` as chairman of the new committee, with Mrs Peggy Stevens and Mrs Linda Smith as treasurer and secretary.

By 1979 the event had grown and the verdict was that the carnival in that year was the 'biggest and best' yet held.

The carnival parade had over 25 floats and 50 walkers, as well as 26 horses and a pack of beagles. The parade itself was described as being very colourful and attracted entries from all over the area, as well as town bands from Totnes and Hatherleigh and majorettes from South Brent, Kingsbridge and Buckfastleigh. The Yealmpton Youth Club brought their float, which they had made for their own carnival and enjoyed it so much that they came along to Brent

Organisations had been planning their entries for weeks. Brent Scouts and Cubs decided on the theme of the slave trade. The parents secretly built a large pyramid which the boys could pull along, but saved it as a surprise until the last minute. Mr. Mike Major, who organised the building, said, 'At least the boys will have a chance to see what is going on this year, because last time they were stuck in a dragon.' The entry won the overall trophy.

At the other extreme, the Male family of Brent, who must have caught carnival fever as it was building up to the time of the parade, decided to enter at the last minute.

Mr Barry Male, with his brother Rodney, two-year-old Michele and Daniel, aged six, only made up

83

For many years one of the carnival traditions has been the Floral Dance. In the early years of the carnival, the band and the dancers would literally weave in and out of the houses in Church Street, going in through the front door and coming out of the back door of one house, then doing the reverse next door. Here the dancers, dressed in their finery, are seen in Fore Street outside South Brent News.
(THE WOODHOUSE COLLECTION)

Another group of runners completes the race. Peter Reed is runner 127.
(THE REED COLLECTION)

Alison Reed completes the carnival long-distance race, cheered home by well-wishers. (THE REED COLLECTION)

their minds to enter half an hour before the parade. They decided to go as haunted spirits.

The 1979 carnival committee secretary, Mrs Linda Smith, was reported as saying that the carnival in that year was, '... the largest and most successful carnival parade Brent has seen. Everyone thoroughly enjoyed themselves and the standard was very high.'

The 1984 carnival got off to a flying start on a warm and sunny day. The atmosphere was festive, with bunting festooning the main street and colourful stalls laden with goodies of all kinds. As the 2p.m. starting time approached, crowds of people gathered to see the crowning of carnival queen Miss Theresa Lake. At 3p.m. Mr J. O'Connor judged the pavement artist competition. Les Andrews organised a Brent Hill run, with over 70 men, women, boys and girls taking part – not a day for strenuous exercise but all gave of their best. The winners were S. Coker, G. Male, M. Mant and J. Frost.

Numerous activities were arranged on each day of carnival week, and on Saturday, 23 June, it all ended with a grand procession at 6p.m. followed by a dance in the Village Hall.

All proceeds of the carnival went to the Village Hall Committee to help with the purchase of a new public address system.

In 1985 carnival week got off to a good start with the street fair, which was opened by TSW personality, Lawrie Quayle. The retiring queen, Trish Lake, crowned carnival queen Louise Ellison. Louise's attendants were Tanya Neal and Rosie Mitchell; the prince was Jonathan Camp and the princess Katie Wall. Jean Sabine made the royal costumes. Although dry, the weather was a little chilly, especially for some of the stall-holders, but there was a good crowd and all the stalls did well. The Anchor Hotel presented a new trophy for the Brent Hill run, awarded to the first South Brent man over 35 over the finishing tape. Guy Pannell won it. The day reached an enjoyable climax with a barbecue at the Glazebrook Hotel, which was attended by over 130 people.

A total of 50 people went to the Sunday carnival service at the Village Hall, which was led by the Plymouth Salvation Army Band. This was followed by the Pip Critten Children's Show, which held the audience of 130 spellbound for two hours, and was a terrific success. After a tea party in the paddock next to the hall, the children went home happy and tired.

Brent is known for it susceptibility to rain. It held off for the football and netball competitions on the Monday of carnival week but, unfortunately, Thursday's children's fancy dress competition in the school field was somewhat dampened by the weather. The rain which had been threatening finally arrived in the evening during the competition, which Len Jackman judged. By the end of the competition, the rain was pouring down, so the floral dance was out of the question. However, the Kingsbridge Silver Band offered to put on a concert in the Village Hall instead, and this offer was gratefully accepted. The

Entrants in the South Brent carnival baby show. Left to right: *Paul Honeywill, Audrey Nicholls with Phillip, Dilys Lilley with Kevin, Shirley Livermore with Andrew, Iris Newman with Beverley, Val Wollington with Darren, Frances Sparkes with Elizabeth.* (THE JULIE TOWL COLLECTION)

concert, which lasted about one and a half hours, was well supported, and a mini floral dance was held in the hall. There was also a demonstration by the Dartington Morris Clog Dancers and their ladies. The rain did not affect Friday's indoor events – the whist drive and the discos.

The committee decided to try another starting point for the procession in 1985, so everyone congregated at the Police Station and surrounding area, with the visiting queens starting from Clobell's. The committee co-ordinated the movement of the procession with the aid of CB radios on loan from Gerald Cleave, and this made their task much easier. The Plymouth City Pipe and Drum Band led the colourful procession, and three other bands were interspersed with the floats – the Ivybridge Marching Youth Band, the Laira Silver Youth Band and the Ambassadors Marching Band from Plymouth. Later in the evening over 100 people enjoyed the carnival dance at the Village Hall, for which the Torbay Trio supplied the music. This proved to be a most successful end to what had been a busy and enjoyable week.

Carnivals, being outdoor events, are often affected by the weather. The carnival of 2000 opened with really hot weather and cloudless skies. Special guest, adventurer David Snelling, and his hinny Henry, who later went on a 2,000km trek across the Pyrenees to Santiago di Compostela to raise money for cancer research and relief charities, carried out the opening ceremony. Henry gave many children rides before they dismounted to enjoy the carnival contests and art competitions.

The midday sun proved too much for some people. The baby competition was almost cancelled, with many tiny tots crying as the sun's rays irritated sensitive skin. Grandmothers were not feeling particularly glamorous with the prospect of their make-up melting, and no-one entered the glamorous granny competition.

The three-mile fun run around the village did not draw its usual number of competitors, as people overheated just standing still! There were events held throughout the week and the carnival culminated in the grand procession on the last Saturday.

The year 2004 saw one of the less clement carnivals, but the wet weather could not dampen spirits. The nine-day event, which ran from Saturday, 19 June to Sunday, 27 June, attracted a strong turnout from villagers and visitors alike. The carnival raised funds for local Cubs and pre-school children, as well as for the Village Hall and the local recreation association.

Television presenter Claire Manning officially opened the carnival, and residents enjoyed a number of competitions, such as the pavement art and best-dressed window events during the first weekend.

Sporting events such as a children's fun run, five-a-side football and cricket matches allowed participants to let off energy, but only a handful of athletes took part in the run around Brent Hill, as it was hit by rain.

However, a bingo evening and a darts competition were keenly contested and organisers felt that the baby competition on the Wednesday morning was a 'screaming success'!

The last Saturday saw the carnival procession wind through the village, and even though there was an extremely heavy downpour midway, those who attended felt that the floats had made a colourful splash.

A family fun day completed the carnival last Sunday and, with a sizzling barbecue on the go, guests were able to enjoy a festival feast in the sultry summer sunshine.

In 2005 there were nine floats carrying carnival queens, with one coming from as far away as Crediton. Despite the light drizzle, there were good crowds.

The Winter Carnival

More recently another of the highlights of the year has been the Winter Carnival. This is the illuminated spectacle that takes place over the last weekend in November and marks the end of the South Hams carnival season. The first winter carnival was held in 1989 and has gone from strength to strength since then. Large floats from as far afield as East Devon and even Dorset, as well as people from Somerset and West Cornwall, have taken part over the years.

The winter carnival in the year 2000 was described in the Ivybridge and South Brent Gazette

A surprising spot of dry weather allowed hundreds of spectators to marvel at South Brent's illuminating carnival on Saturday.

Greg Wall and Richard Hard as 'The Four Aces' in the 1957 carnival.

Laura Murgatroyd (left) *as Mr Funny in the 1981 summer carnival.* (THE MURGATROYD COLLECTION)

The children of Bishopsmead in the 1981 carnival. **Left to right:** *Paul Elms, Debbie Langdon, Scott Evmy, Robert Crannis, Gary Langdon, Colin Hard, Paula Bullen, Lee Bullen, Paul Smith, Rachel Prince.*

(THE BULLEN COLLECTION)

Recycled carnival queens. Margaret Froom, who was carnival queen in 1953, with her 'attendants', Mary Bradford, Dawn McGinty, and Avril Kelly. (THE KELLY COLLECTION)

Left: South Brent Women's Institute always came up with original subjects for their walking entry to the summer carnival. In 1981 they were 'The Wombles'. Left to right: ?, Alice Horswill, Hilda Hard, Anita Perkins, Inez Jordan, Diane Reed, Rosalie Smeeth, Sylvia Warman, Peggy Johns, ?. (THE WOOD COLLECTION)

Below: In 1981 the Football Club, another regular competitor, entered as 'Robin Hood and his Merry Men'. Left to right: D. Stewart, I. Karkeek, P. Bullen, M. Wright, R. Hard, C. Perry, B. Male, B. King. P. Abel was Maid Marion. (THE BULLEN COLLECTION)

About 1,000 people gathered to watch the awesome display of 18 colourful floodlit floats as they wound their way through the streets. The sparkling winter carnival procession stretched at least three miles from Station Bridge to the crossroads and dazzled the crowds.

Marking the end of the South Hams carnival season, it was also staged as a thank you from members of South Brent Carnival Club to villagers for their support.

Due to the uncertain weather leading up to the carnival, six of the floats pulled out and pedestrian entries were low.

Secretary Jennifer Hanney said: 'We were expecting the worst with the weather, but we were blessed with a rare dry spell, and those who decided to take the chance provided a more impressive spectacle than last year.'

Among the most striking floats was Sansindo Warriors from Sidmouth's Gliddon Carnival Club, which took the smaller floats cup from the Dawlish entry, Midnight Magic.

The brightest and possibly the loudest was Show Time, by the Sid Vale Carnival Club.

Boasting some 8,500 light bulbs, it lit up the sky above the village and won the battle of the big floats and the Anchor Shield for the best overall.

Leading the procession was South Brent's own royalty float Swantasia. On board was Carnival Queen Joanne Hanney, 14, and her attendants, Laura Vinnecombe, Lisa IIman and Alison Carr, with princesses Lauren and Holly Senior.

Eight visiting royalty floats produced a strong class for the judges to sort out, with Miss Chudleigh taking first place.

A group of chefs dancing around madly created Kitchen Chaos and gave the Nunsford Nutters Carnival Club a prize for humour.

Cassie Matthews scooped the best local pedestrian with Sew and Sew.

Best local pedestrian with props went to Zodiacs Carnival Club from Crediton, as Defenders of the Dragon.

Miss Ipplepen won the Keith and Barbara Cup for the Queen of Queens.

Treasurer Margaret Beal said that the South Brent Winter Carnival is 'one of the best carnivals in Devon'.

In 2001 the WI turned out 'the Calendar Girls'. **Left to right:** Stella Stickland, Joy Hayman, Rosemary Evans, Eve Stewart, Sylvia Warman, Wendy Woodley, Esther Warnes, Jenny Pike, Pauline Mitchell, Gill Taylor, Pauline Juste, Betty Skinner.

(THE HAYMAN COLLECTION)

CHAPTER 8

Another Look at Church Activities

In this section we trace a year in the life of the three Churches in South Brent, St Petroc's Anglican Church, St Dunstan's Roman Catholic Church and the Methodist Church. One particular feature of all three churches is that they work closely together and many events are ecumenical.

One of the most popular events of Christmas Eve in recent years has been the Christingle Service held in St Petroc's Church in aid of the Childrens' Society. The church is completely full of all generations and it is a case of 'standing room only'.

Following the celebrations of Epiphany, the churches have two events leading up to Passiontide, the Week of Prayer for Christian Unity and the Women's World Day of Prayer. South Brent Mothers' Union has met on the third Thursday of each month for over 100 years, but in March, the World Women's Day of Prayer service is very special. This service, which is organised by a different group of women from all over the world, rotates around the three churches from year to year.

The Church Year beings with the celebration of Advent. St Dunstan's Church holds a Festival of Light on the Thursday after Advent Sunday and Advent crowns are lit in the other churches. Towards the end of Advent both the Methodist and the Anglican Churches hold their carol services, which involve members of all three churches.

The Methodist Church Anniversary

Each year in May, the Methodist Church celebrates the Chapel Anniversary. In 1987 there was a very special 'birthday' celebrating the centenary of the church. Mr Bert Dyer wrote of the weekend that:

... it will commence with a social get-together and tea for the Members Congregation on the Saturday. On the

Midnight Mass at St Petroc's Church is a very atmospheric service, with the church lit by hundreds of candles put up by an army of volunteers. This photograph, taken by Keith Male, was the church Christmas card for 2005.

(KEITH MALE PHOTOGRAPHY FROM THE EATWELL COLLECTION)

The period of Lent culminates with Palm Sunday and Holy Week. Two important events take place outside at this time. The Palm Sunday procession from the Anchor to St Petroc's takes place complete with donkey. Here three generations of the Armstrong family participate – Pat Armstrong leads the donkey accompanied by her daughter, Kate, and her mother, Ann Anderson.

(KEITH MALE PHOTOGRAPHY)

On the afternoon of Good Friday there is a pilgrimage to the top of Brent Hill, where a wooden cross is erected and stands throughout Easter week. This event has been held since 1971, when it was first instigated by Revd Michael Malsom. Our picture shows the procession paused at the junction of Hillside and Hillside Close. In the centre of the picture is Revd David Winnington-Ingram, Vicar of South Brent. To the right, by the cross, is Monty Rogers of the Methodist Church. (KEITH MALE PHOTOGRAPHY)

The great Feast of Easter is celebrated in all churches. In 2004 David Winnington-Ingram dyed his hair to match the church seasons. The normally dark vicar had a gold and white rinse for Easter, he went red for Whitsunday and then green a week later for Trinity Sunday. Here he is seen outside the Parish Church with Cathie Pannell, churchwarden Mardie Everett, Carol Davies, Susan Jozsa and Traudel Pountney, who took part in the Easter Bonnet competition. (THE EVERETT COLLECTION)

Ascension Day is celebrated with fireworks, whilst the ancient tradition of blessing the land is celebrated at Rogationtide. In 2007 the choir led the procession to the new allotment site, where the vicar blessed the plots and the crops growing in them. Gardens along the route were also given a blessing as the procession passed. Shortly after, the churches celebrate Whitsunday, the Feast of Pentecost. (THE ROBERTS COLLECTION)

St Petroc's Day falls on 4 June and at this time an event is held to celebrate the Patronal Festival. In 2003 the vicar and churchwardens travelled by rowing boat from Totnes to St Petrox Church in Dartmouth. On other occasions there have been walks from St Petroc's at Harford to St Petroc's South Brent.

The most ambitious pilgrimage took place in 2006, when the Vicar, accompanied by Bernard Cockfield and Tim Lankester, walked from St Petrox, Dartmouth, to St Petroc's Church in Padstow, where Petroc first landed in Cornwall in the sixth century. It took them a week and they were accompanied by other members of the congregation for parts of the way. (THE PANNELL COLLECTION)

Scenes from the Church Fête

Mr Jimmy Garland has a go at the cork game at a Church fête in the 1950s, watched by Roger Beer, Michael Hard and Beatrice Joint. In the background are Mr Muddeman and Mrs Christine Raikes at another stall. (The Juste Collection)

Scenes from the Church Fête and Flower Festivals

Sunday, our special visiting preacher at 11a.m. and 6.30p.m. will be Revd A. Roberts, a former Minister of our Circuit, now at Exmouth. Throughout the summer there will be other events and further return visits of former ministers of our church to preach. The other churches of our group of the Totnes Circuit will be closing their own churches on Sunday, 9 May to be with us.

Although there has been a Methodist place of worship in South Brent for 230 years, the present church dates from 1812. A century ago it was greatly altered and extended and a new foundation stone was inserted into the front wall of the church. We are celebrating the enlargement and completion of the church as we know it today. The church has been fully restored with new windows and completely redecorated in readiness for this happy very special event.

The Church Fete and Flower Festivals

For many years one of the highlights of the year was the church fête, which took place alternately on Wednesday and Saturday afternoons. During the middle years of the twentieth century, the event

lapsed. The Church Council decided to revive the Summer church fête in 1982. Mrs Olive Dodd, the driving force behind the revival, wrote in the parish magazine:

After such a long interval we want this to be an enjoyable, as well as a successful, afternoon, so planning and preparation has to be done well in advance, and it is proposed the fête will be next year to give working parties a chance to produce some really worthwhile things. Originally the church fête was held in the Vicarage Garden, now the Manor House, and was an event which people really enjoyed and looked forward to.

The intended date is 12 June 1982, and we are making our plans known now so that other events do not clash.

Plans then went on apace, with working parties, coffee mornings and other fund-raisers taking place, and by October it could be reported that £68.40¹/₂d had been raised towards the costs of the fête. As time went on more events were held to boost the coffers, and meetings were held to plan the event so that by Saturday, 12 June 1982, a full programme of events was in place, including a puppet show organised by Mrs Barbara Palmer!

It was estimated that between 500 and 600 people turned up at the Manor ready to admire the garden and enjoy themselves.

After the fête, Olive Dodd wrote:

And enjoy themselves they did, in spite of the weather being so overcast at the beginning of the afternoon. That really seemed a little hard after all the lovely sunny days we've had, but when I took the decision in the morning I somehow felt it would be alright. The various stalls began the afternoon packed with all kinds of goods, and in a short while most of them were half empty and the sideshows were being kept busy. The frequent crashes of crockery told of one that was a smashing success; I have to apologise for not having the children's races, we decided that the grass on the field was too slippery, and the ankle competition didn't materialise either, they were all on their way home. The School Maypole Dancers were a joy to behold as they wove their intricate patterns round the maypole, and I do commend the mothers who troubled to enter the children for the Fancy Dress, we would have liked more but appreciated the few who joined in. I heard the puppets described as 'very professional', and the children certainly loved them. I thought all the children were very well behaved and seemed to be enjoying themselves and the freedom of space.

The final figure raised, after deducting necessary expenses, was £735.6d.

In 1994 Mrs Lucy Moore suggested that a flower festival should be held in the Parish Church over Petroctide with the theme of 'Celebrations', 1994 being the 1,430th anniversary of the church's patron,

St Petroc. This was to be first of a series of flower festivals held in the village churches. In 1997 one was held in the Methodist Church with the theme 'Fruits of the Spirit', St Dunstan's hosted another with the theme of St Dunstan and the culmination came in 2000, when the ambitious festival, 'Jesus, the Light of the World' was held over all three churches simultaneously. It was then agreed that a flower festival should alternate with the church fête and be held in St Petroc's, with the flower arrangers from all the churches taking part.

Summer Outings

At various times church outings have also featured as part of the churches' year.

Lisa Goss wrote of the 1980 Sunday School outing:

At about 10 o'clock on Saturday, 5 July, most of the Sunday school left for Teignmouth. When we arrived at the beach we dumped our gear and then some people sat down whilst others went to the pier. The weather was very good compared to the bad weather we had last year.

Not long after we arrived and a few people had been swimming in the sea, which I found was very cold, it was lunch time. Quite a while after lunch, Mrs Niblett took about eight children swimming in the heated pool. We were there for quite a while enjoying ourselves.

When we got back from swimming, we played rounders to pass the time. After we had been playing rounders for quite a while, we were told it was almost time to go. Everyone started to get ready to walk up to the coach. Almost everyone went home on the coach except for two families that had brought their cars.

I think we all had a thoroughly enjoyable day.

And in 1986 Richard Stevens, now the church choirmaster and organist ,wrote:

On 14 June, the Sunday School went to Dobwalls. We got on the coach at school and there were about 56 children and 20 adults, and we were all very excited. When we got there, we got out of the coach and split up unto groups. First, our group went on a train ride and the train was a diesel train. We had lunch at wooden tables and benches and after lunch we went down to the radio-controlled boats, which cost 20p. Robin and I really enjoyed them. Then we went to a slide, which was a yellow helter skelter. We went very fast down it but we didn't hurt ourselves because there was sand at the bottom. Later we went to the nature display, where we saw lots of animals. When we pressed the button, each display lit up. I particularly enjoyed panning for gold, where I had to get a pot and a sieve and go to the troughs which had sand and water in. We had to find four gold nuggets before we got a medal. Nearly everybody had a turn at doing this. We had a ride on the second train, the steam train, before meeting at the coach to go home. It was a really lovely day.

On occasion the servers have also enjoyed a summer outing. Colin Vallance wrote of the 1986 trip:

On behalf of the servers of St Petroc's Church, I should like to thank Revd and Mrs Niblett for the enjoyable day we all spent on Saturday, 6 September. We travelled to Plymouth by car and spent an enjoyable hour in the Central Park swimming pool. We then made our way to the Hoe, where everyone ate their packed lunches, and later played French cricket. It was then time to make our way to the Drake Cinema, where we saw the film 'The Sea Wolves'. After arriving back at Church House in the early evening we had another game of cricket to finish off our day.

On another occasion, Tim Brierley and Leon Slocombe:

... set forth with the Vicar, his wife and Mrs Baker to Glastonbury for the annual pilgrimage. After one and a half hours, driving (and an unsuccessful stop at a licensed establishment en route), we finally reached our destination and found a car park. To start off our busy day we visited a coffee room, where we all lubricated our voices ready for the main service at noon. After arriving in the grounds of the old abbey and seeing multitudes of other people arriving, Leon and Tim slipped out to explore the town. We met the others at the car and returned to the old abbey to eat our packed lunches. We then donned our vestments and went to the Parish Church of St John's, Glastonbury, for the procession, which took an hour and a half, while the sixty-odd banners paraded the streets for a quarter of a mile. The procession ended in the old abbey ruins for evensong, where 7,000 people turned up. After this service, we joined the mad rush to leave the abbey. This took about 25 minutes. From there we left Glastonbury for the journey home.

Another group of church members who hold an annual outing are the bell-ringers. John Furneaux wrote of the 1981 outing:

On Saturday, 6 June, St Petroc's Ringers held their outing and were accompanied by wives, families, members of the choir, organist and friends. We spent a most enjoyable day, with visits to St Columb Major, St Mawgan and St Nicholas, St Eval, Padstow and St Issey. Lunch was taken at St Mawgan, with an excellent high tea at Padstow.

How refreshing it was having the opportunity of visiting and enjoying the atmosphere of the beautiful Cornish churches and to appreciate the very warm welcome afforded to us all. We, of course, like to reciprocate in Brent in the same way.

Can we now add our thanks to the Ringers' Lord Chief, Fernley Rogers, for the excellent arrangements he made to make our day so enjoyable. We must not forget our Samaritan act, when we 'sighted and righted' five

The annual Civic Service of Remembrance and Rededication now takes place on Remembrance Sunday following a procession from the Anchor Building to the Church. Originally it was held at 3p.m. in the church, where the memorials are housed, and was a British Legion service. At the instigation of Major-General Victor Campbell in the late 1970s it was moved to the morning to coincide with the national two-minutes' silence.

(THE KEITH MALE COLLECTION)

Throughout the year all three churches carry out the offices of baptism, marriage and funerals. Jack Tidball was baptised by the Rev David Winnington Ingram, Vicar of South Brent and Rattery in 2007. (THE TIDBALL COLLECTION)

From top: *In a rural parish Harvest is a very important festival. Traditionally, the weeks leading up to the first Sunday in October have seen South Brent celebrate the harvest initially in the Congregational Church in Plymouth Road, then, on the last Sunday in September, in the Methodist Church, and finally, on the first Sunday in October, in St Petroc's.*

Dartmoor ewes in one field lying on their backs. What a loss this would have been to the farmer but for the Brent Hawkeyes!

During a convenient stop on the 1984, outing, again to Cornwall, the Lord Chief, Fernley Rogers, made a presentation of a mounted miniature bell, together with a suitable card, to a bell-ringer who had given wonderful service to the tower. It read:

Presented from the South Brent Ringers to Jim Goss in recognition and appreciation to a most loyal and regular bellringer at St Petroc's Church for the past 39 years. 2nd June 1984. Well done Jim, you have given a wonderful service.

St Petroc's has a dedicated band of cleaners who make the church fit for the worship of God week after week. This photograph shows Mrs Lillian Wakeley, Mrs Sheila Wall and Mrs Nancy Wright (kneeling), who were affectionately known as the three Ws, with Mrs Edie Davis in a respite from washing the church, which they did on hands and knees! The photograph dates from the late 1960s.

In the latter years of the twentieth century, it was apparent that the parish cemetery, originally opened in 1910, was rapidly filling up and other provision would have to be made. Land behind the Village Hall had been gifted many years before from the parish glebe land for eventual use as a burial-ground and so, on Sunday, 3 June 2001, appropriately Whitsunday and St Petroc's Eve, the then Bishop of Plymouth, Rt Revd John Garton, came to dedicate the new burial-gound. Here he is being led by the churchwardens, Greg Wall and Cathie Pannell, around the edge of the ground as part of the ceremony. The Vicar, Revd David Winnington-Ingram, looks on.

The tower of St Petroc's Church dates from Norman times. After many thousands of years it was found to be leaking badly and restoration work has been undertaken. The top section was begun in autumn 2006.

The former South Brent Congregational Church.

Children in Church

A model of St Petroc's made during the Harvest Mission of 2005.

The Harvest frontal made by the St Petroc's Youth group.

Glass painting done by young people for the Flower Festival, October 2006.

The Methodist Sunday school.

Brent Weddings Through the Years

Mr George Chandler and Miss Lillian Wilkinson married in St Petroc's Church on 20 April 1938. Miss Wilkinson was the daughter of Mr and Mrs George Wilkinson . (THE ANDREWS COLLECTION)

Mr Peter Miller and Miss Jean Uren at St Petroc's Church on 25 July 1959. (THE MILLER COLLECTION)

Mr Edward Fowler and Miss Doris Manning, married in St Petroc's Church. (THE GOSS COLLECTION)

Mr Christopher Smith and Miss Marilyn Langdon with their guests outside South Brent Congregational Church, 12 June 1965. (THE SMITH COLLECTION)

Mr Ernest Wall and Miss Sheila Hard at their reception at the Royal Oak after their wedding in St Petroc's Church on 28 December 1946.

Mr Mark Farrin and Miss Rachel Giles at St Petroc's Church, South Brent, on 31 July 1999.

(THE GILES COLLECTION)

On Being a Reader in South Brent

Mrs Dulce Robertson writes:

A Church of England Reader is a lay person who is trained and licensed to take certain services, preach, assist at Holy Communion and undertake pastoral duties. Bob Brierley and I went forward for training. We spent HOURS and months reading, writing essays and being taught by a patient nun at Denbury convent, and we were encouraged, led and guided, both practically and spiritually, by the Revd David Niblett. In 1990 we stood before the Bishop in St Petroc's Church and were admitted and licensed as Readers, the first in South Brent.

Soon afterwards there was a spate of clergy retirements in South Devon. Readers were in great demand

Mr George Wilkinson and Miss Olivia Hill, married in St Petroc's Church in 1912.   (THE ANDREWS COLLECTION)

to take Morning Service throughout the area. Thus, Saturday became Sermon day for me. On Sunday I took to the lanes and learnt more about South Devon, its churches and, more importantly, its people.

There was always plenty going on in South Brent and Rattery though, from taking ones turn on the service

rota, visiting those at home with Communion, the occasional funeral and many cremations, preaching at Remembrance Services (because I was there!) to the many and varied activities in the two villages.

Busy I may have been, but I treasure the many wonderful friends, past and present, I have made through being a Reader.

A poem written by Marion Jansen, loosely inspired by Brent's church fête:

The Vicarage Fête

The polished sheen of the vicarage lawn
Is reflected in everyone's manners
And modestly aproned charity stalls
Raise Oxfam's tragic banners.

Crimplened ladies flutter about
In pastel pinks and blues
They'll settle soon, like homing doves,
Behind their trellised booths.

Refreshment helpers get up steam
In the billowing marquee
Manning the urns like stevedores
As the crowd sails in for tea.

A babble of Brownies feast their eyes
On a pyramid of hot pork pies
And visiting clergy warm their hearts
On a passing parade of topless tarts.

The vicar, with practised excuses,
Nips back to the house for a while
To knock back a stiff gin-and-tonic
And peel off his Sellotaped smile.

But there's trouble at the bookstall,
Someone comforts Mrs Bee
For among the 'Homes & Gardens'
She's discovered pornography.

The baton rays of the setting sun
Conduct a last tune from the band
The aproned stalls are all defrocked
And the marquee's now unmanned.

Everything went so nicely
Oh, wouldn't it be grand
If this day in the life of our village
Was a day in the life of the land?

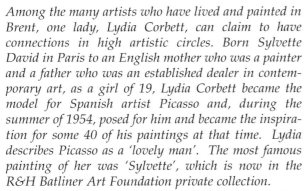

Isobel Coulton, another of Brent's artists, in her Studio in Millswood Lane. Isobel, who is Lydia Corbett's daughter, is an accomplished artist in her own right

Among the many artists who have lived and painted in Brent, one lady, Lydia Corbett, can claim to have connections in high artistic circles. Born Sylvette David in Paris to an English mother who was a painter and a father who was an established dealer in contemporary art, as a girl of 19, Lydia Corbett became the model for Spanish artist Picasso and, during the summer of 1954, posed for him and became the inspiration for some 40 of his paintings at that time. Lydia describes Picasso as a 'lovely man'. The most famous painting of her was 'Sylvette', which is now in the R&H Batliner Art Foundation private collection.

Lydia first started to paint whilst at Dartington Hall, some 26 years after her time with Picasso. She begins her paintings with a pen and ink drawing to which she adds watercolour before again using the pen to add other subjects, thus making up the whole story in paint. Lydia also uses oils and is a potter. She has said of her painting, 'It gives me happiness, it's like a prayer, a healing force. I love doing it. I always want to paint.'

(Photograph by Carol Ballenger, July 2006)

Above, inset: Cover picture for St Petroc's Sunday Worship Service Book, painted by Lydia Corbett.

Lillian Delevoryas, who lives at Three Barns in Aish Lane, was born in Chicopee Falls, Massachusetts, USA. In 1970 she moved to England and has made this country her adopted home. Lillian began her extensive career as a painter in New York in the 1950s, and 20 years later was creating one-off appliquéed garments that proved popular in the world of showbusiness. During this time she also collaborated with fellow-American Kaffe Fassett. From the '90s onwards she was influenced more and more by the icons of Greece and Russia and, for several years, devoted herself to learning the techniques of iconography in order to penetrate its secrets as well as to sharpen her own technique in painting. One of these icons (inset) now hangs in the Lady Chapel in St Petroc's Church.

✦ CHAPTER 9 ✦

Another Look at the Creative Arts in Brent

The Art and Craft Groups

South Brent is blessed with a wealth of talent in the field of the creative arts. There are highly skilled painters in all media, as well as potters, workers in wood, metal, fabric, textiles and photography, to name but a few.

One of the first arts groups to be formed in Brent was the South Brent Arts and Crafts Society. Instrumental in its foundation were Christine Raikes, Margaret Price and Unity Harley. One of the events run by this group is the South Brent bi-annual exhibition, open to artists living in Brent and outlying districts, including Diptford, Harbourneford, Rattery, Avonwick and Wrangaton. This exhibition has been running since the formation of the Society over 30 years ago. The group also arranges occasional talks on art in general, and a feature of the year is the annual Christine Raikes Memorial Lecture, which is held each autumn.

There was another series of exhibitions between 1984 and the late 1990s in the Pack Horse. These were organised by Sylvia Wilkins, Elise Willisson and Jill Ingram. Mrs Wilkins was, from 1982 to 2002, the landlady of the hotel. The exhibitions were run for such charities as the Plymouth Eye Infirmary and, latterly, the South Brent Health Centre Support Group. They were staged in an upstairs room, and in 1984 a comment was made that:

Approximately 200 exhibits from the people of South Brent and district were tastefully displayed to their best advantage, and it was difficult to think of a craft that was not represented.

A children's section in the Exhibition was well represented and of a very high standard. An added interest to the show was the inclusion of two chairs which had been restored by Angela Marshall of Hillside. These chairs had been on show at the first Basketmakers' Exhibition at the Royal Festival Hall, London.

From 1983 several local artists gathered together to 'continue their hobby in the company of others who have similar interests', first under Irene Collecott and later with Elise Willisson. They shared ideas, techniques and skills. That group still continues to meet. Similarly, many people attend the adult education groups which are run in the community.

Another group, which has been going in Brent since September 1991, is the embroidery group set up by Kathleen Stanyon and Joan Noble. It is again a group that exists to further interest and skills of members. The group was responsible for the

Mrs Christine Raikes, one of the leading artists in South Brent in the second half of the twentieth century. She was instrumental, with Margaret Price and Unity Harley, in setting up the South Brent Arts and Crafts Society.
(THE SAVERY COLLECTION)

One of a series of scenes depicting the seasons of the year painted by Mrs Christine Raikes and produced as Christmas cards. (THE SAVERY COLLECTION)

Members of the embroidery group at work in the Church Room. Left to right: *Mavis Moulding, Win Lyons, Marion Newman, Val Meek, Heather Chapple, Joan Noble, Helen Ketteringham, Gwen Holloway, Rosie Mullard, Anne Bailey, Val Chalklin, Bernice Pike, Pauline Juste.* (THE NOBLE COLLECTION)

The Corridor Gallery in the Old School Centre, featuring an exhibition by the South Brent Embroidery Group.

Millenium Tapestry produced in AD2000 and now hanging in the church. This work, featured in *The Book of South Brent*, provided a stimulus for other people to take up the craft.

Following the opening of the Old School Centre, the Corridor Gallery was set up. This was instigated by Diane Gower and is a place where local artists and groups can formally exhibit their work – a variety of people have exhibited here. The exhibitions, which change monthly, have included work by local photographers, artists, emboiderers and South Brent Pre-School group.

The artistic community of South Brent has, since

2003, held the South Brent Open Studios weekend. In 2004 over 30 artists exhibited their work in 10 venues across the local area

Writers

South Brent has often been the home of or base for internationally famous writers. In the late-nineteenth and early-twentieth centuries William Crossing lived here. Eden Phillpots wrote one of his novels based in Brent and, in more recent times, another Brentonian to achieve a name for himself in the world of literature is John Van der Kiste, who has lived in South Brent since the age of 15. At school he wrote and performed in a one-act comedy, and contributed regularly to the school and house magazines. He edited the students' journal at library college in London, and then contributed historical articles and book and record reviews to local and national journals while writing his first book, *Frederick III*, published in 1981.

Since then he has written over 20 historical biographies, mainly on British and European royalty, from Stuart times to the twentieth century. He has also written books on true crime, starting with *Devon Murders*, as well as a novel set partly on Dartmoor and in the surrounding area, *The Man on the Moor*. He has also edited a Gilbert and Sullivan Christmas anthology, contributed to the *Oxford Dictionary of National Biography* and produced titles on rock music. He was historical consultant for the BBC TV documentary 'The King, the Kaiser and the Tsar'. At the same time he has also worked in public and academic libraries, written songs, played in rock and folk groups, including the South Brent Folk Club, and worked locally as a disc jockey.

South Brent Amateur Dramatics Society

We have seen in *The Book of South Brent* how the fortunes of SBADS have come a long way from its original 'foundation' by such worthies as Mr Arthur Manning in 1935, including many award-winning productions in the 1980s and 1990s.

In the year 2000, as part of the South Brent millennium celebrations and to celebrate 75 years of drama in the village, the group, with the help of the Brent Singers and supported by the Parish Council, undertook a trilogy of events during May. It began with 'Verses versus verses', a chance for local poets to promote their own work and for others to share their favourite poetry. The musical group Concentus shared the programme. The second part of the trilogy was a youth production called 'Looking for a Rain God'. Described as 'an exciting piece of theatre', this was produced by Sue Burgess with some original songs by John van der Kiste. The third part of the trilogy was an 'extravaganza' of entertainment entitled 'Millennium Moments', and consisted of a

variety of drama, music and dance through the ages. Once again, it involved the Brent Singers. To complete the year the group performed a series of one-act plays in November under the umbrella title 'A Trio of Titters'. The programme consisted of

Debbie Plummer, Alan Prince and Paul Wonnacott at Hallsands for Shifting Sands. *Also in the cast were Barry Cummings, Robin Willoughby and Michael Murphy.* (STEVE CLEAVE COLLECTION)

The cast of Shifting Sands *on location at Hallsands.* Left to right: *Mike Roberts, Paul Wonnacott, Debbie Plummer, Anthony Hope-Johnson, Robin Lee, Alan Prince* (seated) *and Margaret Cuthbertson.* (STEVE CLEAVE COLLECTION, MAY 2004)

103

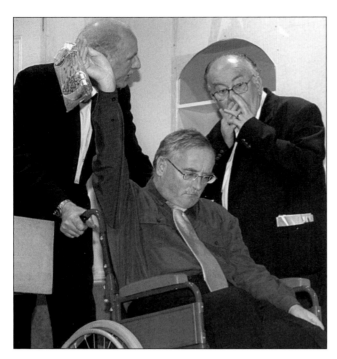

How to dispose of a dead body! A crisis for two of the residents in Old Dogs. *Left to right:* Paul Wonnacott, John Giles *and* Clive Mays. *Also in the cast were* Alan Prince, Tom Cuthbertson *and* Robin Willoughby.

A scene from Old Dogs. *Left to right:* Paul Wonnacott, Clive Mays, Jacqui Lyons, Donna Warne, Greg Wall *and* Val Meek. (THE SBADS COLLECTION, NOVEMBER 2006)

'Dinner for One', starring Paul Wonnacott and Stella Gillingham, 'Joining the Club', by Davis Tristram, starring Vickie Jones and Robin Willoughby, and 'Last Tango in South Brent', starring Steve Melia, John Gower, Val Meek and Sue Burgess. And to top it all, in January 2001 the pantomime *The Sleeping Beauty* was performed.

Between 2004 and 2007, SBADS produced no fewer than three world premieres.

In 2004 came *Shifting Sands*, an original play written by local author Steve Melia, adapted from his book *Hallsands, a Village Betrayed*, published in 2002, which described the events around the destruction of

Top and above: *The cast of the musical* The Ballad of Tippling Down.

Carol Davies produced Robert Boult's A Man for All Seasons *in November 2007. This classic play featured John Palmer as Sir Thomas More and Sue Burgess as Lady Alice More, shown here in the Catherine Chapel of St Petroc's Church.*

(KEITH MALE PHOTOGRAPHY COLLECTION, NOVEMBER 2007)

Sir Thomas and Lady Alice More and Matthew, Sir Thomas's steward, played by Peter Brown, welcome King Henry VIII, played by Tim McGill.

(PHOTOGRAPHED IN ST PETROC'S CHURCH BY KEITH MALE)

the village of Hallsands on the South Devon coast in January 1917. The play, directed by Kate Stubbs was a 'fictional story spun around those real events'. Some of the characters were totally fictional, some very real and some amalgams of real people. The production received great acclaim and was a triumph for all concerned.

In 2005, another new work was performed, this time the adult comedy *Old Dogs*, by Plymouth writer and former Royal Marines Commando Steve Raw. It was directed by Mary Wonnacott. The play, set in a residential care home, involves the hilarious antics that happen when matron is away and three elderly gentlemen residents befriend a 'lady of the night'. Once again, the play was performed to packed houses. Mary then took the play to Teignmouth, where it ran for the summer season before being accepted for publication!

The third world premiere produced by SBADS was *The Ballad of Tippling Down*, an ambitious musical written locally by Tony Simister and with a cast of over 30. The director Mike Roberts described the play in his synopsis:

The Ballad of Tippling Down is based on a small rural village deep in the South Hams of Devon. It is 1944 and the locals are anticipating the arrival of several evacuees and American GIs... There are over 20 original songs, which aptly describe those turbulent times. Tragedies, triumphs, loves, losses, rivalries, reconciliations are emotions which are cleverly brought to light by very skilful writing and music. It is one of two South Brent entries for this year's South Devon Drama Federation Festival.

Sue Burgess, the Society's chairman wrote of the production in the June edition of 'Much Ado', the Society's newsletter:

They came, they saw... We conquered!!

The news around the village from the people who came to see Tippling Down *is of great achievements, brave production and congratulations on the whole event.*

After a longer than usual gestation period, this production has set the community talking and one of the main comments is... 'What a feat!' From the inside, we always knew that it was one of the biggest challenges that SBADS had embarked upon, and now that it's done and dusted all of the production team, cast and technical crew, and in particular Tony and Lucy Simister, can deservedly pat themselves on the back.

The adjudicator, Richard Clarke, said that the community of South Brent is envied by many other societies for the range of expertise and ages of performers, and for the support, the village gives to each production. He commended several individuals on their performances, including the youngsters, and also the front of house team (which was a whole production by itself).

He highlighted some areas for us to think about in the future, as he always so sensitively does, but told us to remember that our audiences give us the most important feedback, and in the case of Tippling Down *they enjoyed it.*

May 2007

Paul Alexander

During the late 1980s Brent was fortunate in having actor Paul Alexander give his recitation of the Gospel of St John, both in the Village Hall and in St Petroc's Church. Paul Alexander, the son of the late Mr and Mrs Rex Smith, who lived at Ladieswood, was trained at the Rose Bruford College of Drama, has acted all over England, Scotland and Ireland, and was in *Beau Brummell* at the Edinburgh Festival. His recitation of the Gospel was broadcast at Easter in the same year, from the Holy Land, at prime time on Sunday evening.

St Petroc's Five Lost Souls
written by Peter and Sheila Finch in 1995

When the Church Choir went out to sing!
'Twas the week before Christmas and all through South Brent,
The homes were a readying, the message been sent.
The choir will be coming some carols to sing,
Excitement for residents, await doorbells ring.

The first night they sang in the homes closer by.
Leaze, Paddocks and Windward their spirits quite high.
To sing unaccompanied was their intent,
With David's strange whistle, the note was well meant.

Some sherry was served to lubricate voices.
Mince pies, sausage rolls, such were the choices
At eight thirty, back with their robes and their tomes
'Tomorrow we'll sing in the outlying homes.'

On Wednesday, the choir travelled further afield.

Four carloads to Pinewood and then Merrifield.
At Pinewood they sang to an appreciative group
Who smiled, and even joined in with the troop.

'Now on to Merrifield,' the choirmaster said,
'To give them some carols before they're to bed.
Downhill to the bridge, turn left, then turn right,
Follow the first car, keep it in sight.'

The first car arrived, the second close behind.
Out piled the juniors all ready and fine.
Third car decided to wait and be guide
To the driver who had the choirmaster inside.

They waited and waited but nobody came.
It was cold, dark and wet with plenty of rain.
Where were Kate, David, Sally, Richard and Paul?
A broad span of voices, they needed them all.

So the third car to Merrifield, Where are the rest?
Surely not lost, is this some sort of jest?"
Then car lights were seen in the valley below
Could it be – is it them – No.

They could wait no longer, so a much reduced choir
Sang carols to Merrifield for quarter of an hour
As they left to return home, they all asked each other
'How could they get lost, oh what a bother!'

So if on the Moor at Christmas you hear ghostly howls
Just direct the car to Merrifield for 'tis only five lost souls!

Another Look at the Musical Tradition in South Brent

The Church Choir, 2007. Left to right, back row: *Anne Wise, Fiona Harvey, Gill Taylor, Sarah Mules, John Mules;* middle row: *Sarah Roberts, Ursula Reid-Robertson, Richard Stevens, Stella Gillingham, Roger Cockings, Ann Anderson, Shirley Eatwell, Jane Tuson, Greg Wall, Paul Gibbons, Kate Born, Linda Chadburn, Catherine Roberts, Hilary Cockings;* front row: *Eleanor Mules, Katie Armstrong, Kerri Dardis, Henry Mules, Chloe McNulty, Olivia Mincher, James Kendall.* (PHOTOGRAPH BY NICK KENDALL)

Another Look at the Musical Tradition in South Brent

The Pack Horse has become a centre for folk singing in South Brent following the traditions of earlier years. The Tuesday night singers in the Pack Horse meet to keep alive traditional folk music.

Another group meets on Wednesdays and includes young musicians who will keep the tradition of live singing going. Left to right: Tony Simister, Martin Fenton, Mick Bramich, Caren Parke, Caroline Cleave Colin Vallance, Steve Cleave. Geoff Caplan is seated at the front.

The Packhorse Folk Festival broom-dancing competition. The children have a go at an old Dartmoor tradition, having been taught the skill by Frank Noble.

(THE STEVE CLEAVE COLLECTION)

Miss Val Trinder, organist at St Petroc's Church.

(CHOIR COLLECTION)

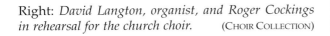

Above: The Church choir assembles for service. Richard Stevens, wearing the medallion, is the current church organist and choirmaster. (THE GILES COLLECTION)

Right: David Langton, organist, and Roger Cockings in rehearsal for the church choir. (CHOIR COLLECTION)

These two studio portraits are of Miss Elizabeth and Miss Beatrice Carew, the daughters of Sir William Carew (1807–1874) and Ann Taylor. The Carew family lived at Marley in the neighbouring parish of Rattery but were influential within South Brent. The name Carew is still remembered in the Carew Service Station on the A38, and in the former name of the Woodpecker Inn – the Carew Arms. (THE COLLIER COLLECTION)

✦ CHAPTER 10 ✦

Another Look at Health Matters

A Nineteenth-Century View

South Brent is served today by a top-quality health centre with a team of doctors, nurses and other medical practitioners who look after the health of the community. However, this would appear not to have always been the case.

In the latter years of the nineteenth century, Dr Parson's report to the Local Government Board on typhoid fever in the Totnes Urban and Rural Sanitary Districts noted:

South Brent. – In this village typhoid fever is almost endemic; it has not been absent any year, as far back at least as 1875. About 30 cases were heard of, occurring in 19 households. South Brent is situated on a high and open site, but the cottages are many of them old and dilapidated, built in confined situations, and as regards sanitary condition wretched in the extreme. The inhabitants are employed, some in agriculture, others at a flock manufactory. The main street is drained by two stone sewers, one of which discharges into a brook, the other upon a meadow; the outfall of the latter was formerly close to a house, but on the occurrence of several cases of typhoid fever in this house pipes were laid to carry the outfall to a greater distance from it.

There is a public supply of water brought down from a reservoir to taps in various parts of the village. The reservoir is supplied by a spring which rises in a water meadow on the hillside above. This water meadow is irrigated partly by a stream which receives the contents of the privy of a farmhouse, and the drainage of the farmyard; but the portion immediately above the spring is watered by another stream, though it would be possible to divert the stream from the farmyard over it. No fever has occurred at the farmhouse during the many years that the occupier has lived there. The overflow of the reservoir runs in an open stone channel down the side of the street. Dirty vessels, vegetables, offal, &c. are washed in this stream, and the Medical Officer of Health has seen children on their knees drinking out of it; he has recommended that it should be diverted into the sewers in order to flush them.

Privy accommodation is scanty, one privy being sometimes shared by five, six, or seven houses. In such cases either the privy is allowed to get into a filthy condition, through disputes as to the responsibility for its cleanliness, or else it is not made use of, the men resorting to the fields, the women using utensils in the house, and throwing the contents of them on dung heaps.

A number of cases of typhoid fever occurred in 1877, in a group of wretched cottages in Fore Street, and behind the 'Anchor' inn. One of these, then inhabited by a man, his wife, and 10 children, but now empty, has a living room of 1,670 cubic feet, and two bedrooms of together 1,450 cubic feet. The lower floor, of rough stone, is below the ground level; the bedrooms are only 6ft 6in. high to the roof, which is not ceiled, but merely plastered on the underside of the slates, and does not keep out the rain. One bedroom has a window of 10 square feet, of which a third opens; the other has only a skylight which will not open. There are no back windows, and the front of the house looks into a narrow passage, bounded by a high wall; 8 feet from the front door was the untrapped inlet of a stone drain, since trapped and piped. Close to this are six back-to-back houses, in two of which fever occurred about the same time; the stone drain above mentioned runs under one of the houses in which fever occurred, and there are untrapped gratings in the backyard close-to the doors and windows.

Water Supply

South Brent in 2007 gets its water supply from the Avon Dam, constructed in the mid-1950s.
Long before the construction of the dam a reservoir was constructed in Hillside. Anthony Hope-Johnson writes of the reservoir mentioned by Dr Parsons:

In the 1870s South Brent decided to harness the copious amounts of fresh water soaking out of Brent Hill. An area in the south-west corner of a seven-acre field was set aside to build a reservoir next to Hillside Lane, by the cottages. This field was part of Underhill Farm, which was owned by the Carew family. The Carews gave the water authority at the time permission to drain the natural springs into a culvert. The open culvert ran across from Underhill Farm and joined a second stream coming down from the hill on the top side of the old cricket field.

As well as a right to drain, the Carews also granted a right of collection into the reservoir that was created for the purpose. The size of the granite-lined tank measured approximately 11m by 8m and was 4m deep, holding in the region of 350,000l. The open reservoir was sunk at ground level within a 3m concrete apron. Around the edge of the apron the water board erected a 2m granite wall about 18in. thick.

The tank was set back from Hillside Lane and on two sides, towards the road, there was an area of land later

The notice on the wall of the Royal Oak, where the leat from Hillside emerged into Station Road.

The valve house on Hillside. The inscription over the door reads 'As a token of gratitude to Sir W.R. Carew Bart, this tablet was erected January 1873'.

used for private allotments and chicken sheds.

The reservoir tank was filled from a sluice gate in the field behind the reservoir. The overflow from the streams continued along the old leat to the rear of all the properties on the north side of Hillside Lane. This leat, or stream, eventually flowed through the pipe next to the railway bridge and down towards the Royal Oak.

The supply from the reservoir to the village was controlled from within the valve house, which still exists in form rather than function, outside the property suitably called Freshwaters.

From the valve house the pipes ran down to the village in the road.

Unfortunately, the supply which fed the Hillside reservoir was too inconsistent for the needs of the growing village, and within 20 years the water board had to bring a second major supply from Splatton. This was a 9in. pipe which again crossed the fields to Hillside Lane just above the old reservoir. This continued right on until the building of the Avon Dam. With the supply from the dam now crossing that same field behind the old reservoir, the water board were able to feed a spur to the Splatton reservoir, which now supplies the village with all its water. The 18in. main feeding the rest of the entire South Hams crosses Hillside Lane at the 30mph limit. Here there is a simple manhole for a sampling and inspection point.

When the second supply came from Splatton the local water board ran down the Hillside reservoir, which became abandoned. It is known that during the 1950s and '60s, Stan Stevens, at No. 2 Hillside Cottages, had the use of the allotment area, which was then rented from the water board for the princely sum of 15s. a year. This arrangement continued with John Reynolds in the 1970s and '80s. The tank lay dormant as a trap for foxes and the first seedlings of a sycamore forest gradually took hold, splitting the apron and floor of the tank, but the granite walls remained fairly well intact. After John Reynolds moved to Totnes, the South West Water Authority was approached with an offer to buy the tank and surrounding land.

The water board agreed terms and then went silent. Their own legal department discovered that the water board had never owned the land in the first place. The only right they had was the right to collect water there. However, the purchaser took a conveyance in any event, bought the land and registered the title with the Land Registry. The Land Registrar queried the title to the property and was only satisfied by a declaration on behalf of the Carew family, stating that, as the family had sold their entire Brent estate in the 1920s, the family had no interest whatsoever in any land in South Brent, nor the rest of Devon, for that matter.

Having acquired a full title, the purchaser then applied for development for a single dwelling. The planning authority lost the appeal on the grounds that development could not be denied on a piece of ground that had already been previously developed.

The St John Ambulance Association

The South Brent St John Ambulance Brigade was formed on 22 February 1972 under the leadership of Mrs Anne Wakeham. One of the first activities it undertook was a sponsored walk, on Sunday, 30 April, which proved to be very successful. The money raised was spent on badges, berets, first-aid kits, bandages and other equipment and to pay half the cost of transport to take the cadets to the Golden Jubilee Camp of St John Ambulance Cadets No 7 region and was held around Sunday, 30 July 1972 at Dunster.

The ambulance and nursing cadets had their annual inspection in the Congregational schoolroom. The inspection officers were Miss M. Best; Mr D. Quinnell; Lt-Col C.M. Townsend (Area Commissioner South Devon), Mrs Cleasby (Area

Marion Stephens and Teresa Wakeham are presented with awards. Looking on is Anne Wakeham, leader of the South Brent St John Ambulance Association.

(THE JULIE TOWL COLLECTION)

Superintendent) and Mrs Grisbrook (Divisional Nursing Officer, Cadets).

Mrs M. Price, president of the cadet division, opened the proceedings, and the prayers of the Order of St John were said by the Vicar of South Brent, Revd L.M. Malsom.

Warrants were presented to Mrs A. Wakeham (Divisional Officer, Cadets), Mrs Price (President) and Mrs Waddams (Vice-president).

In 1980 Barbara Sparkes wrote a second pantomime, *Snow White*, which was produced to provide funds for the ambulance and garage funds. The group were also very active in such things as the Village Hall Show.

The ambulance had come into service in 1978 after two years of fund-raising. RRL613G, as it was registered, came second-hand from Cornwall Health Authority in Truro. Initially, the vehicle had to be kept in the station-yard car park as there was no garage available for it. Officially handed over by Rear Admiral W.A. Haynes, it was commissioned by the Area Commissioner and blessed by members of each of the churches in the village at the time. Revd David Niblett represented the Parish Church, Revd Charles Holgate the Methodist Church, Fr Sebastian Wolff the Catholic Church and Mr Albert Dyer represented the Congregational Church. A celebration in the Village Hall followed in the best of Brent traditions.

It was reported that 'many who hoped to buy tickets at the door on Friday were disappointed, for all 200 tickets for First-aid Fairy Tale *were sold out. The tale, located at South Brent, was written and produced by Barbara Sparkes, with more than 30 people taking part. These included cadets and their parents. With the family at the fair and the romance between Annabel, played by Teresa Wakeham, and Robin, played by Julie Sparkes, it had a real pantomime atmosphere, with many popular songs and a comedy spot, with Vic Newman providing the laughs. Sally and Ray Luscombe produced more laughter with their. 'Two Little Boys' act. It all ended happily and lots of praise came from Revd L. Malsom, who thanked all who had-taken part.*

(THE JULIE TOWL COLLECTION)

Walter Wicks, Anne Wakeham and Jackie Newman in a St John presentation. (THE JULIE TOWL COLLECTION)

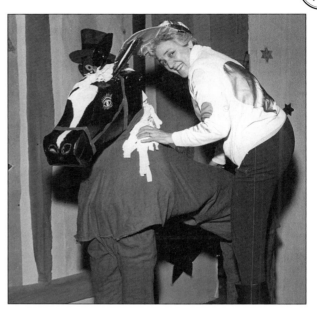

Pauline Grisbrook looks after the cow.
(THE JULIE TOWL COLLECTION)

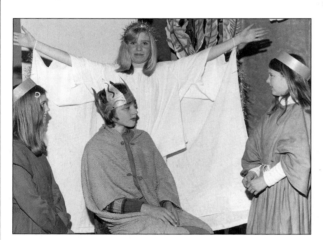

Sarah Harley, Delwyn Wallace, Linda Warman and Susan Towl perform. (THE JULIE TOWL COLLECTION)

Above: *Wendy Mumford, David Luscombe, Teresa Wakeham and Julie Sparkes.* (THE JULIE TOWL COLLECTION)

Left: *Gay Waddams, Anne Wakeham, Walter Wicks and Barbara Sparkes pose for a photographic shoot.*
(THE WADDAMS COLLECTION)

Nicola Crosbie, Denise Webber and Hilary Hannaford receive their St John awards. (THE JULIE TOWL COLLECTION)

In May 1976, the South Brent St John's was praised as one of the very best. Many parents went along to the Village Hall on Saturday to watch the annual inspection and the demonstrations of first aid and nursing techniques which followed.

Mr H. Trevains, the area staff officer, carried out the inspection, accompanied by Miss E.M. Grant, (Assistant County Staff Officer, Cadets); Mr Hoarer, an inspecting officer; Mrs G. Warrens (Cadet Vice-president)and Dr J. Wildman (Divisional Surgeon).

Miss Grant was delighted with what she saw and was full of praise for the South Brent unit. 'I go all over the county and see many cadets,' she said, 'but I can really say that South Brent is one of the very best – full of enthusiasm and very smart. Mrs Wakeham is to be congratulated.'

Mrs Anne Wakeham, the divisional superintendent in charge of South Brent, saw her daughter, Teresa, presented with the highest award for a cadet, the Grand Prior Badge. Marion Stephens also received the Grand Prior award and a special service star for 200 hours of voluntary work. Mrs M. Cox, the cadet president, declared the ceremony open and welcomed new juniors Anya Cockings, Hilary Hannaford, Maria MacArthur, Alison Warman, Julie Froom, Clare Shield, Judith Blackmore, Gary Warn and Gregory Phillips. Suzanne Mugridge, Susan Towl, Karan Pearse, Lorraine Bass, Jane Widdicombe, Tracey Miller, Denise Webber, Melina Fox, Doreen Hannaford, Nicola Crosbie, Joe MacArthur, David Bayliss and Paul Stone were enrolled as cadets. Certificates in road and home safety, handicrafts and first aid were presented to Lorraine Bass, Jane Widdicombe, Tracey Miller, Denise Webber, Melina Fox, Doreen Hannaford, Nicola Crosbie and F. Stone. Prayers of the order were said by Mr Dyer of the Congregational Church.

Ambulance and nursing cadets gave enthusiastic demonstrations of how to cope with sudden accidents, including broken legs, scalds and burns, all of which they dealt with confidently. Mrs Wakeham and Mr Walter Wicks told the *Gazette* they were

South Brent St John Ambulance cadets. Left to right: *Susan Towl, Nyree Doye, Karen Skinner, June Wicks, Pauline Wicks, Carol Newman, Louise Hannaford, Angela Hoare, Jackie Towl, Pauline Towl.* (THE JULIE TOWL COLLECTION)

113

Didworthy Hospital

The opening of the new wing in the Plymouth and South East Cornwall Hospital in 1905 or 1906. William, the 4th Earl of Mount Edgecumbe, who took a great interest in the hospital, is in the centre of the photograph wearing a light hat. On the right of the drive are the children of 'A' block.

(THE BATEMAN COLLECTION)

Charge Nurse Cross and Dr A.T. Bettison. Dr Bettison came down from the Brompton Hospital as as locum in 1924. Shortly after he had returned to London, the committee wrote to him to say that the person for whom he had locumed would be leaving, and to ask if he would like the job on a permanent basis. Hence he returned to Didworthy. (THE BATEMAN COLLECTION)

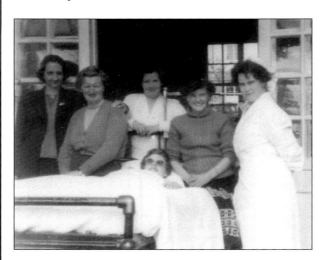

Sister Cross with Dr Bettinson outside the Womens' 'B' block. Dr Bettinson was always willing to talk to any of the patients whenever they wished, especially so when there was anything that was troubling them.

(THE BATEMAN COLLECTION)

Above: *The male patients' recreation room at Didworthy Hospital, possibly the only surviving photograph of this part of the hospital. Men who were allowed to be out and about could play billiards and take part in other recreational activities here. There was also a 'tuck shop' selling ginger beer, etc., to the patients. Mrs Bateman recalls nipping down to the tuck shop to get some ginger beer for herself.*

(THE BATEMAN COLLECTION)

Left: *A group of female patients outside 'B' Block.*

(THE BATEMAN COLLECTION)

Didworthy Hospital

The men's dining-room at Didworthy.

(THE GOSS COLLECTION)

The Lord Mayor and Lady Mayoress of Plymouth often paid visits to the hospital. Here they observe children at work in the schoolroom. Miss Wright was the schoolteacher. (THE BATEMAN COLLECTION)

Most of the photographs featured here are from the collection of Mrs Bateman, Dr Bettison's daughter, who lived at Didworthy.

Above and right: *The Didworthy May Day fancy dress parade. The patients at Didworthy were often in the hospital for a considerable period of time and so various 'entertainments' were provided for them, such as the celebration of May Day and St George's Day.*

(THE BATEMAN COLLECTION)

St John Ambulance Grand Prior Awards in the presence of HRH The Princess Margaret, Countess of Snowdon, at Lympstone Barracks in 1977. Included in the photgraph are Angela Hoare, Colette Crosbie, Wendy Mumford and Susie Towl. (THE MUMFORD COLLECTION)

Chris Miller, Denise Webber and Michael Tidball with a celebration cake. (THE JULIE TOWL COLLECTION)

grateful to parents and friends for supporting them so well with their interest and practical help.

The 1985 annual inspection of the St John cadets and juniors took place in the School Hall on Saturday, 8 June, during the afternoon. The 30 cadets and juniors were inspected by visiting officers from Torquay, Newton Abbot, Ashburton and Brixham, and an assortment of certificates were presented for clerical ability, hygiene, first aid and home nursing. Two new juniors, Clarissa Barrow and Michelle Male, were welcomed, and two cadets, Michelle Popham and Nicola Male, were enrolled.

The boys put on a display featuring evacuation from a burning house and treatment for burns, while the junior girls presented a dance routine and the senior girls did country and western dancing. The afternoon finished with refreshments for the parents and friends who had attended

By 1986 the St John's were meeting in the Church Room from 6.30 to 8.00p.m. on a Thursday evening, and were keen to welcome new members from eight years of age upwards. The group was particularly looking for adults who would care to join either in the brigade (uniform section) or as an auxiliary. There were 14 cadets, two of whom were competing in the South Devon area junior competition.

Unfortunately, despite all the hard work and enthusiasm that had been put into the organisation, in March 1988 it was announced:

It was with great regret that at a meeting with Mrs Wollacott and members of the Division on Wednesday, 3 March, it was felt necessary to close the Division for the present. The Division was down in numbers to seven cadets and three adult members and unfortunately, there appeared to be no prospect of finding a volunteer for divisional officer.

I would like to express my thanks to all members of the Division and supporting adults who have tried so hard in the past year or so to make a going concern of St John's. As it happens, our bank balance is healthier than it has been for a long time! It has been suggested that anyone interested might like to join either the Lee Moor or Totnes Division. Will all those who did not return their uniforms on 3 March please bring them to Church House soonest.

Elisabeth Niblett (President)

South Brent St John Ambulance on the occasion of the presentation of the Area Cup in 1975. Left to right, back row: Alfred Honeywill, Doris March, Shirley Livermore, Renee Aston, Cpl Walter Wicks; *front row:* Nursing Officer Julia Carroll, Divisional Superintendent Barbara Field, Area Superintendent Mrs Cleasby, Pat Levitt.

(THE FIELD COLLECTION)

✦ CHAPTER 11 ✦

Another Look at Horticulture

Brent's Weather

South Brent has a reputation for being one of the wettest places in the county of Devon. Many people who move into the village have noted that you can be in Ivybridge or in Buckfastleigh, our two nearest neighbours along the Devon Expressway, and the sun might well be shining. Come those four or five miles to Brent and it will often be raining, or at best cloudy! Brent has its own version of the weather saying which runs, 'if 'ee can't see the Beacon (Ugborough Beacon) tiz rainin', if 'ee kin t'will zoon be.'

The rainfall figures bear testimony to the fact that Brent is wet. To take but one example, the figures for rainfall in 2006 show that Brent had 1,619mm of rain and was only outrained by Cherrybrook, in the heart of the moor near Princetown, which had 2,020mm. Even Widecombe, in the centre of the southern moor, only managed to record 1,529mm, and Buckfastleigh only had 1,449mm. The higher than 'average' rainfall can be explained by the community's position at the southernmost point of Dartmoor, between Ugborough Beacon and Brent Hill and below Whittaburrow, which is often the wettest location on the moor.

In the 1970s Cdr Collier recorded the following information from the rain gauge at Whinfield, which he considered to have been a record for this district, at any rate for the last 30 years.

24 hours ended 0900 on 10 March: 2.20 inches of rain
24 hours ended 0900, on 11 March: 2.41 inches of rain
Total rainfall: 4.61 inches of rain

The weather can sometimes have very dramatic results, as illustrated by this extract from a newspaper report of 15 March 1914:

A serious accident which may have been of a far more serious nature occurred on Saturday afternoon near South Brent to Mr F. Moores, foreman for Mr R.H. Gill,

A view of Ugborough Beacon from the mid-twentieth century. This was sent as a postcard from Brent to Scotland in December 1941.

(THE SHARVILLE COLLECTION)

117

general merchant, etc. Mr Moores was carrying out his usual delivery of goods with a horse and trap in the Shipley district, returning by the Downstow road to Lutton village. The road approaching Downstow is the highest in the neighbourhood and comes in for the full force of the storm from the Dartmoor hills. It was so fierce at this place on Saturday that the driver had to hold on to something to prevent his being blown off the box of the trap. Just as he was about to descend the hill in Downstow Lane, a terrific storm of wind, hail and rain struck the horse, which gave a plunge and dashed off at a fast rate. The driver did his best to pull it up, but with numbed hands he was only able to keep in the centre of the narrow lane. Just as he turned the bend of the lane at Downstow gate a flock of sheep being driven by Mr T. Smerdon and his two sons, of Downstow farm, was approaching. The horse dashed into the sheep and fell with such force that both shafts broke and the trap was cleanly telescoped over the sheep and the driver thrown a distance of 20 yards down the hill. Mr Smerdon and his sons had a marvellous escape from being killed, but saved themselves by clinging to the roots of a tree under the hedge. The horse was free some distance from the trap.

Periodically, Brent experiences extreme periods of weather. Mrs E. Catt wrote of the winter of 1947:

The Winter of 1947
Wind, rain, frost and snow,
Food scarce, fuel low;
Greens rare with one potato,
Indeed men reap just what they sow

God teaches a lesson men will not learn,
To keep lamps trimmed, that they may burn;
Were we prepared in case of need,
Then these bad times would not have been.
Foresight, forethought, men doth need,

But in women, they are strong indeed;
They plot and plan and fill their stores,
Getting things done as ne'er before.

This lesson learnt, will bring release,
In times of war, and times of peace;
Learn it men, without delay,
While we women weep and pray

Robert Savery recalls the heavy snowfall of 1963:

The snow began to fall on Boxing Day 1962. Four inches of snow fell on ground which had already been hardened by frost before Christmas, and so the root crops that had been grown for forage were destroyed. The snow continued to fall for the next eight weeks, filling the roads and the lanes and burying sheep which, although they can survive under snow for quite some time, all had to be dug out by hand. Drinking troughs

and streams froze over in the 32 days of continuous frost, and even the wild rabbits were known to enter farmers' barns to graze on the hay stored there.

In 1982 this report appeared in the parish magazine:

In the absence of Hazel Millington, who certainly chose the right time to visit Australia, I have undertaken to fill in for a month or so, but, as like most people, I have been kept indoors for the last two weeks, news around the village is a little scarce. We did, however, get off to a really rousing start to 1982, with a peal of bells from St Petroc's tower. We are lucky in South Brent to have both the bells and the ringers, although I have never asked those residents in the immediate vicinity how they feel about them. I guess Ray Wakeley, as a former ringer and captain, is in no position to grumble. I'm not sure about the others, though.

Snow, biting winds and power cuts are, to say the least, very inconvenient and frustrating, and tend to be unsettling too – even the children tire of the snow when their hands start to ache. But for our 'Milk Persons' I feel the village should have nothing but praise. They worked long hours in appalling conditions to ensure that everyone had their deliveries, and to them and their helpers we must say a very big 'thank you'. I heard stories of vans and lorries being stuck while trying to deliver in the village and I feel we must consider ourselves very fortunate that we were not more inconvenienced. Brent was very lucky and we are grateful to all the people who helped to keep things nearly normal.

A number of bookings in the Village Hall had to be cancelled, the School, the Art Club, Cubs and the SBADS rehearsal, also the Seniors' rehearsal for the VH concert. Mrs Nosworthy went ahead with her Whist Drive in aid of the Agricultural Society, but of course attendance was very sparse, as it was held on 8 January. Mrs Herd was able to cancel her Whist Drive in aid of 'Cancer and Leukaemia Research'. Instead it was held on 13 February,

Allotments

In 2006 the South Brent Parish Council purchased the old tennis courts on Vicarage Road with a view to them being transformed into allotments for local people with the proviso that, when required, some of the land could be used as a cemetery extension.

The land was suitably cleared and graded and in the autumn of that year 42 plots were made available, meaning that over 200 people could be involved in the growing. There were 48 paid-up members in the first instance, with more on the waiting list.

But there have always been allotments in Brent. Many people will remember such men as Mr Norman Hard walking from the cottage he shared with his wife Evie and daughter Melba to his allotment garden on the land that is now occupied by Churchside Villas, or even further to his other allotment in the field above Crackhills, with watering cans to feed the vegetables growing there. He was far from being the only one. There were allotments at Quarry Park, the site of the village tip. Mr Stephens, Mr Pulleyblank and Mr Foale all had holdings there, indeed Mr Foale eventually built a bungalow on the site. Derrick Pulleyblank remembers digging the allotment for his father. He recalls that there was a

The allotment site in Vicarage Road prior to its transformation. The banks on which stood the old tennis courts can be clearly seen and were preserved when the allotments were created. (THE GILES COLLECTION)

A general view of the Vicarage Road allotments in their first year of operation.

Mr John Sparkes preparing his allotment plot for the first time. (THE KEN SMITH COLLECTION)

hose reel there just in case the tip needed damping down when it overheated. There were also allotments on the sides of the Kingsbridge branch-line tilled by railwaymen, and Mr Mark Roper had some ground along Harwell Lane. There were also plots of land on the site of Ashwood and on the site of Brookwood Close. Here Mr Pinhey had his allotment and also kept chickens. The water for these allotments came from the stream that ran from Hillside and finally emerged under the Royal Oak before being piped down to Stockbridge Lane, where it entered the town leat and eventually ran into the Avon at Brent Mill.

South Brent Produce Association

Norman Hard, a leading light in the South Brent Produce Association, was for many years the show secretary.

The Association was founded in the mid-twentieth century, and in 1955, under the presidency of Cdr A. Penrice-Lyons and chairmanship of Mr

Mr. Paul Honeywell won the Hawes Cup for the best exhibit in the flower-arranging class.
(THE KEITH MALE COLLECTION)

Mrs. Margaret Eales with her winning narcissus and camellia. (THE KEITH MALE COLLECTION)

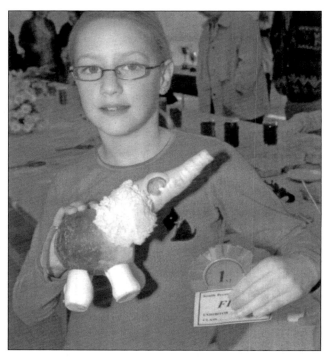

Ellie Ford won first prize with her vegetable elephant in a spring show. (THE KEITH MALE COLLECTION)

From top: Exhibits in a Spring Produce Association show.
(THE EALES COLLECTION)

George Hannaford, 60 members attended the annual general meeting held in the Primary School on 14 April. The report of the 1955 show reads:

The Horticultural Section was a great success, with 450 entries, 30 more than the previous year. The judge remarked that the standard of exhibits were on the whole very good. The Association Challenge Cup for the highest points went to R.V. Hard, with 18 points. The runner-up was Mr D. Vallance, with 15 points. Members attaining 1st prizes in Division A and qualifying for the 2s.6d. for each 1st prize from the Association were Messrs Vallance, Teague, Jefford, N. Hard and R.V. Hard.

The Association originally held shows three times a year, one in the spring, another in the summer and a third in the autumn. Until 1964 the Spring Show was known as the Bulb Show. In the early years, as well as Cdr Penrice-Lyons and Mr Hannaford, Maj-Gen Jameson held the posts of both chairman and president. This was between 1964 and 1973. Mr W. Halfyard was chairman between 1968 and 1976 and Mr Mike Major became chairman in 1978 and held the post until 1995.

It was reported in 1970:

Nearly all the main trophies and class awards at the South Brent Produce Association's autumn show were carried off by Mr Fred Wakeley, one of South Brent's most popular gardeners. He took the Association Challenge Cup for most points in the show, the George Hannaford Cup awarded to the member who gained most points in the three shows held by the Association during the year, and the special prizes for the best exhibits in the flower section and pot plant classes.

Runner-up to Mr Wakeley was Mr A. Terry, who also won the special prize for the best exhibit in the vegetable section. Mrs P. Juste won the Hawes Bowl for the best exhibit in the decorative section, and the special prize awarded in the same section.

Entries were down on last year's figure but, nevertheless, the judges were impressed with the quality of the exhibits, particularly in the vegetable and floral arrangement sections.

Again in 1972, the judges. Messrs G. Webber, B.J. Key,

Mr John Eales congratulates Mrs Nancy Wright on her success. (THE EALES COLLECTION)

M. Perring and Miss J. Howell. described the show as 'the best autumn show' they had seen in South Brent.

In 1974 it was reported that Mr John Eales won 19 of the 45 classes, while Mr Arthur Terry won eight classes in the vegetable section. Indeed, Mr Eales won the Didboy Shield for the most points in the chrysanthemum classes, the Association Autumn Cup for the top marks in the flower and vegetable sections and the George Hannaford Cup for the most points in all three shows for that year. Mr Terry was the runner-up for the Autumn Cup.

Mrs Pauline Juste wrote of the 1985 Summer Show:

A poor summer does not stop the gardeners in South Brent winning cups for their prize produce. At the Summer Show, on 27 July, Mr and Mrs Jonas not only won the cups for entries in the show, but also a cup for the best front garden in the village. Mrs Jonas also made a winning impression on the judges in the domestic section. Other cups were won by Mrs Bromley in the cut flowers section; Mr Terry in the non-members' section; Mrs Moore for the most points in the flower arranging, plus a Blue Ribbon presented for the first time this year by Mrs Ashton, a regular summer judge – this she decided to present to the best exhibit in the flower arranging, which was Mrs Moore's interpretation of 'The Barn-yard'. Mr Mercer had the best

Mr John Eales with his prize-winning vegetables.
(THE EALES COLLECTION)

bottle of wine and won the B&G Trophy. I am sure that the rest of the bottle was used to celebrate. Mrs F. Sparkes had the best exhibit in the handicrafts. As usual, the children entered an interesting display of work, and many were rewarded with prizes.

Each year the Association runs an outing to a place of horticultural interest.

South Brent in the Snow

Matthew Carroll and David Carter enjoy playing in the heavy snow. (THE CARROLL COLLECTION)

Heavy snowfall in Hillside (THE WONNACOTT COLLECTION)

Children of South Brent pre-school enjoy playing in the snow. (THE PRE-SCHOOL COLLECTION)

The heavy snowfall of 1975, looking from Kerries Road across Sanderspool Cross to Totnes Road.

(THE MAJOR COLLECTION)

Sledging in not just for children! Val Meek, Jill Sparkes, Judith Crannis and Marilyn Bullen enjoy the snow of February 1986 in Weir Path Field.

(THE BULLEN COLLECTION)

CHAPTER 12

Another Look at Sporting Activities

The Cricket Club

The South Brent Cricket Club played between 1976 and 1995, adopting as its colours old gold and blue. The club played first at Underhill Meadow, moving to Palstone Park when that facility became available. The club was affiliated to the Devon Cricket Association and the National Cricket Association, as well as to the Devon Playing Fields Association and the Devon Umpires' Association.

The annual general meeting of the South Brent Cricket Club was held on 9 March in 1981. The attendance was recorded as poor:

The reports by Maurice Rush, the Chairman, Graham Jordan, the Secretary and Dick Norrish, the Treasurer, were all received with thanks. All reports spoke of a successful 1980 season, with 32 senior playing and non-playing members, 29 juniors and 28 vice-presidents. There was a healthy balance in the accounts, though there were unpaid bills.

All the Officers were re-elected and Dick Norrish was re-elected captain, with Malcolm Cowper his vice-captain. Dick and his family had found the demands of cricket too time-consuming during 1980 and much committee time was spent in trying to persuade Dick to

remain captain and in trying to lighten his load. The committee did succeed in taking the teas off him and the responsibility for equipment – much more help was needed in ground maintenance. Mondays in April were put aside to work on the ground.

Sid Mercer reported on the Colts and the under-16s. They had four matches in the 1980 season and it was hoped to increase this number in 1981. The fixture list

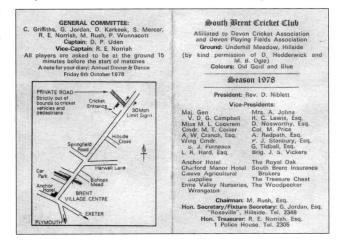

The 1978 Cricket Club membership card,

(THE JORDAN COLLECTION)

South Brent Cricket Club at Underhill in 1978. Left to right, back row: *Peter Drake, Gary Griffiths, Paul Wonnacott, Eddie Bristowe, Nick McCaig, Alan Pickering;* front row: *Brian Male, Dick Norrish, Don Uden, Graham Jordan, Brian Thomas.*

(THE JORDAN COLLECTION)

South Brent Cricket Club in 1976, the first year it was re-formed. Left to right, back row: *R. Norrish, P. Bullen, ?, ?, D. Karkeek, D. Stewart, P. Wonnacott, D. Newman;* front row: *D. Goss, M. Rush, B. Male, B. Thomas.*

(The Bullen Collection)

Graham Jordan in action at Ilsington, 1980.

(The Jordan Collection)

for Colts matches will be inserted into the Senior Club's fixture list.

Graham Jordan promised to inform all last season's members of the decisions of the meeting and in particular to appeal for help in working on the ground.

In 1981 the under-16 cricketers started their competitive season on 9 July with a home fixture against Dartmouth at 6.30p.m. They then had eight other fixtures during that summer. Any boy keen on cricket was welcome to the practice nights on Tuesdays at Underhill Meadow at 6.30p.m.

The 1982 season began as quite a promising one, both weatherwise and by results. Highlights of the season were the defeat of both Cornwood and Keyham in the first two rounds of the Devon Cricket

Association Corinthian Knock-out Cup. Graham Jordan, the club secretary, wrote:

The machine for cutting the outfield has meant that Underhill is looking 'a picture', and many visitors have complimented us on the wicket. A feature has been the number of ex-Colts who are 'coming through' to the first team. We are indebted to many people who help to keep the club 'ticking over', and special mention must be made of Sid Mercer, Maurice Rush, Brian Stone, Mrs Stone, Malcolm Cowper and, last but by no means least, Viv Mant, who prepares our delicious teas. All in all, Underhill is a splendid place to watch cricket, and we extend a welcome to anyone to join our many regulars at home matches.

There was another good start to the season in 1984, with the team winning 10 matches, losing eight, and drawing two, and there was one tied game. That year also saw the visit of Woodchurch Cricket Club on their tour of Devon. Woodchurch is a village near Ashford, in Kent. Brent progressed to the third round of the Corinthian Cup, Totnes just defeating the team in a thrilling and high-scoring match. A milestone was reached on 14 July, when Nick Hawkins became Brent's first century maker, while in June 1985 South Brent Cricket Club hosted a team from TSW.

Graham Jordan wrote of the 1987 season:

In 1987 there were quite a few new milestones in the

South Brent Cricket Club, July 1982. Left to right, back row: *Jeremy Niblett, Mike Goss, Mike Worden, ?, Tim Pett, Bryn Taylor;* front row: *Peter Brown, Brian Stone, Malcolm Cowper, Graham Jordan, Peter Drake.* (THE CRICKET CLUB ARCHIVE)

history of the Club. The move from the Underhill pitch to Palstone Park resulted in some high-scoring matches, due in large part to the excellent playing surface there. Despite the remainder of the country apparently not seeing much in the way of sunshine, it is now history that this 'neck of the woods' did very well for weather, with the result that we played all but six matches on the fixture card. Another milestone was passed when Brent won their 20th game, passing the best record ever. We lost 11 matches and drew three. Two centuries were hit (by Keith Bullock and Mike Baines), and Peter Bird was only three short of his maiden century when he was caught! All in all, a wonderful season under the captaincy of Peter Brown.

During his time as Vicar of South Brent, Revd David Niblett was one of the leading lights of the club. As a member of the MCC, he was able to get tickets for international matches. On one such occasion Dick Norrish and Graham Jordan went to watch England play a one-day match against Australia:

The match, although not a classic, had many flashes of brilliance – not least the sheer athleticism of David Gower. He surely is going to be an England ' ever present'.

We were able to look around Lord's, the Mecca of World Cricket, during the lunch and tea intervals – and

what a fascinating place it is. Anyone with only a passing interest in the game could spend an intriguing day there, even when no match was in progress:

We witnessed many amusing incidents and met many friendly people during a memorable day.

We rounded a 'sporting day' with a look around Wembley Stadium (the car was parked at the tube station there) and Brent hove into view at 2.15a.m.

The Football Club

The South Brent Football Club was founded in the early 1920s and has been an important part of community life since then. The team played on the old playing-field, now Pool Park, from 1946 until 1967. At this time problems arose over the widening of the A38 and the erection of a fence to prevent the ball going into the road. The team then moved their home matches to Kerries, but the need of the farmer for the field for agricultural purposes left the club with more problems.

However, the problem was resolved when the Club moved to a new venue at The Marsh. But the troubles were not over just yet. It was reported:

South Brent football club's pitch, new last season, is called The Marsh. And for very good reasons. During the last few weeks, Mr Alf Sabine, the club secretary,

South Brent Football Club, 1982/83. Left to right, back row: P. Baker, A. King, S. Sparkes, P. Bullen (Manager), D. Stewart, I. Karkeek, C. Heath, E. Chapple; front row: R. Martin, N. Cockings, C. Hannaford, P. Soper, B. Headon, C. Jones. (The Bullen Collection)

The South Brent Football Club team that played Plymouth Argyle football team in 1944. (Francis Sparkes Collection)

and a few dedicated helpers, have been working hard to drain and resurface the pitch. Mr Sabine put an advertisement in the South Brent Post Office calling for volunteers to bring their own spades and help spread topsoil evenings and weekends. But his appeal brought no response. 'I expect they are all out courting on these summer evenings,' said Mr Sabine. 'They are good boys, but they are naturally more interested in playing football than in helping to prepare the pitch.'

In home games during their first season at The Marsh the club scored 43 goals. Only 13 were scored against them.

Then another ground crisis arose. As a result of the work to construct the new sewage disposal system the pitch had become a 'churned-up mess'.

South Brent Football Club 1st XI 1920/21. Left to right, back row: G. Cullem, ?, W. Elliott, A. Manning, G. Wilkinson, ?; middle row: H. Bunker, B. Chapple, A. Drew, E. Catt; front row: A. Jefford, L. Fox, R. Andrews, R. Staples, G. Wakeham. (The Football Club Archive)

The players and officials tried very hard to get the pitch back into condition. Mr Alf Sabine was hopeful that, 'Weather permitting, we'll complete our restoration when we hope to have turf ready to lay.' Things did not go quite to plan, and the teams were forced to think about playing all of their games for the rest of that season away. Yet, by Christmas, the team had managed to get a new pitch at West Cannmore at Wrangaton. The club finally returned to The Marsh, where they continued to play until moving to Palstone Park Recreation Ground in 1985.

South Brent Football Club 1st XI 1981/82. Left to right, back row: *B. Male, C. Heath, P. Eastley, D. Stewart, C. Hawkins, T. Winsor, B. Lake (Manager);* front row: *D. King, D. Goss, P. Soper, E. Chapple, S. Sparkes, I. Karkeek, K. Stephens.* (THE FOOTBALL CLUB ARCHIVE)

South Brent Football Club 2nd XI 1966/67. Left to right, back row: *D. Ayres, H. Honeywill, R. Hard, M. Goss, D. Perry, B. Langdon;* front row: *C. Smith, ? , S. Witheridge, M. Wright, A. Honeywill.*

(THE FOOTBALL CLUB ARCHIVE)

South Brent Football Club 1st XI 1945/46. Left to right, back row: *F. Smallridge, D. Newman, R. Tucker, J. Andrews, G. Chapple, E. Male, C. Wilkinson;* front row: *C. Joint, R. Parsons, E. Sowden, M. O'Connell, V. Newman.* (THE FOOTBALL CLUB ARCHIVE)

South Brent Football Club winners, 1974/75. Left to right, back row: *T. Skelton, B. Lake, G. Langdon, ?, C. Smith, ?, C. Hawkins, Alf Sabine (Manager);* front row: *J. Skelton, N. Rooke, P. Bullen, P. Soper, R. Stephens.* (THE BULLEN COLLECTION)

South Brent Football Club Cup winners, 1973. Left to right, back row: *Graham Bloomfield (sponsor), Stephen Towl (Manager), Richard Male, Michael Woods, Joseph Clarke, Shaun Clarke, Alan Caldwell, Lee Kirk, John Chapple, Stephen Snell (Asst Manager).* Front row: *Richard Wilson, Colin Jones, Alan Eyles, James Andrews, Shaun Biddis. The mascot was Ben Towl.*

(THE STEPHEN TOWL COLLECTION)

South Brent Football Club Ronald Cup winners, 2006/07. Left to right, back row: *Paul Soper (Manager), Nick Errington, Simon Parsons, Paul Underwood (Captain), Lee Soper, Mark Vinecombe, Martin Hill, Gareth Hughes, Dave Skelton, Mark Watson (Assistant Manager);* front row: *James Watt, Neil Vinecombe, David Marrah, Rob Heveran, Sean Biddiss, Mike Nicholson, Andy Underwood, Jason Pratt.*

(THE FOOTBALL CLUB ARCHIVE)

Left: *South Brent under-14s at The Marsh. The team was sponsored by Tom and Doris Crawley.* Left to right, back row: *Doris Crawley, D. Chapple, Pat Bullen (Manager), L. Bullen, P. Smith, J. Ramsden, J. Chapple, C. Lake, S. Popham, Tom Crawley;* front row: *A. Ramsden, P. Reed, M. Toogood, K. Hodge, R. Bradshaw, G. Hodge, M. Carroll.*

(THE BULLEN COLLECTION)

In 1986 it was reported that: 'Brent Football Club's presentation evening turned into a family affair when Chris Smith and his two sons, Andrew and Michael, collected awards for the season's top performances. Veteran centre-half Chris, making his comeback and playing regularly in the past season, was chosen second team player of the year; teenage winger Andrew was the runner-up in the second team and, for the second successive year, took the under-16 trophy. And if all that wasn't enough, 12-year-old Michael won the top player's prize in the under-14 team. The first team trophy went to Eddie Chapple, who edged out Ian Karkeek, the winner for the previous two seasons. Peter Eastley was the first team's top goal-scorer and the second team's chief marksman was Tim Winzer. Colin Jones became the first winner of a trophy presented to the club's most improved player of the year. Colin began the season in the second team and later became a first team regular. Treasurer Malcolm Wright was awarded the trophy for the club member of the year. Brent's chairman, Peter Moore, urged players to take part in a wider variety of club activities when he spoke at the annual meeting. Mr. Moore's words reflected the poor attendance by players at the meeting and he emphasised the need for the players to become more involved in aspects of the club "other than those on the field". However, he added that the atmosphere within the club was good and the year had seen its successes.'

(THE STEPHEN TOWL COLLECTION)

Above: *A team from the mid-1990s. Left to right, back row: Stephen Towl, Mike Frame, Richard Perry, Matt Carroll, Gary Langdon, Mike Gosshawk, Mark Nicholls (Manager); front row: Andy Honeywill, Steve Hannaford, Mark Langdon, John Burnitt, Roger Bowhay, Shaun Beer, Phil Harler.*

(THE STEPHEN TOWL COLLECTION)

Left: *Carnival Five-a-side Football, 1981. Left to right, back row: Darren Wollington, Lee Bullen, Joe Lyne; front row: Andrew Bird, ? Mant, Mark Norrish.*

(THE BULLEN COLLECTION)

The team sponsored by 'The Friary'. Left to right, back row: Dean Edwards (kit supplier), John England (Manager), David England, Neil Brooks, Joe Langford, Kevin Hare, Phil Atkins, Mike Frame, Matt Hellyer, Malcolm Tidball (sponsor), Mike Smith (Coach); front row: Paddy Wellens, Gareth Davies, Peter Miles, John Currie, Richard Saunter, Chris Bailey, Lee Ryder.

(THE ENGLAND COLLECTION)

Above: *Not only did the Football Club enjoy success. In 1977 Mr John Eales's five-a-side soccer team appeared at the Empire Pool, Wembley, on 29 May, their reward for winning the Devon and Cornwall newspaper delivery boys' championship. The competition was sponsored by the National Federation of Retail Newsagents and the* Western Morning News, *and the boys' success meant that, apart from the Wembley trip, they were the proud possessors, for one year at least, of the* Western Morning News *trophy. The boys were: Neil Cockings (Captain), Richard Headon, Steve Hannaford, Benny Headon, Mark Nicholls and Steven Sparkes. Ian Karkeek was also involved with the team.*

(THE BULLEN COLLECTION)

The South Brent Football Club has had its share of success. In 1973 the club had its most successful season so far and received the congratulations of the Parish Council for winning the South Devon League Division 3 Championship and the Ronald Cup. Unfortunately, their first match in Division 2 was threatened with postponement due to the non-appearance of the referee, whose car had broken down. There was nothing for it. Brent and Beesands accepted Mr Alf Sabine's offer to referee the match. In 1974 the club was again congratulated by the Parish Council when they won the Lidstone Challenge Cup for the second year running.

In the 1977/78 season, the club became Division 3 champions and so winners of the Ronald Cup. They were also Devon Intermediate Cup finalists, losing to Axminster Town after a replay.

The team was captained by Pat Bullen alongside Richard Hard, Colin Perry, Eddie Chapple, Duncan Stewart, Howard Milton, Paul Shalders, John Frude, Tim Winzer, Norman Rooke, Colin Hawkins and, last but not least, Paul Soper, who went on to manage the team in the 2006/07 season and won the Ronald Cup – their first trophy for 29 years.

A report on the 1984/85 season by Bert Field which appeared in the April 1985 edition of *The Marsher*, the official programme and news-sheet of South Brent Football Club, read:

Here we are once again at the end of another season for our two senior teams. Our first team has had a satisfactory season which will see them finish in the midway mark of Division 2. Many thanks to Steve Sparkes, the first team manager, for his efforts. He has worked hard with his players and is a popular member of the football club. Our second team are not having a very happy time this season and they have to win their last game against Channings Wood on 4 May to avoid the

drop into Division 5, provided the team immediately above them in the league lose their last game. This is due to no fault of the team manager, John Palmer, and his assistant, Mark Nicholls. The team has had many changes in the season due to players who are members of HM Services not being available every week, also to two players who are under 16 years of age. It is hard for players of their age to be playing in the senior teams. Many thanks, John and Mark, for all your hard work and dedication to the game of football. May good fortune be with you today to help us get out of this very difficult situation.

Now to our two youth teams. The under-14s team have had an excellent season, winning the Tony Rogers Cup for the first time ever, and with one more game to play on 5 May against Kingsbridge, success in this game will see them on top of the league. Many thanks to team manager Pete Kelly and his assistant, Jim Anthony, for their persistent hard work in motivating these lads to final success.

And now to our first ever under-12s team in South Brent. Team manager Francis Sparkes has worked wonders with these lads, some of them only nine years old, ably assisted by Pat Bullen and Ken Foot, who took them to the final of the Pearson Cup but were beaten by a bigger and more robust team, Torquay Hungarians. However, these lads did not disgrace themselves or Francis – they played their hearts out. They have two more games to play and, with a little luck, I think they could achieve third place in the League.

The Judo Club

Richard Cleave writes:

The club was formed on 17 April 1970 by Mr Roy Warnes and his wife Esther, with 17 members, at South Brent Primary School. To start the school managed to borrow a judo mat from Newton Ferrers School, which gave us a good start. Over time, enough money was raised with the help of Devon County Council to purchase some of our own. Members paid 2d. a week !!

Two years later the *Western Morning News* reported that South Brent was 'a judo stronghold'. It went on to say:

At this year's Devon Schools Judo Championships five out of 20 gold medals were won by youngsters from the village of South Brent, where two years ago an ex-Marine Commando started giving instruction at the Primary School. Now the village boasts a judo club with over 80 members, ranging from eight to 32 years.

The club also took part in competitions with Brent's French twin town of Châteauneuf-du-Faou.

In August 1985 Roy Warnes wrote:

Thirty-six children ranging in age from seven to 14 years, took part in the training weekend and grading session which was run by Devon County coach Roy Voisey on 29 and 30 June at the Village Hall, and each one gained at least one stripe (there are three stripes in between each colour belt). Members who did particularly well included eight-year-old Ian Stannard, who gained three stripes, Ross Pannell, who gained three stripes and is now an orange belt, and Ian Sparkes, who also gained three stripes to earn a green belt. One girl who did well was Anna Hall, who gained two stripes, as did Rupert Prince, aged 14 years, who is a blue belt, the second highest which can be earned by juniors (black belts cannot be awarded to under-16s). Unfortunately, one accident marred the weekend – nine-year-old Neil Hart broke his ankle.

Richard Cleeve continues:

Roy and Esther retired in 1985. For a few years we had several coaches until 1990, when a committee was

Alan Tout with Jackie Horswill at a training session.
(THE JUDO CLUB ARCHIVE)

Richard Cleeve and Roy Warnes.　(THE JUDO CLUB ARCHIVE)

formed under the chair of Mr Alan Tout, with home-grown coaches Mark Nicholls and Richard Cleave.

The club moved to Palstone Recreation Park, new mats were needed and with a lot of fund-raising we were able to purchase 30 new ones.

When Mark retired from Judo in 1994, the main coaching was taken on by Peter Ash, Lee Hard and Gary Craig.

Richard Cleeve carried on coaching at the club until 2003 when, unfortunately, after suffering a stroke, he retired from coaching at the club.

The members of South Brent Judo Club who competed in the British National Team Championships, five of whom returned with National Amateur Judo Association awards. A total of 14 fought their way through preliminary rounds to qualify for the championships at Poole. There, representing the Western Area, they had to fight in teams of seven. Black belt Jim Cutts and brown belts Jeremy Eastley and Mark Nicholls were part of one team which, handicapped with a 20 point deficit because they numbered only five instead of seven, gained bronze medals. In the 16–18-year-old group, Richard Bishop won a silver trophy as his team came second in its section. Other members in the championship were Beverly Edgson, Jane Lonsdale, Glenn D'Conceicao, Jackie Steer, Susan Ryder, Gary Langdon, Julian Lyne, Rachel Cousins and Rupert Prince. They were instructed by Roy Warnes. (THE JUDO CLUB ARCHIVE)

We still use the hall today, with the whole room as a mat area. We currently have a large membership of juniors and many adults.

Racing in the Brent Area

Many people new to the community are surprised to hear that horse-racing once took part in Brent. Peter Wakeham recalls:

In the latter part of the nineteenth century Devon boasted seven licensed National Hunt Racecourses – Plymouth, Totnes and Bridgetown, Torquay, Buckfastleigh, Newton Abbot, Devon and Exeter and South Brent Devon and Cornwall Hunt (the Devon and Cornwall Hunt part being discarded in later years), of which only two, Newton Abbot and Exeter, remain.
The first fixture credited at South Brent took place on Tuesday, 4 June 1889 on a course at Horsebrook Farm,

approximately two miles from the town. Six races were on the card, of which four were run over banks and two over the 'flying course' (fences similar to those in use at the present time). The first race to be run was the Maiden Hunters Plate, over banks and at a distance of 2½ miles, in which all but the winner fell in a six-horse field. It is not precise as to how many years the meeting was housed at Horsebrook, but in all probability it was only a short stay, as later meetings were held at Palstone Farm, then owned by Mr J.W. Wakeham. A left-handed course, approximately a mile in circumference, was constructed, which was bisected by the A38 Plymouth to Exeter road in two places. An annual one-day fixture was held in either late May or early June. Fields were small and rarely exceeded seven runners per race, which were all steeplechases. Hurdle racing was introduced into the programme in 1901, when prizes varied between £24 and £33 to the winner. Many of the participating horses were locally owned and trained, but others were carried by rail from further afield, disembarking at Brent Station. According to press reports the attendance figure for 1890 was 'about 1,000', but there do not appear to be any existing records, which indicates that that number was maintained or exceeded. Two local professional jockeys, Robert 'Bobby' Gordon and Edward 'Ned' Southwood, rode their fair share of winners, Bobby Gordon being successful in three of the five contests in 1908. In 1901 the programme listed a race for half-bred horses, and another notable feature was the fact that Mr G.D. Bondon's Horicon won the opening race, a two-mile handicap hurdle, and ran again in the third race, a three-mile handicap chase, in which it did not finish! This was by no means unique in the annals of racing at that time, and even as late as the 1950s two well-known performers in point-to-point races, Diana II and Juno III, not only ran twice on the same day, but won both races. A most unusual event occurred at the same 1901 fixture when the owner of Henry II, who finished first in the Dartmoor Hunt Selling Chase, reported that his jockey failed to draw his weight at scale after the race and that a discrepancy was found to exist in the scales themselves, also that one of the stewards who was called in to adjudicate was a disqualified person. The stewards of the National Hunt subsequently investigated that matter and decided that Henry II should be disqualified. It was not recorded what happened to the steward! It was clear that not everything ran smoothly, as racing calendars of the era reported such comments as, in 1903, an objection made to the placed horses in a race on the grounds that they went the wrong course was overruled. Other objections for crossing and/or boring were not infrequent. The stewards of the day needed to be vigilant and, of course, had to operate without all the present-day technology. It would seem, however, that most objections were overruled, so either many were spurious or it was a case of 'what the eye doesn't see'! The stewards whose names appeared on the Brent panel were Captain Parlby, Mr H.F. Brunskill, Mr G Hext, Mr W. Coryton, Mr W.J. Phillips, Mr G. Crake, Mr R. Fox, Major Boyd, Mr R.H. Hughes and Mr D. Potts-Chatto. Two of these, Messrs Brunskill and Coryton, were Masters of Foxhounds.

Selling races were always featured on the race-card, most meetings including both a selling steeplechase and a selling hurdle. The winner of such a race was then offered for sale by auction, with a minimum opening bid of £50. When sold, most animals realised a sum of between £50 and £100. Any bid in excess of the latter amount would have been considered to have been an excellent result. However, in 1911 the five-race card, in addition to the two usual sellers, offered an additional optimal selling race. This was the penultimate year before the cessation of South Brent races and the five races yielded a total of only 13 runners, which included one walk-over and two two-horse contests. The final year, 1912, saw a slight increase in numbers when a total of 17 faced the starter. It is not easy to ascertain

why Brent races ceased when they did, but rumours have since prevailed that the crossing of the main road presented problems to motorists who were delayed, although the passage of traffic would have been insignificant then. It is more probable that the small fields and, in particular, the poor race card of 1911, signalled the end of the road to racing at Palstone due to lack of support for a course which, in comparison to its other Devon neighbours, was probably always the poor relation.

South Brent lies in the midst of the Dartmoor Foxhounds hunting country, so it is hardly surprising that the area featured prominently as a venue for its annual point-to-point meeting, point-to-point being an amateur sport as opposed to its professional counterpart on licensed racecourses.

Early history records that the first Dartmoor Hunt point-to-points were held in the nineteenth century on a course at Battisborough Cross, Newton Ferrers, and were still there in 1905. However, by 1908 they had relocated to Cannamore, Langford, and Lady Down farms at Wrangaton. Both courses held banking meetings, as indeed did nearly all others during that period. Five races were run per fixture, at which most of the horses were half-bred hunters with substance and bone and eminently suitable to negotiate the large Devon banks over which they competed. All races were over a minimum distance of three miles, during which they encountered both grass and ploughed underfoot condi-

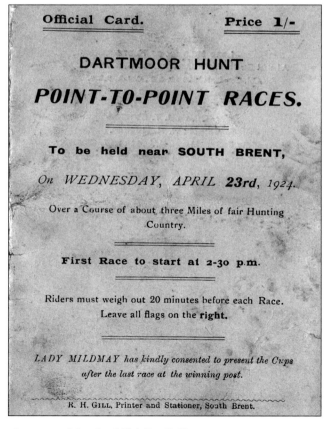

A race card for the 1924 South Brent races.

(THE WAKEHAM COLLECTION)

The Dart Vale Harriers 1946 Adjacent Hunt Ladies' Race at Stippadon. Winner (centre) Delight II (Miss E. Simms, No. 5), 2nd (far left) Moonlight (Miss J. Depree), 3rd (far right) Channon (Miss A. Coaker), then Workman (Miss P. Hyett, in bower hat) and Double Time (Miss A. Pascoe, No. 3). (THE WAKEHAM COLLECTION)

Dartmoor Hunt Point-to-Point Adjacents Hunts Pony Race. Left to right: Copperknob (Mr D. Fuller), Golden Rhapsody (Mr F. Ryall), Timer (Mr J.P. Gardner), Juno III (Mr C. Martin). (THE WAKEHAM COLLECTION)

tions. One curiosity which appears in the racing calendar for 1909 is a listing of two April dates, 24 and 29, for the Dartmoor races, when a hunt was only permitted one day's racing per year. Could there have been a postponement? Following the First World War point-to-point racing resumed in 1920 at Wrangaton and the venue remained the same for the next year, but in 1922 the Hunt races were held on a Moorland course at Dunnabridge, near Hexworthy, before returning to Brent and a new course at Kerrydowns, where they raced in 1924. The utilisation of this track was short-lived, probably for only a couple of years, for the Dartmoor Hunt had re-established again at Wrangaton by 1926, remaining until 1936. The following year saw a new course constructed in Brent, at Stippadon and Thynacombe in the shadow of Brent Hill.

A powerful lobby for the conversion from bank racing to birch fences was instigated by the fatal fall of the Earl of St Germans at Wrangaton. The inherent risk of serious injury to a rider whose mount falls at a bank is enhanced by the horse rolling on its jockey. Coupled with the increasing demand for more speed, the typical half-bred hunter was becoming infiltrated and replaced by the pure thoroughbred, whose extra pace at the obstacles translated into more jumping errors. The Dartmoor point-to-point of 1937 heralded the beginning of the end of banks, although this mode of racing did continue on an ever-decreasing scale until the final rites were administered in 1964.

Although this proved to be the end of the Dartmoor Hunt's association with Wrangaton, the course was re-opened in 1952 by the Modbury Harriers, the banks having been replaced by birch fences, and was in use for the next 11 years, after which the final curtain fell. Undoubtedly the red-letter day at Wrangaton occurred in April 1928, when, among the entries for the Nomination Open Race, was a six-year-old mare from the Belvoir Hunt who was to be ridden by HRH The Prince of Wales, later to become King Edward VIII. The horse's name was Miss Muffit and a large crowd turned up on the day to witness the spectacle in anticipation of a royal victory. Alas, it was not to be, as HRH. was beaten into second place by Mr T.P. Lawry's Ladder, an eight-year-old gelding ridden by Mr A.C. Hext, an invader from the East Cornwall Hunt. A total of 14 runners went to post, the largest field of the day. Newspaper reports of the event stated that HRH put up a competent performance but that he was considered to be more of a horseman than a jockey, which, reading between the lines, indicated that perhaps his mount had not received maximum assistance from the saddle. Nevertheless, HRH did ride a career total of 14 winners between the flags.

The intervention of two world wars had interrupted the point-to-point scenario and, when racing resumed in 1946, the Dartmoor Hunt held a joint meeting with Mr Spooner's Harriers at Dunnabridge before retuning to Stippadon to share the course with the Dart Vale Harriers, who had used the track in 1946, this being their first venture into point-to-point racing. This hunt remained at Stippadon until 1948, then moving to Drybridge Cross, Rattery. The Dartmoor remained in situ until they were rejoined by the now renamed Dart Vale and Haldon Harriers, who shared the course before relocating again in 1957. Final closure came in 1963, when the more attractive proposition of a move to Buckfastleigh racecourse was irresistible.

Two days at Stippadon of particular note are, firstly, the winning appearance of Mr Jack Cann's Prince Blackthorn in 1951, who, although by now a veteran, had been a horse of fine calibre when racing in his native Ireland, winning races and competing at the highest level, including being paced third in the Cheltenham Gold Cup in a 12-horse field. The second occasion of note had happened the previous year, in 1950, when two peers of the realm, Lord Mildmay and Lord Roborough, were on opposition in the Dartmoor Hunt members' race. Lord Mildmay was at the time a leading amateur rider under National Hunt rules in the country, having come close to winning the Grand National on Davy Jones and coming fourth on Cromwell in the same race in 1949. On the day, Lord Mildmay was riding Mrs Mary Douglas-Pennant's Double Time II, this combination having been successful in the corresponding race in 1949, whilst Lord Roborough was aboard his own grey gelding, Alight. However, the party was spoiled then by Mr Denis Ferens on Orson, a prolific winner, who defeated Double Time II with Alight third. Tragically, Lord Mildmay was to lose his life the following month, an inestimable loss to English racing.

Point-to-point racing has seen its fair share of unusual personalities. A tipster often appeared on the course at Stippadon and plied his trade under the name of Little Tommy. He dispensed his selections to all who proffered a half-crown (25p). As he returned to the scene in successive years, he must, presumably, have tipped some winners or else relied on the amnesia of race-goers. However, he was a less colourful character than either Gulli Gulli or Ras Prince Monolulu, who were part of the professional racing establishment both before and after the Second World War. Tricksters, card-sharps, con-artists and pick-pockets were all part of the racecourse scenario in the years between the wars, and at least one continued to operate at Stippadon. Arriving on course, he would assemble a crowd and visibly place a number of pocket watches in individual packet envelopes, which he then placed into a container which held a number of dummy packets. He then invited customers to part with 2s.6d. for a packet which he drew from the pile. Upon opening their purchase the packet was always a dummy, but if his offer was refused, when opened the packet contained a watch. There were many takers who fell for this sleight of hand.

So where horse once galloped and jumped and spectators cheered, the countryside around South Brent, which at least once a year became a hive of activity, is now at peace (if one can forgive the cacophony of modern-day living). The show has moved on. Point-to-point racing continues to thrive, although the nearest courses to South Brent are at Buckfastleigh to the east and Flete Park to the west.

Blarney – a poem by Tom Anderson

An Irishman walked through the streets of South Brent
On holiday here from Killarney.
As he went in the shops he stocked himself up
And paid for it all with his blarney.

A bottle of Guinness I think I shall have
'Tis only one bottle I need,
But the size of the bottle that I have in mind
I think the five thousand would feed.

As he leant on the bar his braces gave way,
At Wakeleys he bought three pairs more.
When asked why he needed so many he said,
'To be sure, to be sure, to be sure.'

Three pubs in the village look after my soul –
The London, the Oak and the Pack.
Three Churches there are to pick up the bits
When I am flat out on my back.

When the pubs throw you out it's downhill all the way
You sail like a cloud up in heaven,
You drift in a haze past the Churches all three
And cool yourself off in the Avon.

What a wonderful place is this village of Brent
But it's time to go back to Killarney,
For the folk who live here all beat me for sure
When it comes to pushing the Blarney.

A triumphant London Inn Darts team. Left to right: Dave Lockyer, George Bishop, Rodney Male, Tim Sings.
(THE R. MALE COLLECTION)

Stephen Towl with Eric Bristow at the Sportsman's Arms in Ivybridge. (THE STEPHEN TOWL COLLECTION)

Representatives of South Brent voluntary groups, 2007. Left to right, back row: *Nick Kendell, Fiona Harvey (Scouts), Christine Morgan (Rangers), Marion Wiseman (Guides), Jane Maunder (Brownies), Pauline Juste (Produce Association), Helen Ketteringham (Table Tennis Club), John Shepherd (Conferences), Ron Akehurst (Community Library);* third row: *Pam Honeywill and Winnie Sparkes (Senior Citizens' Club), Anne Marie Kendall (Beaver Scouts), Pat Stewart (Twinning Association), Val Meek, Carol Davies and John Wakeham (SBADS), Sally and Ray Luscombe (Friday Games Club), Phil and George Mumford (Monday Dance Club);* second row: *Beatrice Campbell (Moor Trees), Eileen Blockly (Ivybridge and SB branch Devon Wildlife Trust), Ruth Noble and Ross Kennerley (Sustainable South Brent), Mike Roberts (Brent Island Trust), Don and Rosemary Stansbury and Margaret Eales (Village Hall), John Meek (Dartmoor Lodge);* front row: *Mary Shepherd (Conferences), Joan Jenkins, Maryann Ford and Philip Ward-Green (Action & Community Group), Sue Burgess (Community Centre), Greg Wall (Parish Council), Brian Thomas and Stephanie Bromley (Village Hall), Peter Hopwood and Stephen Hanney (Carnival), Val Stanley (Community Library).* (THE KEITH MALE COLLECTION)

Left: *Pictured at the dedication of the new Masonic Hall are* (left to right, standing): *Messrs C. Back (Asst PG Secty), S.L.E. Pitman (PG Org), V. Thompson (PSGW), W.A. Clegg (PJGW), Revd G.H. Greeslade (PG Chap.), H.J. Stamp (PGDC);* (seated) *Mr H.H.G. New (APGM), Mr J.J. Gerry (WM of Dartmoor Lodge No 4604), the Bishop of Crediton (PGM).*

(THE MASONIC COLLECTION)

CHAPTER 13

Another Look at Some More Organisations

The Freemasons

Mr Reg Hard outlined the early history of freemasonry in a booklet published in 1983 entitled *The First Twenty Years*.

Although freemasonry was not established until 1924, its roots might go back into the mid-nineteenth century, when Revd William Spear-Cole came from Chiltington, Sussex, to take up the living at South Brent.

He was among the founders of Pleiades Lodge No. 710, Totnes. At the same time another reverend gentleman, Thomas Russell, a contemporary of Mr Speare-Cole, was priest at Avonwick. Mr Hard suggested that they instil Masonry into the minds of a group of men in Brent. Two of these gentlemen, Mr R.H. Gill, the postmaster, and Mr W. Hull, the schoolmaster, had thought about bringing freemasonry to Brent as early as 1904. The inaugural meeting took place on 23 April 1923 at the Pack Horse Hotel, with 19 people attending.

With the Vicar of Diptford, the Revd T. Parry, in the chair, the outcome of the meeting was that:

It was decided that a Warrant be applied for, from the Grand Lodge of England, for the formation of a Lodge at South Brent, with as little delay as possible. Their petition received the assent of his Royal Highness The Duke of Connaught, The Grand Master, and a Charter was issued.

There were two suggestions as to where meetings should be held, the Pack Horse Hotel being proposed by Mr Sandsford, who was the landlord at the time. The Vicar's Hall was proposed by Mr R.H. Gill.

As they already knew the Pack Horse Hotel, they decided to visit the Vicar's Hall in Church Street.

It was agreed that the Vicar's Hall would cater for all their needs, and the tenancy was applied for, the cost being £5 per annum. Some alterations were needed to the hall and it also required painting. Together with furnishings, this was to cost £150. It was agreed that the work would be carried out by Jervis Veale builders, South Brent.

It was also necessary to find a name for the lodge. It could not be called the Brent Lodge because the lodge at Topsham had this name. There were two suggestions – St Petroc's, after the patron saint of South Brent, and Dartmoor. The result of the subsequent ballot was Dartmoor 12 votes and St Petroc's eight votes.

On the afternoon of Wednesday, 30 April, the consecration of the Dartmoor Lodge of Freemasons No. 4604 took place. The ceremony, performed by the Provincial Grand Master, Major G.C. Davie, was followed by a banquet at the Anchor Hotel. The first meeting took place on Thursday, 8 May 1924.

The early progress of the lodge was everything its founders had hoped for and, at a meeting held on 10 March 1927, it was hoped that a permanent home could be found for the Dartmoor Lodge. One of the members made an offer to give the necessary money for the immediate purchase of a suggested site:

... if the WM (Worshipful Master), in the name of the lodge would accept the offer, with the definite purpose of establishing ways and means for a Masonic Hall, say within the years 1927/28/29.

With the stipulation that, should the site not be used within the time stated, it would automatically return into the hands of the donor, the WM agreed to accept the offer.

No further action was taken until 14 November 1929, when a 'building fund' was opened. The site was fenced off and a gate and pillars were erected to comply with the terms of the offer made. A scheme put before the lodge on 12 December 1929 did not find favour, and discussions about the building lasted until 16 August 1939, when the foundation stone was laid. Reg Hard wrote of the occasion:

The Brethren met and opened the Lodge in the Church Hall. Then by virtue of a special dispensation, they marched clothed in Masonic Regalia, to the site, each Brother carried his appropriate 'Working Tools' which were used for the Ceremony. The weather was perfect. Just pause for a moment, think of the procession coming up the street, one hundred Freemasons in full regalia, the sun shining on sleepy South Brent, and the colour of the brethren. The only other occasion that so many people would be seen was on Brent fair days and then it usually rained! It was a unique occasion.

The Stone was laid by the Provincial Grand Master of the Province of Devonshire, the Lord Bishop of Crediton the Rt Revd W.F. Surtees MA.

Despite the declaration of the Second World War, the building of the Masonic Hall continued, and, after all the trials and tribulations, it was completed in 1940 and subsequently consecrated by the Bishop of Crediton.

The Senior Citizens' Club

South Brent Senior Citizens' Club has been meeting on Wednesday afternoons since its inaugural meeting on 13 September 1967. Their activities are varied. At the regular meetings over the 40 years of its existence the members have enjoyed talks and activities such as the weekly game of bingo. On one occasion it is reported that:

Mr Wootton, from our local Antique Shop, will be our guest speaker on 14 July. He will give his comments on members' antiques, so please turn up with all your treasures.

And at another time:

Last month the Citizens heard a very interesting talk on the breeding and keeping of bees by Father Abbot Leo Smith, to whom we extend our grateful thanks. Another such meeting dealt with Crime Prevention and, as a result, it was hoped that the members would be more watchful and careful in the future;

As well as meetings in the Village Hall, the members enjoyed many trips to shops, both locally in such towns as Newton Abbot and Kingsbridge and on organised day trips further afield to such places as Cardiff, Stratford-upon-Avon and Bournemouth, and there were many visits to Cornwall, North Devon and Somerset. Then there were the trips to the theatre, which, according to Anneliese Stephens, writing in the Parish Magazine, were 'thoroughly enjoyed by all'.

In addition, there were the Senior Citizens' holidays. It was reported in June 1980 that a coach-load of members returned from their week's holiday in Whitby tired but happy. The weather had been kind, the service and the catering at the hotel first rate and these facts, coupled with the warm companionship of the South Brent Club and overall stewardship of Peggy John, made for a vacation to be happily remembered.

During the day, trips were made to such local places of interest as the city of York, Scarborough and Castle Howard, and in the evenings they joined in the competitions held among the various Senior Citizens' Clubs staying in the same hotel.

It sounds as if Brent walked off with a goodly share of the honours. Olive Mortimore received a very nice prize in the talent competition, in which she sang. She was also proclaimed 'Personality Granny'. Mr Tommy Andrews followed her example, with Mr Carpenter coming a close second. The choir also gained first place in their class, winning a shield which they proudly brought back to the village.

The seniors were at large again a year later. For once, the sun did not shine for the whole of the senior citizens' holiday; usually they were very fortunate with the weather. Olive Dodd wrote of the trip:

Setting out in the rain didn't dampen any spirits, though, and by the time we stopped for lunch in Carnarvon the sun was shining. Our reception in Tenby was a little mixed. We were confronted by a very militant looking traffic warden, who told us we shouldn't be where we had stopped and to move on, but eventually she made friends with Richard, our driver, and all was well. Our hotel was fine, everywhere was warm, the beds were comfy, and the food very good, served up very hot by friendly restaurant staff.

About 18 of us went to early service in the nearby Church of St Mary the Virgin, the largest Parish Church in Wales, which dates back to 1210 and is very beautiful. Later, many of our Methodist members went to the Methodist service – their Church was also close.

We spent a lovely sunny afternoon in a wildlife park at St Florence, and another at Stacks Rocks, where we saw hundreds of seabirds on the rocks. This is a very rugged, wild coastline and we saw, very sadly, many dead lambs who hadn't made it through the previous bad weekend.

Unfortunately it rained on the two days that we had longer excursions, but St David's Cathedral more than made up for the rain, and so did Pembroke Castle on the other day.

The museum at Tenby was very interesting, and everyone who went on the boat trip round Caldey Island in perfect sunshine thoroughly enjoyed it.

In the evenings the hotel had an organist who played for dancing and singing – and we sang! We held a talent evening and a quiz, and the unexpected arrival of two very glamorous Hawaiian dancers (Bill Lang and Percy Bramble) reduced everyone to tears of laughter.

On our final evening we had a fancy dress competition, with 18 taking part, and everyone had a prize. And of course we had some bingo!!

When we came to leave on Saturday the sun was shining again and Tenby looked very pleasant, with the sea washing against the promenade and the little boats dancing in the harbour. We had a very pleasant drive home.

It was a good holiday and our thanks are due to Peggy John and Richard Hard, who planned the outings and who saw that things went smoothly. I somehow think that the Royal Gate House Hotel is a bit quieter since we left.

Those are but two of the reports from the many trips that they made over the years.

The senior citizens have played their part in raising money for local activities. They have taken part in both the Village Hall concert and the fête during their 40-year life, as well as joining in the street fair to raise money for the carnivals, and have raised money for other national causes, just one occasion being in 1987, when 'members took a collection

Another Look at Outings

A 'pub jolly' to Okehampton in 1965. Left to right, standing: Bill Clough, Dick Oliver (landlord), Tom ?, Len Webber (driver), Bob Ellis, Tom Corbett, Mervy Maye, Maurice Manning, Keith Neale, Eddie Rush, Rufus Murphy, Patrick Williams, Tony Moore, Jin Cansdale, Norman Langdon; front row: ?, Eric Rush, Robin Chandler, Mike Gimlet, Arthur 'Tiddler' Heard.
(THE NORMAN & LORRAINE LANGDON COLLECTION)

Robin Wells, Matthew Carroll and Ross Pannell with the South Brent banner on a church servers' trip to Glastonbury. (THE CARROLL COLLECTION)

The senior citizens on a tour in Scotland.

A trip to Weymouth on 12 June 1952.

A 'pub jolly' to West Devon in August 1950. The group visited Lee Moor, Yelverton, Tavistock, Milton Abbot, Launceston, Camelford, Delabole, Doublebois, Torpoint and Ivybridge before returning home!

Included here are Maurice Manning, Jock Lang, Bill Endacott, Phil Luscombe, Cyril Gove, Albert Elliott, Percy Sparkes, Jack Hard, Archie Fare, Ken Fox, Dick Reynolds, and (kneeling) Dick Stancombe and Roy Manning, enjoying a day's relaxation.

to be sent to the Zebrugge Disaster Fund'.

Each September the members have held a 'birthday tea'. In 1980 they also helped fellow member Mr Fred Mitchelmore to begin celebrating his eightieth birthday on 20 September. His daughter, Esther Warnes, had secretly liaised with the committee to provide a super tea for the 90-odd members, along with Mr Mitchelmore's sisters, brother and brothers-in-law. She also provided a very large birthday cake. At the meeting:

... a further surprise came in the form of a letter from HM the Queen Mother in reply to a message from the club congratulating her on her birthday. In her reply, the Queen Mother expressed her good wishes for a very happy afternoon, and her interest that all the members were to receive commemorative coins to mark her birthday – that was another secret.

The whole afternoon was enlivened by the presence of an old friend of the club, Vic Hughes, who came from Tavistock to play his portable organ, so there was dancing and a sing-song. It was altogether a memorable afternoon.

Not only did the group have parties for local events, there were national celebrations that warranted an event:

The club had its own little party to celebrate the forthcoming marriage of HRH The Prince of Wales and Lady Diana Spencer. At a well-attended meeting over 90 members were pleased to welcome the Revd David Niblett, a much-loved and frequent visitor, who, after joining members for tea, complete with 'wedding cake', very kindly distributed commemorative coins to each member on behalf of the club committee.

Another such party was held to celebrate the anniversary of VE Day, prior to another foray to Clacton-on-Sea.

The senior citizens also hold their own Harvest Festival service in October. It has been conducted both by members of the South Brent clergy from all denominations and also by members themselves.

The Winemakers' Guild

The South Brent Winemakers' Guild was formed after a meeting held in the Village Hall on Tuesday, 23 September 1980 under the chairmanship of Mr Ken Woodhouse and attended by 28 people. At that meeting, members of the Brixham amateur wine-makers' guild, Mr Dickson and Mr Sampson described how their guild worked. Following their talk, it was agreed to form a steering committee to draw up a format for the formation of a guild in South Brent. The committee consisted of Mr. Woodhouse, Mr Michael Evens, Mr O'Connor, Mrs Puddifoot and Mr Grieves.

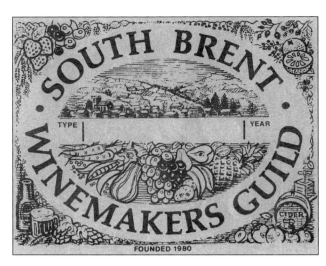

The Winemakers' Guild wine label.
(THE WOODHOUSE COLLECTION)

The aims of the group were listed as:

1. to keep alive the country tradition of wine-making, brewing and cider-making
2. to discuss methods and exchange ideas for the mutual improvement of home-made wines, beers and ciders
3. to assist beginners in the art
4. to encourage viticulture
5. to study the showing and judging of wines and beers and to train members in wine and beer judging
6. to foster good fellowship amongst wine lovers and wine and beer makers

The programme was varied and interesting and aimed at a mixture of educational and social activities. The first annual general meeting, held in November 1981, described the year's activities as 'beer making, cooking with wine by member Jenny Christmas'. Another member, Darrold Angus, gave a talk on vermouth and his 'vino collapso', and there was a talk on the hydrometer by a Plymouth circle member. The members had a barbecue and there were other enjoyable evenings. The group attended the street fair in July and all enjoyed the sun and the carnival atmosphere. Beer and wine were given when recipes were bought. They joined the South Western Amateur Winemakers' Federation and some members went to Brixham and Plymouth wine circles. Members were encouraged to participate in competitions at functions organised by the local produce association, and several members have enjoyed success there.

The meeting for May 1982 was a quiet one. Due to unforeseen circumstances, the films ordered for the evening failed to arrive and, after the business side of the meeting, teacher Mr Ken Woodhouse showed cine films he had taken on an exchange visit to America. Ken and his wife had bought an old Hillman Minx and travelled from one side of America to the other. In June Mrs Wallace of

Richard Cleave samples some of the wines on offer at the street fair stall of the South Brent Winemakers' Guild.
(THE WOODHOUSE COLLECTION)

Always popular, the Winemakers' Guild stall does a roaring trade. (THE WOODHOUSE COLLECTION)

Plymouth came to judge the competition, which was for the best dry red wine. In her comments afterwards she declared presentation good, the clarity and colour of the wines very good, but added that the wines were 'young and could do with keeping longer'. Even so, in 1983 several members entered into various classes at the South Western Counties Wine Show in Newton Abbot and come away with one third place, one highly commended and two commended certificates. This was described by the chairman as 'a very good result', since there had been over 700 entries of wine.

Meetings then followed a pattern: wine evenings, guest speakers and social events. In September 1985, at an evening of wine tasting, members were challenged to identify and name six home-made and six commercially produced wines. The two categories of product were generally identified, and there was a high degree of accuracy in identifying the types. Comments on each wine were invited and it was interesting to note that some of the more disparaging remarks were directed towards the purchased wines.

The following month, October, members' thoughts begin to focus on Christmas and its festivi-

ties and, with that season in mind, the subject of the guest speaker was 'Making Liqueurs'. We were glad to report an upsurge in membership and offered a warm welcome to the members

At the first meeting of 1987, the guild saw two films – *Bellamy on Beer* and a Sandeman film about port, and in February the meeting had a German theme, with food cooked by the ladies accompanied by appropriate wines.

The group also endeavoured to draw new people in, not only by participation in village activities but also by way of an open evening. One such was held in June 1986 and, as Mr John Warman wrote:

... can be said to have been a great success. With membership dwindling for various reasons, it has been a positive effort by the Guild to show just how easy it is to make your own wine and beer, and at far less cost than buying commercial varieties. Mr Tony Beaumont gave an interesting and informative demonstration on beer making. Mr Braunton, a lecturer and wine judge, showed just how easy it is to make wine from any of the fruit juices on the market. Two of our members, M Woodhouse, and Mr R. Cook, showed their expertise in cooking with wine, with two very tasty recipes, which all members enjoyed tasting.

In 1984 Mr Guy Pannell was the guest speaker at the meeting. Guy, a Brentonian, worked as an editor for Television South West news. He started his career as a reporter for a local paper in the Home Counties and gradually progressed to his editorial position. He gave a most interesting talk on the many facets of newsgathering for the daily programme, explaining that ITN had the main news programmes and that the smaller companies were allowed time for their own local news items. Sometimes ITN bought big news items from the smaller companies. Although TSW and BBC South West were different channels, they sometimes used each other's films of events when, for some reason, one channel was unable to film the event. Following his talk, Mr Pannell answered numerous questions from the members.

Mr Sconce, a Customs and Excise Officer, gave a talk on his work. He started by explaining the origins of the Customs and Excise Service, when and why it was founded and what are its many duties. Quoting figures, he told us how many officers were then in the British Isles and how much money they collected in a year. At the time of the talk, VAT was one of their latest revenue boosters. Their duties were many and varied and he told of the many happy memories he had of the time he spent working in the whiskey distilleries in Scotland and the breweries in Staffordshire. His work had also taken him to Northern Ireland, where he still had many friends. He touched on the subject of drug smuggling and said that the continuing increase in this traffic was causing much concern.

Mike Ramsden of the Handchime Co. based in Moretonhampstead gave:

... a delightful talk and demonstration on handchimes and handbells. Then much to our surprise, Mike proceeded to involve us all, with the aid of prepared charts, in a double act of ringing, first with the chimes and then with the handbells, which were exquisitely made. By dint of some extraordinary concentration on our part we managed to produce at least some recognisable tunes on the chime bars, which gave us heart for our second act – the handbells. With these we rendered several well-known tunes, from 'Yankee Doodle' through 'Scarborough Fair' to the 'Ash Grove' with a full vocal backing.

According to Mr A. Beaumont, the secretary at the time, the group also enjoyed:

... a very interesting and entertaining evening. The subject, a complete change from our normal type of activity, was entitled, 'Hypnotism and Hypnotherapy'. The talk and demonstration, by Mr 'Mitch' Mitchell of Torquay, gave us a fascinating insight into the techniques of hypnotism and its possible uses in therapeutic applications. We await with interest to see whether one of our lady members has been cured of her nicotine addiction after gamely volunteering to participate as a demonstration subject.

Social events played an important part in the Guild's life. One July, on the eve of American Independence Day, the group held an American-style barbecue for their July get-together. Good food, good wine and good company, including welcome friends from wine circles throughout South Devon from Teignmouth to Yealm, made this a festive occasion:

A mouth-watering rice with salad, and a certain gentleman's exquisite homemade rolls, plus a selection of desserts fit to grace the pages of Michelin, were provided by our ever-willing lady members. The finale to our evening was a jig in the Village Hall. We danced, and some ladies were swept off their feet. After a very successful gathering we wended our way home.

Another highlight was the summer barbecue held at Didworthy House. In 1986 it was reported:

Thanks to a beautiful July evening and the hospitality of our hosts, club secretary Tony Beaumont and his wife Sheila, our annual barbecue held at Didworthy House was again a most enjoyable event. Our thanks to the Chef at Didworthy Hostel for providing all the salads, to Win O'Connor for all the preparations beforehand of the meats etc, and to all the ladies for the superb sweets. Members and guests from other wine circles were welcomed by our Chairman, Ken Woodhouse, after which we all did justice to the lovely food, and of course

the wine. Some of our members even managed to go for a swim.

Visits also provided highlights for members. In August 1985 guild members enjoyed a visit to Thompson's Brewery at Ashburton.

This small but efficient brewery was the brainchild of the son of the landlord of the London Inn at Ashburton, Mr Thompson. The brewery is located at the rear of the inn in the old billiard and social rooms, with certain storage functions in the old coach house, in which Mr Thompson junr intends to create a new and larger production plant over the next year. The output from the brewery, predominantly bitter and lager, is sold in the London Inn and also through a limited number of other hostelries in the area – the planned increase in volume will enable additional outlets to be established. At the conclusion of the tour around the plant, conducted by the younger Mr Thompson, who gave most interesting description of the brewing processes and an insight into the setting up of the brewery, we retired to the bar of the inn to sample the products of the house.

Members also went to Buckfast Abbey for:

... a lighthearted guided tour by the Father Abbot, who took about 20 of us around the honey-making plant with a most interesting talk on the history of the Abbey, beekeeping and honey-making. From there we found ourselves amongst wine vats, with the Abbot explaining how the Abbey came to be in the winemaking business. The Abbot, being a benevolent man and not wishing us, metaphorically speaking, to be in the orchard but forbidden to taste the fruit, most generously allowed us to taste the fruits of the monks' endeavours.

During the latter years of the 1980s the membership of the Winemakers' Guild dwindled and so, in 1989, the viability of the club was called into question. There was concern about the 1990 programme of events. The AGM held on 6 November 1990 proved to be the last – only 12 members attended the meeting. The secretary reported that the club had been going for ten years but that for the past two the membership had dwindled to the point that there was very little hope for the future of the club:

After some discussion from everyone it was decided that the club should cease and no longer continue. The proposal was made by Dave Simpson and seconded by John Warman and unanimously carried.

The final function was the 1990 Christmas party.

The Women's Groups

The Women's Circle was set up originally as the

The Women's Circle perform 'The Birdy Song' at the Village Hall Concert in 1980, with Esther Warnes as the bird (centre). Left to right, back row: *Lyn Thorn, Lucy Moore, Caroline Hedges, Linda Wall, Caroline Jefferys, Diane Vooght, Ena Wells, Sue Rooke, Julie Andrews, Sally Luscombe;* front row: *Susan Norrish, Diane Reed, Esme Saunter, Sue Neale, Jill Sitch, Joy Hayman, Margaret Eales.* (THE HAYMAN AND WARNES COLLECTIONS)

The Women's Circle taking part in a carnival procession, date unknown. Among those pictured are Judy Crannis, Marilyn Bullen, Di Reed, Inez Jordan and Jill Elms (THE BULLEN COLLECTION)

Young Wives' Group by Vivienne Malsom in 1974.

Regular meetings took place in the Church Room. The programme was very varied, with many activities and guest speakers.

Well into their autumn programme, the Women's Circle had already had their enthusiasm raised for such diverse activities as the renewing of rush and cane seats on chairs, basket and mat weaving, etc., and also an insight into the art of 'writing for fun and profit'.

Over the years that the Women's Circle met, their speakers included Dartmoor National Park warden Robert Steemson whose talk was entitled 'Dartmoor and the National Park Role'. 'There was something new for everyone in his talk and the beautiful slides which illustrated it made us all feel like donning walking boots and setting off for the moor.'

Commander Ivor Thorning, who spent some years working as a police officer in royal service, also came to talk to the group. On another occasion Audrey Price of Rose Cottage, Harbourneford, a talented and infectiously enthusiastic potter, demon-

Mary Steer, a former branch leader of South Brent Mothers' Union, pictured outside Exeter Cathedral with the Bishop of Exeter, the Rt Revd Michael Langrish, after her installation as Diocesan President of the organisation in March 2007. Many of the members of the South Brent branch went with her that day and witnessed the Bishop being admitted as a MU member.

(THE MOTHERS' UNION COLLECTION)

strated some of the technicalities of her craft and displayed pieces of her beautiful, distinctive work.

After another meeting Mrs Carol Reid reported:

On the roads around South Brent there is a confident group of women motorists who feel able to deal personally with their car's maintenance. This group – about 75 per cent of the Women's Circle members who attended Richard Hard's comprehensive and knowledgeable demonstration of car maintenance at Avonwick Garage – now know how to deal with routine tasks and minor breakdowns. As for the other 25 per cent of the group – no names given – thanks for trying, Richard! We are grateful to Mr Cousins of Avonwick for the use of his garage facilities, and of course to Richard.

On another occasion she wrote:

Tuesday, 22 May saw the Women's Circle on safari. Neither pith helmets nor mosquito nets were required, however, as we were no further afield than Harbourneford. The occasion was, in fact, the closing event of this year's programme – a most enjoyable Safari Supper. Liz Hoare got the evening off to a flying start with sherry at Springfield Terrace, then it was off to Lyn Thorne's at Harbourneford for an appetising paté. Back in Brent, Esther Warnes (ably assisted by Roy) provided a delicious main course, which was followed by a mouth-watering selection of sweets at Audrey Pawson's. On to Pennaton, where Janet Ayres provided a tempting cheeseboard, and finally to Val Meek's for coffee. Our thanks to all who organised the evening – it was a great success and we hope to repeat it in the future.

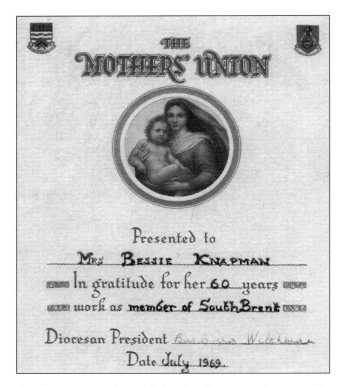

The banners of visiting branches in the Totnes Deanery gather outside St Petroc's Church on the occasion of the centenary celebrations of South Brent Mothers' Union. Cathie Hamblin is holding the South Brent banner.

(THE STEER COLLECTION)

South Brent Mothers' Union has been meeting monthly since its creation in 1902. Despite its title, it is a group of women and men who support the concept of Christian family life. Mrs Bessie Knapman joined in 1909 and in 1969 was presented with a 'long-service' certificate in recognition of her 'diamond jubilee'. (THE STEER COLLECTION)

The Women's Circle also participated in various village activities, such as the carnival and Village Hall fête, and were very active in raising money for the Leonard Cheshire Foundation.

The Women's Institute, which was founded in 1920, continued to meet in the Village Hall in the early years of the twenty-first century, but dwindling numbers meant that, at the end of 2006, 86 years on, the Institute would disband – the end of a Brent Institution. Another women's group based at the Methodist Church was the Women's Guild

Some of the volunteers who staff the Community Library. Left to right, back row: Dennis Hall, Elise Willisson, Naomi Gibson, Eileen Blockley, Helen Ketteringham, Vera Allen, Ron Akehurst; front row: Val Stanley, Shirley May, Margaret Eales, Poppet Hall, Molly Harvey, Doe Mason. (THE MASON COLLECTION)

The only women's organisation still functioning in Brent is the Mothers' Union. Even that has changed, and now admits male members, Brent's branch having three!

South Brent Community Library

When South Brent Primary School moved into its new home in 1997, there was a lively debate in the village – and beyond – as to what should happen to the vacated old school buildings. Numerous people gave their time and skills to establish the Old School and they continue to do so today.

Ideas were legion: a business centre, affordable homes, a care centre, executive homes, a community centre, etc. A committee formed to look into possibilities produced a questionnaire asking people for their opinions.

Two requests constantly recurred – permanent premises for the pre-school group and a library. As far as the library is concerned, the layout and system were designed by Caroline Martin. The day-to-day running was, and is, the responsibility of Doe Mason.

At the start, the library held 200 books and opened one day per week. Today there are 4,000 volumes, donated by generous individuals, and 25 volunteer librarians. The library is open five days a week – morning and afternoon – and Saturday mornings. There are no fines, no fees and books may be borrowed for as long as required.

South Brent Conservative Club

Colin Perry writes:

How could anyone imagine that the cosy, comfortable Conservative Club tucked away in Stockbridge Lane used to be a garage, complete with an inspection pit! This was in the 1930s, and it has gone from strength to strength since its conversion. One of its past chairmen, Mr Roy Cockrem, sadly lost his life when his ship was

Members of South Brent Conservative Club in a winter carnival. Pictured are Francis Sparkes, Pat Bullen, Neil Toogood and Peter Cornish. (THE TOOGOOD COLLECTION)

sunk during the Second World War. He was a brilliant all-rounder, especially at cricket and apparently some sort of 'one-man team'.

Maidie Cockrem (Roy's sister) was a staunch member, organising whist drives and bridge drives. Other past officers of the club have included Les Hard, Sid Ashton, Les Fox, Sid Ayres, Ken Hickey, Malcolm Tidball, David Ayres, Neil Toogood, Shaun Crannis, Malcolm Wright, our current chairman, Colin Perry, and president Graham Jordan.

The club was extensively refurbished in 1996, when the office and snooker table were transferred upstairs, creating new and larger facilities downstairs. The club was officially reopened by Anthony Steen, MP, and Les Fox.

Many great characters used to play billiards here when the club used to open during the day-time.

The three Bills (Smith, Tucker and Endacott) spring to mind, and where they got their stamina from at their age, heaven knows. Bill Endacott was great at 'malapropisms', for example Aston Villa always became Ashton Villa. The club has had numerous stalwarts over the years and it would be impossible to name them all.

The South Brent and Avon Valley Society

The South Brent and Avon Valley Society was an environmental group formed in the 1960s by a number of people concerned about the development in the upper reaches of the Avon Valley around South Brent, Avonwick, Diptford and beyond. One of their earliest concerns was the registering of rights of way, bridle paths and green lanes, and they 'fought the cause' to ensure that they were kept open. The society, under the chairmanship of Tom Anderson of Higher Downstow, was also active in the maintenance of the river bank and the cleaning of the river, as well as monitoring the otter population along the Avon.

The society also had an educational strand, giving several series of lectures, many of them in association with the Extramural Studies Department of Exeter University. These often involved fieldwork, and ranged from Dartmoor archaeology through West Country history and looking at the architecture of Devon churches to weather and forecasting.

The group went into abeyance when its initial 'raison d'être' became subsumed, and members began to join other groups

The Action Group

Joan Jenkins, a founder member and vice-chairman of the Action Group, writes of its activities:

The Action Group (as it was originally known) was formed in 1973 at the instigation of Joy Carnochan, a

head teacher who lived in Hillside. Joy was responding to concern among villagers about a development that was to take place on the Vicarage Road fields. The concern was that extending the village into this quiet lane to the north of the railway line would spoil a pleasant country walk into the Dartmoor National Park, and lead to further intrusions into this unspoilt area. Joy was a member of the Avon Valley Amenity Society, but neither the Society nor the Parish Council felt able to help. They had been told that to remove the existing planning permission would involve Totnes Rural District Council in paying a large sum in compensation to the landowners. Various people living nearby were approached by Joy to see if they could form an action group. Thus the Action Group was born.

The Group quickly made an important discovery: on examining the planning permission in the Council Offices, they found that it had in fact expired by several days and would have to be re-applied for!

Here was a chance to do something about it. After much lobbying, the Totnes Rural District Council was persuaded to refuse the new application. Some years later the developers decided to go to appeal. By then the group had grown considerably and enlisted the help of Colonel Peter Lodge, who had recently retired and come back to live in the village. The appeal, held before a full audience in the Village Hall, was rejected.

Since then the field has been used for grazing. When it eventually came up for sale in 2005, everyone was pleased that the Parish Council decided to buy it for allotments, much needed in the village. The Group made a contribution towards the work needed to make the land suitable for horticultural use.

Another key event occurred in 1976 when the Lord of the Manor offered the Toll House in Church Street for sale. The group decided to buy the Toll House with the help of loans from some members of the group. The building was in a poor state of repair, but the group felt it would be an asset to the village if they could save it. The group raised the money to repay the loans by holding a weekly market at the Toll House, organised and run by Mrs Elsie Way, with goods, mostly fruit and vegetables, provided by members. The National Park helped finance the repairs and the group suggested that they might like to use the building as an Information Centre. The Park agreed and undertook to pay an annual grant towards its upkeep. Interestingly, when Sidney Hobbs was re-hanging the bell during the repair work, he discovered the name 'Thuell' engraved on it, the name of a churchwarden who lived in Brent early in the nineteenth century.

At this stage the group decided to add the words 'and Community' to their title, as they felt that they were going beyond the original concept of an action group. A logo depicting Brent Hill was designed by Phoebe Stanton, who lived at Splatton Cottage, and the motto 'the price of amenity is eternal vigilance' was also adopted.

To mark European Architectural Heritage Year in 1975, the group produced a heritage trail leaflet to guide visitors round the village. Greg Wall edited the history. It was a free handout available in the Toll House – the National Park paid for the printing. The leaflet was eventually included in a book of Devon Heritage Trails.

The group continue to comment on planning applications and village plans and also take part in appeals where they feel it is appropriate for the well-being of the village. Sometimes they are successful, but other times not so. As long ago as 1980 the group started trying to persuade the National Park, and later the Department of Environment, to move the park boundary up to the new dual carriageway, so that the whole village would be included under one planning authority. They felt that the area that was still in the South Hams was particularly vulnerable to housing development without the protection that park status gives.

To celebrate the millennium, the group donated a garden seat for use in the extension to the cemetery.

A recent legacy left to the group by a late member has enabled them to use the money towards a new children's garden in the Primary School and to make a contribution towards the building of a skate park shelter in the recreation ground.

During 34 years the group felt it necessary to act against the wishes of the Parish Council on occasions and to take a stand, which perhaps the Parish Council felt unable to do. Today the group works amicably with the Parish Council, and they still feel able to act independently. The group's latest project, with help from the Parish Council and the National Park, is the production of a Village Design Statement for use as a guide in any future development in the village.

Sustainable South Brent

Sustainable South Brent was a new initiative that began life in 2006. The aim of the movement is to involve as many people as possible in taking positive action to combat climate change and declining energy resources. It began when several local residents were inspired to start a group after attending the South Brent Action and Community Group annual meeting, which had a talk given by David Kelf a representative from the Devon Association for Renewal Energy (DARE).

As a result, they invited villagers who felt as they did to join the group and discuss ways of making the village a greener, more sustainable environment. With a great deal of interest from those present at the meeting, it was hoped that a group in the village could capitalise on this. Indeed they believed that the close-knit community spirit in South Brent could make it a perfect venue for community-wide renewable schemes and noted at the time that renewable energy schemes had appeared before the Parish Council planning committee. As a result, Sustainable South Brent (SSB) was launched.

The poster announcing the abolition of plastic bags from South Brent Co-op. (COURTESY OF THE PLYMOUTH & SOUTH DEVON CO-OPERATIVE SOCIETY)

One resident, Judy Davy planned to have 12 photovoltaic cells, which capture energy from sunlight, on the roof of her property in Clobell's, while Lt-Cdr Tom Anderson installed a 15-metre high wind turbine on his land at Higher Downstow on the outskirts of the village. The wind turbine was connected to the National Grid for domestic household use but also, on occasion, pumps electricity back into the grid. He noted that 'several people have expressed a great interest in the idea'.

The SSB group also carried out a survey of what the community felt and found that the three most significant projects were the promotion of local produce and services, home insulation and energy efficiency and the generation of energy from water.

At the same time that the SSB was beginning, another initiative was introduced in the South Brent branch of the Plymouth and South Devon Co-op. Following on the back of the ban on plastic bags in Modbury, the Co-op ceased to use plastic carriers in the South Brent branch and gave every household a cotton bag in which to carry home their shopping.

The Twinning Association

South Brent's association with Châteauneuf-du-Faou began in October 1975, when a public meeting was held in the Village Hall to discuss the foundation of a Twinning Association. That meeting was addressed by Mr F. Claxton, the County Twinning Secretary.

In 1986 Mr. Peter Moore, the chairman, wrote of the association in a booklet published to celebrate the tenth anniversary of the twinning:

South Brent has been twinned for ten years now with the small town of Châteauneuf-du-Faou, beautifully situated above the River Aulne in the Department of Finistère in the western part of Brittany, and within easy reach of many delightful coastal and inland beauty spots. There is a twinning Association here in South Brent, and also one in Châteauneuf, whose prime purpose is to encourage and facilitate contacts and exchanges of all kinds between the two communities.

Châteauneuf-du-Faou was known and recommended by Guy van der Kiste, a founder member of the Association, and a visit was made by the chairman, secretary and treasurer to explore the possibilities of twinning. The English party were given such a warm welcome and found such a genuine desire to know more about England that arrangements were made for a visit to South Brent of a party of Chateauneuvians the following spring. This in turn led to the formation of a Twinning Association in Châteauneuf under the chair-

The signs at the entrances to the two communities declaring the twinning link. (THE TIDBALL & GILES COLLECTIONS)

manship of M. Jean Citeau, and a Constitution, setting out the aims of the two Associations was drawn up.

In essence, the aim of the two Societies was to provide, by means of exchange visits of children and interested groups, a means by which social, cultural and economic exchanges could take place between the two communities, leading to better understanding of a different nation with different customs, habits and conditions and by so doing, to foster the ends of peace, harmony and understanding between those nations. Charters were signed and exchanged by M. George Le Meur, mayor of Châteauneuf-du-Faou and Peter Moore, chairman of South Brent Parish Council.

The Society is celebrating its tenth anniversary this year, followed next summer by a celebration in Châteauneuf-du-Faou. To mark the occasion the Association arranged two events in Carnival Week – a light-hearted evening with music and entertainment by local people, 'Music Léger' and a more formal performance by a string quartet followed by a 'champagne buffet supper', Soirée Musicale. Both these events were well supported, and funds raised went to the Carnival Committee and from them to CLIC (Cancer and Leukaemia in Children).

To celebrate the tenth anniversary of the French linking, the Twinning Association presented a glass plaque and engraved goblets to the citizens of Châteauneuf-de-Faou, at a ceremony held in South Brent Primary School which was well attended by Parish Councillors, the Mayor of Chateauneuf-du-Faou, members of the two Twinning Committees and representatives of village organisations. A buffet luncheon was provided by the Parish Council.

In the parallel ceremony held in the Marie of Châteauneuf on 28 August 1987, the Twinning Association presented the mayor and citizens of Châteauneuf with an oak priest's chair and received in return two specially commissioned vases and a large oak plaque made by Yann Moulin, a local craftsman, and

The oak priest's chair and plaque presented at the tenth anniversary celebrations of the twinning on 28 August 1987 in the Marie of Châteauneuf.

(TWINNING ASSOCIATION COLLECTION)

using the Breton version of the town's name, Kastell-Nevez-ar-Faou The vases are now kept in St Petroc's Church and the oak plaque is in the Village Hall.

The 1986 carnival also had a French flavour, with several floats in the carnival procession entering into the 10-year celebration spirit by adapting to a French theme.

Since the formation of the societies, there have been numerous visits and exchanges between the communities. Initially, the association arranged holiday exchanges of groups of up to 50 children and since then many groups have made visits, with reciprocal visits coming back across the Channel.

Olive Dodd wrote of her experiences on a visit to Châteauneuf in August 1977:

The days and months seem to fly by, but I am sure no weekend ever passed as quickly as the one we spent in Châteauneuf at the end of August. We had rather an inauspicious beginning to the adventure because the crossing by ferry was decidedly rough, the ship pitched, tossed and rolled, and I do not think many people had much sleep. However, we were all bright – well, fairly – when we arrived at Roscoff to be greeted by the President of the Châteauneuf twinning committee and M. Le Meur, the mayor of Châteauneuf.

We drove in two coaches through the awakening countryside and gradually collected ourselves together. I noticed that the fields were full of artichokes and broccoli plants, most of which will presumably soon be passing along our dual carriageway to Covent Garden. Our welcome in the town itself was very warm, and we were whisked off for coffee and croissants before being despatched to our various hosts.

My hostess was Madame Breton, a doctor's widow, about my age. She has a delightful house in the grounds of what had originally been her home. The big house is now occupied by her daughter and son-in--law, M. and Mme Le Goffe. I just had time for 20 minutes on the bed and a bath before leaving for the twinning ceremony at 11a.m. This was held in the Village Hall, or its equivalent, and when we arrived we found several other Brent people there, including, of course, the schoolchildren who had been visiting for several days. The actual ceremony followed almost exactly the lines of the one held here, and the two historic documents were signed by M. Le Meur and our Parish Council chairman, Peter Moore.

Some dancing followed, performed first of all by some of the local people in their national costumes – you may remember that two of the young people came over for our carnival last year, and they were wearing their picturesque embroidered black clothes. After the three national Anthems had been sung, English, French and Breton, the dancing developed into a form of conga, and then everyone really needed the drinks we were offered.

The official party then moved down the road and across a bridge to have lunch in a delightful hotel which could have been lifted from anywhere in Devon.

Now, I think the French really have the right idea about food. They take their time, both in eating and serving, they don't fill your plate too full, they wash it all down with good wine and they save on the washing up. This, I am sure, would have appealed to the school-children – it certainly would have done to me at 14 years old. The one plate, knife, fork and spoon are used throughout the meal, quite a saving in energy.

We had a delicious meal, finishing with fruit, cheese and, of course, coffee, and now I can hardly remember what we ate. There were a couple of brief speeches and we all trooped off again.

The change of time, lack of sleep and sheer excitement eventually caught up with me, and when we embarked on two launches for a cruise down the river I had lost all idea of time. The launches chugged slowly through green landscape, again very like our own, and the sun shone. Conversation in two languages flowed around me and I closed my eyes. I still insist I didn't sleep, but I felt much better when I woke up!

When we arrived back at the landing stage, Mme Le Goffe whipped Nancy and Guy Van der Kiste, who were staying with her, and I, back to the house for tea. Another quick wash and change and we were off again to M. Le Meur's house for drinks and snacks in his charming garden. On the move again, this time away from the residential area into the town to a 'Crêperie', where we squeezed behind tables and ate crêpes with delicious fillings and drank Breton cider. If you think the day was all eating and drinking you are right, it was. Eventually, replete, we started singing. The Bretons sang some of their songs and South Brent responded with a spirited rendering of 'Widdicombe Fair'; fortunately, Nancy knew all the words and we all knew the chorus. Maybe it was the cider, but I thought we did pretty well!

At 11p.m. I was quite ready to concede it had been a full day, but some of the hardier members of the party went on to a dance. My bed was welcoming and comfy and I certainly needed no sleeping tablets, but at 8a.m. I was enjoying coffee and French bread and was ready to be picked up at 9a.m. for a tour of the surrounding country and a picnic.

My main impression of the Brittany countryside was how much more ground each house had, and how little traffic there was for a warm sunny Sunday morning. For the first, well, of course, France is a big country, and I guess that is the answer to the second also. We drove through quiet villages to Landisiau, where we stopped in the town square while Madame went shopping for fresh bread.

M. Le Goffe, Nancy, Guy and I went into the big church and then looked at the memorial. M. Le Goffe explained that vandals had damaged many of the statues which adorned the exterior of the church; the missing fingers and noses on many of them were not due simply to the ravages of time and war, so that is one problem we share.

On the road again, we drove to Santec, where the Le Goffes have a seaside house, a barn that has been cleverly and tastefully converted into a charming cottage. Madame did things with saucepans and the stove while we admired the view: then we were off again to visit a couple of nearby châteaux at Trontoiy and Kerouzere. In both cases, the families were in residence but did not seem to mind us walking around the grounds. Then it was back to Santec for our picnic which, in fact, turned out to be a very sumptuous lunch, and by the time we had finished it was time to return to Châteauneuf for the football match.

I do not think much needs to be said about the match. Châteauneuf proved themselves much the superior team, and they had a very impressive ground to play on, altogether in a different league from our village football. South Brent did their best and really ran their legs off, but in the end class told.

Then it was back home for a quiet evening meal 'en famille', with some Breton music on the record player and some quiet conversation, and a respectable bedtime.

Next morning it was very dark at 5a.m. when I packed my suitcase, and at 6a.m., we climbed into the coaches again for the drive back to Roscoff and this time a quiet sunny crossing to Plymouth.

I feel we left behind people who consider us friends, even if, as in my case, conversation was a bit difficult.

During my drive through the villages I had noticed many memorials with the dates 1943, '44, '45 and the word 'Résistance', and I remembered the many, many, men, women and children who had gone on fighting in their own way long after France had capitulated, and I think that well sums up the Breton people – resistant and unyielding – but so friendly and generous to those they like.

Most definitely, it was a trip well worth taking and one long to remember.

To mark the first visit by the French football team to South Brent, Brent Captain Pat Bullen presents his French counterpart, Andrea Lebrun, with the South Brent crest as referee A. Hill looks on. (THE BULLEN COLLECTION)

The veterans' football team in Châteauneuf- du-Faou in 2003. (TWINNING ASSOCIATION COLLECTION)

Presentation of gifts at the tenth anniversary celebrations, Châteauneuf, August 1987.

(TWINNING ASSOCIATION COLLECTION)

On another occasion, the chairman of the association and four members accepted an invitation from Ivybridge Twinning Association to join their visit to St Pierre-sur-Dives, Ivybridge's twin town, during the 40th anniversary of the D-Day landings in 1984. They were well received and reported on the very genuine and profound gratitude still prevalent among the French people for their liberation in 1944. A local result of this visit was that a young lady from Lisieux found an exchange family in South Brent, which proved to be very satisfactory, and a son of the South Brent family was due to visit Lisieux in 1985.

In the spring of 1984 John Wain and Grahame Blackwell walked from South Brent to Châteauneuf, a total of 70 miles (not counting the wet bit across the

Channel). They spent 20 hours walking and, like other travellers, got somewhat confused by the new road layout west of Morlaix, where the map makers had not caught up with the road engineers. When they limped into Châteauneuf at 11.30p.m. they received a warm welcome. Their efforts realised a very worthwhile contribution of £200 for the Judo Club and £350 for Derriford Hospital.

There can be little doubt that the full value of the twinning links are best appreciated when exchanges such as those involving groups take place, and many of them have become regular features.

In 1982, when the association hosted a very successful weekend with the Judo Club, 38 visitors from Châteauneuf-du-Faou descended on Brent early on Friday morning for a packed programme of entertainment and judo. When they left on Sunday night, the Twinning Committee chairman commented, 'When they left I am not sure who was the most exhausted, the French or the English.'

Football matches have been a strong focal point of twinning activities and were arranged and played in an excellent sporting manner, many South Brent footballers forming firm and enduring friendships with their opposite numbers in France. The 1982 football visit was a memorable occasion; even more so as South Brent recorded an exceptionally fine win. The football exchange in 1984 was the ninth since the association was formed, and took place when Châteauneuf came to Brent in June and, as always, resulted in two wonderful weekends producing many more friendships between the young people of the two towns. The return tournament followed in August, the result of the match being a four-all draw. However, South Brent retained the trophy by winning on penalties. November saw the first exchange of the veteran football team (over-33s). Châteauneuf's team had been waiting for this exchange for some time. Over 15 couples made the

Celebration twinning dinner in South Brent Village Hall. Amongst those at table are John and Gwen England, Francis and Jill Sparkes, John and Val Meek, Sean and Jill Crannis. (TWINNING ASSOCIATION COLLECTION)

trip and all had a good weekend. Several couples made their first trip to France and forged new contacts with Breton friends. As for the score – South Brent just lost, which was not too bad considering many of the South Brent players had not played football for some years.

Other sporting connections in 1984 included an exchange of the South Brent table tennis and the Châteauneuf ping pong teams

On the back of the Brent twinning with Châteuneuf, exchange weekends of firemen from Buckfastleigh, with their French opposite numbers - *sapeurs et pompiers* – provided enormously successful, and links with the police were initiated

In 1984 came the first exchange between a small group of 10 young farmers with a number of committee members. It was a most interesting trip and thoroughly enjoyed by all.

In 1977, not to be outdone by the other organisations who had entertained visitors from our proposed twinning town, the senior citizens prepared to meet about 30 of their opposite numbers from Châteauneuf-du-Faou. The visitors spent the weekend in South Brent and the seniors invited them to join in the dancing on 13 June, when they also gave them tea.

Another activity enjoyed by the Twinning Association was playing pétanque, the predecessor of English bowls, and is commonly believed to be the game that Drake played on the Plymouth Hoe before fighting the Armada. Mike Temple provided the association with a permanent pétanque court at the Woodpecker. In 1984 a new trophy, the South Brent Twinning Trophy, was generously presented to the association by John Wain and was won by a team consisting of P. Moore, R. Pike and J Meek. In 1985

The Chairman of South Brent Parish Council, Cllr Mrs Irene McNevin, is seen presenting a silver salver to her French counterpart on the occasion of the 25th anniversary of the Twinning Association.

(TWINNING ASSOCIATION COLLECTION)

the South Brent team scored a notable success by winning the South Devon Pétanque League and the NatWest Trophy.

The presentation was held on 12 October at Moretonhampstead, where the trophies were presented to Dave Hannaford and the rest of the team, at the league's annual dinner and dance. They won the NatWest trophy again in 1986 for the fifth time in six years.

A group of South Brent singers went to Châteauneuf on the occasion of the tenth anniversary of the twinning and their singing was greatly admired by the French, both for its technical merit and for its content and programme. These visits have continued to the present day.

The cast of over 50 pose for the camera during a break in rehearsals for the St John Ambulance Cadets' Jesus Nativity *in the Village Hall in 1974.* (THE CARROLL COLLECTION)

The refurbishment of the Village Hall, originally constructed in 1910 as the Coronation Church Hall.
(THE HAYMAN COLLECTION)

✦ CHAPTER 14 ✦

Another Look at the Village Hall

Rosemary Stansbury has documented the history of the Village Hall. She writes:

South Brent Village Hall was built in 1911 for the village by the church, which also owned the land. Previously entertainments such as shows, dances and films were presented in the Vicar's Hall, built in 1861 in Millswood Lane, and then from 1904 in a hall in Millswood Mill (also in Millswood Lane), generously provided by Mr Hawke of the Mill.

The new hall was originally called the Coronation Church Hall, as this was the year of the coronation of George V, but it soon became known to everyone as the Church Hall. The new hall was basically the main hall we have today, with large windows on both sides, a high ceiling, a good stage and two dressing-rooms; also the main entrance and the small meeting-room. There were very sparse kitchen facilities in the basement, and gas lamps on the walls. Heating was by a few coke-fired heaters, which had to be frequently stoked and were very smoky. The floor was then very good, and has often been described as the 'best sprung dance floor in South Devon'. Together with the stage facilities, it was a hall to be proud of at the time.

During the First and Second World Wars the hall had other roles to play, not only in entertainment and relaxation. In the First World War prisoners of war were billeted there, and in the Second World War, when there were 671 evacuees living in the village and the school was very overcrowded, the hall served as an extension to the school for the younger children. The Produce Association was set up as part of the Dig for Victory campaign. American forces were billeted there during the build-up to the Normandy landings. After the war the hall was found to be in such a bad state of deterioration that it was closed for six months for renovation.

In the 1960s the Church sold the hall to the village and it was renamed the Village Hall.

The hall needed a lot of work, there was no money available and, because facilities were rather primitive, lettings did not bring in sufficient funds to start improvements – a vicious circle. So it was necessary not only to find the money to buy the hall in the first place, but then to get it to its present high standard. Rosemary Stansbury continues:

On 19 July 1968 the South Brent Gala and Trades Fair was held at Wrangaton in aid of Village Hall extensions. This was a great occasion and it was estimated that over 3,500 people attended. In true South Brent

manner the morning was wet, but just as the fête started the sun came out and all was well. Among the many attractions were the Dagenham Girl Pipers, the Royal Marine Band, the Mercury Motor Cycle Stunt Riders, the Thunderbird roller-coaster, three hours of professional wrestling, judo, sheep-dog trials, clay pigeon shooting, Punch and Judy and the Paignton Zoo Chimps' Tea Party.

Shortly afterwards a large extension was built, containing the kitchen, side hall, toilets, chair-room and longer entrance lobby. Oil-fired central heating was installed throughout the building. The famous dance floor was so worn it was dangerous and, after much debate, it was covered with a layer of industrial hardboard. In 1982 the Scout Room was built under the flat roof, and further refurbishment was carried out.

Although the hall stood up very well to all the changes and demands, further problems arose, particularly incurable leaks from the flat roof, and it was decided that more radical action was needed - either a completely new Village Hall on this site or drastic and extensive refurbishment. At a public meeting on 13 September 1999, the decision was made by a small majority to refurbish, so the solid old structure remained, together with fond memories of past celebrations, activities and friends. A slate pitched roof was built above the flat roof, allowing for a comfortable meeting-room with tea bar, an up-to-date stage lighting room, a storage room for the scouts and a costume store for SBADS; also a lift for the disabled and inside and outside staircases. Downstairs a fine maple floor was laid, ideal for dancing, and (with new supportive structure) a completely level surface to extend the short-mat bowls facilities. Improvements to the stage, double glazing, a new heating system and a toilet for the disabled improved the atmosphere and facilities considerably. In the summer of 2005 the side hall was refurbished with a fine new bar and modern lighting, and the kitchen benefited from new equipment, notably a commercial dishwasher, cooker and larder fridge. The two dressing-rooms were also renovated and equipped.

The history of the hall is an on-going story, and during 2006/07 the basement was changed from a dark and grotty hole to a well-lit and carpeted area with improved storage facilities. The hall benefited from paving round the building and paved areas for the Scouts and Brownies (in memory of Miss Cranch). A new seat was given by Dave and Sheila Cockings, beds were prepared and planted and other areas improved.

During the life of the hall there must have been many red-letter days. In recent years the stage appearance of

Each year the Village Hall is the venue for the South Brent Amateur Dramatic Society's productions. In 1979 the group won the South Devon Drama Federation Spring Festival for the second year running with the production of Love on the Dole. *This followed the 1978 production of* Relative Values. *Both plays were produced by Jane Tuson.*   (THE CARROLL COLLECTION)

Dora Bryan with the one-woman show she has given in many parts of the world, to contribute to our refurbishment and to delight all those present with her abilities and charm, was definitely a red-letter day. SBADS celebrated the 50th anniversary of their last production of The Sleeping Beauty *by staging a new production of the pantomime and inviting members of the previous cast to join the audience.*

In 2011 it will be the centenary of the Village Hall, and future generations will, we hope, continue to enjoy the facilities and care for the hall as the village has done over the past 100 years.

Two of the main events in the life of the Village Hall are the Spring Village Hall Concert and the Autumn Fair, or Fête.

The Village Hall Concert

In March 1977 it was noted that:

Once again, the wit and talents of the village have combined to give two packed audiences a thoroughly good evening's entertainment. Outside the Hall, the weather was doing its worst, pouring and blowing. Inside all was amusement, movement and music, and a general feeling of warmth and pride – this was 'Our Village Concert', and a jolly good one, too. Apart from the fun (and worries and problem of taking part), all the organisations will take pleasure in the knowledge that their efforts resulted in £170 going into the hall funds – a case of congratulations all round.

And again in April 1981, the concert was deemed to be:

... another great success. Playing to capacity audiences each night one would be hard put to it to decide whether spectators or performers enjoyed the evening more. The concert was a wonderful exercise in co-operation between many of the village organisations and succeeded in raising approximately £300 for Village Hall funds – all of which is used to help pay for the upkeep of the hall and consequently to keep hire charges as low as possible.

Indeed the AGM in June of that year reported that:

At the recent AGM of the Village Hall Committee those present were told that for the rest of this year it was felt it would not be necessary to increase the Hall charges. The books had balanced but Mrs Goss, the treasurer, pointed out fuel and electricity costs are still rising and although hall lettings had come to £2728.05 in the year to 31 March, one organisation (the Brownies) had pulled out from using the hall, and in the future the Youth Club hoped to have their own premises. The Village Hall Fête and Concert had been successful, both socially and financially, but the New Year's Eve Dance, although enjoyed by those who attended, had lost money, and would not be repeated this year. Nevertheless, it had been a good year for the hall.

In the year 2000 the concert had a cast of over 100

The 1978 Village Hall show, featuring (left to right) Sandra Cockings, Gillian Meade, Mr Bristow, Marion Stevens, Wendy Mumford, ?. (THE MUMFORD COLLECTION)

The 1957 Carnival Concert with Tanner Shields, Rose Watts, Peter Jensen, Valerie Catt, Michael Wright and Margaret Hard, Paul Roberts, with Len Watts on the drums. These events were always well supported and encouraged local talent to take part each year.. (THE MILLER COLLECTION)

The Womens' Institute at the 2001 Village Hall Fête. Left to right: *Maggie Taylor, Joy Hayman, Stella Stickland, Sylvia Warman, Eileen Honeywell, Margaret Catt, Rosemary Evans, Pauline Mitchell, Vera Jordan, Margaret Herd.*

(THE HAYMAN COLLECTION)

people and included the debuts of the new Vicar, David Winnington-Ingram, reciting the poem 'The Vicar of Bray', and SBAD's own Karlos Fandango Junior, alias Carl Heslop, with his highly original stage routine. The programme was described as 'a medley of dance, drama and song with contrasting vocal offerings from Wild Harmony and the Brent Singers'. In 2001 the show was described as 'the best ever', and had a cast of over 130. It raised £650 for the refurbishment fund.

The Village Hall Fête

The Village Hall Fête is another way in which the community at large has helped to maintain the Village Hall to its high standard:

The Fete held in August 1981 was a very successful function and resulted in £230 going to the funds. This is an all-in effort to keep the charges for hiring the hall as reasonable as possible.

As always, it was a very generously supported by the village. In 1984 there were a number of urgent repairs needed to the fabric of the building. The committee was pleased to be able to announce in that year that approximately £200 was raised at the Village Hall

Fête, which was held on 15 September.

In 2001 came the ninetieth 'birthday' of the hall and 8 September saw the fête with an 'Upstairs, Downstairs' theme to mark the occasion and the reopening of the building after major refurbishments. The festivities not only looked at the past but also at the future of the hall, which was built in 1911. Parishioners aged over 90 years and those who were one year old were special guests at the event and included Miss Naomi Cranch, whose father helped to construct the hall in 1911. They all received a commemorative gift. The stalls and entertainments at the fête raised more that £1,000 for the Hall which went towards future work to the upstairs facilities.

Don Stansbury, then secretary of the Village Hall Committee said: 'We had a brilliant day and everybody was very pleased with all the work that has been carried out.'

The Fire at South Devon Furniture, 1979

Traders and villagers in South Brent banded together to help a local firm get back into business after its workshop was destroyed by fire. Thousands of pounds worth of equipment and export orders were lost in the blaze, which gutted South Devon

156

Furniture in the station yard in late August 1979. The building was originally the goods shed at Brent Station and is only one of two remaining parts of that important junction. The cost was estimated at £48,000. But there were no temporary job losses and stopping in production when offers of help came flooding in. The managing director, Mr Anthony West, said:

We have had a fantastic response. It has been marvellous. We are very fortunate to have the offer of alternative premises with most of the necessary equipment. This means that we will be able to carry on almost immediately. I hope that near the end of next week production will be back to almost 75%.

The firm specialised in hand-made reproduction furniture and had offers of storage space and the loan of sanding equipment. William Slade and his two sons, Peter and John, from Great Aish, gave time to clear up the fire debris. The records were luckily in another building, as all that was left of the workshop were the walls. Sadly, some of the staff

had lost woodworking tools that they had had for a long time.

William Morris, whose father worked there, wrote at the time:

The fire happened in August 1979. My Dad was woken up at 3 o'clock in the morning to tell him that the factory was on fire. He could smell the burning when he opened the front door. It was very frightening. The fire was seen by a train driver as he was passing the old railway station.

The factory was in the old goods shed. Several fire engines came to try and put out the fire. They were there a long time. The flames were very high. All that was left of the building were the walls. The machinery and the furniture were destroyed. It was very sad to see it after the fire was out. Everything was black, wet and very, very smelly. There was a lot of clearing up to do. Some of it was done using a tractor. This was written about in the newspaper. The present South Devon Furniture is back in the goods shed. If you look carefully at the outside of the building you can still see evidence of the fire of 1979.

Another Look at Fires in Brent

Kate and Helen Dahill with the teddy bears rescued from the Anchor Fire.　　(THE DAHILL COLLECTION)

Above: *Another look at the fire which devastated the Anchor in 1990.*　　(THE DAHILL COLLECTION)

Left: *A few months after the Anchor disaster a fire broke out in the chimney of the Pack Horse. Here the Buckfastleigh fire crew deal with the aftermath.*

(THE WILKINS COLLECTION)

Another Look at Fires in Brent

Crowds gather to see the devastation caused by the fire at the bottom of Church Street on 23 February 1901. Four cottages were totally gutted. When the new buildings were constructed by Mr Fred Veale for Mr C. White, the White brothers exchanged the ownership of the properties. Hence they are now call Nos 1–4 The Exchange.

(The Anderson & Cranch Collections)

Subscribers

Ron Akehurst, Village Crier
Paul and Steven Andrews, South Brent, Devon
Mrs Julie Andrews, South Brent, Devon
James and Nicholas Andrews, South Brent, Devon
Ray Anstis, Bray, Berkshire
Roger Anstis, Bishop's Waltham, Hampshire
Roy Austin
Linda and Kenneth Austin, Packhorse, South Brent
Mer Baker
Robert L. Barclay, Yonder Cross, South Brent, Devon
Mrs Mary Bateman, South Brent, Devon
Leslie Bell
Aminah Benaceur, South Brent
Patrick Benaceur, South Brent
John and Valerie Bevan, Underhill
Eileen Blockly, South Brent
Judith Blowers, South Brent, Devon
Kate Born, South Brent
Mrs G. K. Brooks (née Jones), Epsom, Surrey
Peter and Veronica Brown, South Brent
Anya Budden (née Cockings), Plympton, Devon
Mr and Mrs P. Bullen, South Brent
K. J. Burrow, Bucks Cross, Devon
Mr I. Burrows, Plymstock
Dr B. Campbell, South Brent
Richard D. Carroll, South Brent
Tich Chapple, South Brent
E. Chapple, South Brent, Devon
Jan and John Clark, Galmpton, Devon
Cindy L. Clarke, Wokingham
Gerald and Jean Cleave
David Cockings, South Brent, Devon
John and Anne Collier, Whinfield, South Brent
Mike and Val Copley
Keith Corner, Barton on the Heath, Glos
Coulton Family, South Brent, Devon
R. O. Cranch, South Brent, Devon
Peter and Maureen Crimp
Tim and Sue Currant, South Brent
Evan and Anthea Davies, South Brent
Mrs Margaret Eales, South Brent, Devon
John and Shirley Eatwell, South Brent, Devon
Barbara Edge (née Lang), Shrewsbury
Paul and Caroline Edginton, South Brent
Jilly and Roger Elford, South Brent
Bernard and Jill Elms, South Brent, Devon
Angela J. Endean, Totnes
Mrs G. England, South Brent
Rosemary Evans, South Brent, Devon
Wendy and Bill Evemy, South Brent
Dick and Mardie Everett
Tim and Felicity Ferry, South Brent
Su and Ken Field, Torquay, Devon
B. E. Field
A. and J. Field

Godfrey H. and Margaret C. Foot (née Cranch),
  Kingskerswell, South Devon
Simon Fox, South Brent; Andrew Fox, Launceston,
  Cornwall; Sally Scanlon (née Fox), Cheltenham
Stella Gillingham, Didworthy, South Brent, Devon
Rupert Gillingham, Malton, N. Yorks
Emma Gillingham, Kingston-upon-Thames, Surrey
Mike and Jan Goss, South Brent, Devon
Robert Goss, Tokyo, Japan
Frank and Phyllis Gove (née Fox)
Derek Grills, South Brent, Devon
Olive Guinn, South Brent, Devon
Mandy and Tim Haley, South Brent
Christine Halstead, Riverside, South Brent
Stephen and Jennifer Hanney, South Brent
Lester and Tina Hard (plus Tizzy)
"Knocker" Harmsworth,
Miss Gillian Hawes, South Brent, Devon
Bill and Joy Hayman (née Lang), South Brent
Mr C. and Mrs E. Hocking,
Pamela M. Honeywill, South Brent
Eileen Honeywill (née Joint), South Brent
Joyce and Ralph Howitt
Joint Family, South Brent, Devon
Peter Jones, Barrydale, W. Cape, South Africa 6750
Ginny Jones (Murgatroyd), South Brent, Devon
The Jozsa family, Aish, South Brent
Peter and Avril Kelly
John and Maggie King, Aish, South Brent
Graham Korner, South Brent
Doug Langdon, Eckington, Worcester
Bernard and Mandy Langdon
Doug Langdon and family, Worcestershire
Brian and Liz Lavers, South Brent, Devon
Denise Leaning, Swindon, Wilts
Barbara Lodge, South Brent
Mrs and Mrs A. Major
M.W. and E.A. Major
Mr R. Major, Newquay
E. G. "Eggie" Male, South Brent
Mr M. Male, Pangbourne
Mrs L. Male, South Brent
Barry Male, Totnes. Devon
Mr and Mrs R. A. Male, Ivybridge
Elizabeth and Robert March (née Wright), Ivybridge
Mona Marshall (née Lang), Woodley, Reading
Doe and Roland Mason, South Brent, Devon
Jon Mason, St Margarets, Twickenham
Paul Mason, Malmesbury, Wilts
Lionel and Vicky Mayling, South Brent
Tim McGill (King Henry), South Brent
John and Margaret Mead, South Brent
The Merriman family, South Brent and Bristol
Peter and Jean Miller
Hazel Millington, Perth, Western Australia

Subscribers

The Mitchell Huggins Family, formerly of
  Shipley Bridge
Lucy A. Moore, South Brent, Devon
Peter A.W. Moore
Andrew and Christine Morgan
S. J. and W. Morris, South Brent
Betty Morris
Sheila Morrish, South Brent
Kay and Patrick Mullen, Ivybridge, Devon
Phyllis and George Mumford, South Brent, Devon
Miss Jasmine Mumford
Richard and Jane Mumford
Hannah Murgatroyd, London
Trevor Newman, South Brent, Devon
Peter and Joan Noble
Old School Centre Library, South Brent, Devon
Stuart and Margaret Orr, South Brent
Betty Osborne, Dartington, Devon
Ann Packford, Boars Hill, Oxford
Ruth J. Peard, South Brent
Zoe Pedrick, Buckfastleigh
Norman Perkins
Jennifer Pike, South Brent, Devon
Gaynor and Adrian Platt, South Brent, Devon
John and Jill Poulton, Torquay
James and Michael Prickett
Derrick and Mary Pully Blank, Leigham, Plymouth
Diane and John Reed (née Wright), South Brent
Ursula Reid-Robertson
Bernard and Mary Rice, Eltham
Patrick and Heidi Rice, South Brent
Marky and Pat Richards, Westleigh, Devon
Dulce Robertson, South Brent, Devon
Monty Rogers, formerly of Aish
Marilyn Roper, South Brent, Devon
Annie and Martin Ross, South Brent
Phyllis D. Rundle, South Brent
J. K. Shepherd, South Brent, Devon
Mrs S. Shepherd (née Major), Paignton
Tony and Lucy Simister
Mark Simmons, Liskeard, Cornwall
Tommy and Maureen Simmons (née Hard),
  Pensilva, Cornwall
Mr Tim and Mrs Kathy Sings, South Brent, Devon
Mr Frank and Mrs Joyce Sings, South Brent, Devon
Pamela and Sarah Sitton, Morgana Cottage,
  South Brent
Betty M. Skinner
Marilyn Smith, South Brent
Gilly Smith, South Brent
Miss Charlotte Soby, South Brent
Margaret and Mary Soper

L. and N. Soper South Brent Parish Council,
Mr and Mrs J.E. Sparkes
Win and Roy Sparkes, South Brent, Devon
Mrs M. M. Spence, South Brent, Devon
Mr and Mrs N. Steer, South Brent, Devon
Margie and Peter Stevens, South Brent
Richard Stevens, South Brent
Duncan, Pat, Kirstie and Callum Stewart
Eva B. Stewart, South Brent
Fred Stone, Ivybridge
Gill Taylor
Pete and Sadie Tempest, South Brent
The Rockey family, Aish, South Brent
Paul and Sue Thomas, Melbury
Brian A. Thomas, Clobells, South Brent
Roderick Thomson, South Brent
Rod and Patsy Tidball
Sue Timmins
Janet and Neil Toogood, South Brent
Joan Towl, South Brent, Devon
S. Towl, South Brent, Devon
Doris Trundle, South Brent, Devon
Jane Tuson
Colin J. Vallance, South Brent
Betty C. Vallance, South Brent
John and Kim Van der Kiste, South Brent, Devon
Mr and Mrs Peter Wakeham, Rattery
Phillip Ward-Green, Millswood, South Brent
Roy and Esther Warnes, South Brent
Ann Warren, Lutton, South Brent
Pauline Richards and June Watts, South Brent
Christine Webber (née Joint), South Brent
Mr and Mrs J. Wells, Wrangaton
Carole Whittard, Frome, Somerset
Marjorie Wicks, South Brent
Bob and Elise Willisson, South Brent, Devon
Mr E. J. Wilson (Deceased), Born in Brent
Revd. David R. Winnington-Ingram,
  South Brent, Devon
Brian and Val Wollington
Simon Wonnacott, South Brent
Paul and Mary Wonnacott, South Brent
Nano and Clive Wood, South Brent, Devon
Simon Woodhouse, Hordle, Hants
Mark and Dawn Woodhouse, South Brent
Adrian Woodhouse, Canberra, Australia
Ken and Marian Woodhouse, South Brent
Malcolm and Cindy Wright, Totnes
Michael and Stella Wright (née Manning),
  Stoke Poges
Kenneth R. Yabsley, Plympton, Devon